The Complete Guide to Writers Groups, Conferences, and Workshops

Wiley Books for Writers Series

The Elements of Storytelling: How to Write Compelling Fiction, by Peter Rubie

Book Editors Talk to Writers, by Judy Mandell

Networking at Writer's Conferences: From Contacts to Contracts, by Steven D. Spratt and Lee G. Spratt

The Complete Guide to Writers Groups, Conferences, and Workshops

Eileen Malone

John Wiley & Sons, Inc.

New York • Chichester • Brisbane • Toronto • Singapore

Library of Congress Cataloging-in-Publication Data

Malone, Eileen.
    The complete guide to writers groups, conferences, and workshops
/ Eileen Malone.
      p. cm. — (Wiley books for writers)
    ISBN 0-471-14217-4
    1. Authorship. I. Title. II. Series: Wiley books for writers
series.
PN145.M246   1996
808'.02—dc20   96-14684

Contents

3   Group Expectations of You   43

4   Receiving Criticism   59

Introduction

One Group's Story: The Writers' Bloc

It's 7:30, and the Oakland evening is balmy. As we enter the open doorway of the cottage, the smell of French roast coffee and the sound of energized conversation greet us. I am introduced all around as Joe's guest and warmly welcomed. One by one, the writers settle into sofas and chairs. Some kick off their shoes, and others place pillows behind their backs. A marmalade cat enters and stretches out in the middle of the living room floor. As if this were the gavel that starts the meeting, it begins.

All attention is focused on a woman sitting on the far sofa. While shuffling some papers on her lap, she gives a short synopsis of her story thus far, enough to jog everyone's memory. Then she sits up and proceeds to read aloud from her manuscript. As she continues her smooth, clear recitation, everyone vigorously scribbles notes. She pauses once to put a check mark on something she wants to fix later. There are no interruptions as she completes the reading of her thirty-page chapter. When she is finished, she leans back and looks around.

A distinguished-looking man with graying hair sitting opposite me is moderator this month. He calls on a young woman who signals that she is prepared to comment. Using her notes, she delivers her critique. She throws out terms like *protagonist* and *conflict resolution* and *the sense of consequence*. The moderator makes sure that she is finished speaking before moving on. I am astounded at how carefully everyone listened to what was read. I am also impressed by the apparently effortless flow of professional, technical terms in this informal, laid-back group. No one is showing off or one-upping others in a display of expertise. Weak areas are pointed out, and several ways to remedy the flaws are suggested. Exceptionally well-written segments are also acknowledged. As the discussion progresses, everyone speaks, even if only to agree with what has already been said; however, most group members submit new ideas for consideration. One suggestion is debated quickly, and then the pace of the piece is discussed.

Throughout the entire critique, the reader does not defend or explain what she has written. Once she asks the critiquer to be more specific, and another time she rereads a sentence in question. Otherwise, she rapidly writes down notes to herself in the margins of her manuscript and once in a while on the backs of pages. After the last person has contributed, she thanks the group. Later, she will review the comments and make whatever changes, additions, or deletions she deems appropriate.

Another man reviews the group's calendar. It's up to him to keep track of who is going to read a month or two in advance, and he reminds them that should something unavoidable arise, the person scheduled must call around and get somebody else to substitute. Each and every meeting must have a reader—no exceptions.

The moderator interjects that he will not be attending the next two meetings. He has tickets to the opera. There is no problem. Informing the group ahead of time of meetings that will be missed is an expected courtesy.

The woman sitting next to me passes out photocopies of her chapter. She is struggling with character development in this particular scene and encourages everyone to write comments in the margins. Typed critiques would be gratefully received, too.

The treasurer, wearing one earring and a Hard Rock Cafe T-shirt, gives his report. He takes a moment to explain to me that everyone pays $10 per month and that the money is held in a bank account. It is used for birthday cakes and cards and a huge annual party. At Christmas, the members pick names out of a hat for presents and have a marvelous dinner in a San Francisco restaurant—open bar, whatever they want, all on the treasury. The money also helps pay for guest speakers and scholarships.

Sitting in front of the window is a woman with a lovely southern drawl who has received partial funding from the group's treasury for a writing class she is attending at a local university. In exchange, she has agreed to bring back to the group what she learns in the class. Tonight she explains that each person in her class reads five or ten pages, two or three people make comments, and then someone says, "Next," and on they go. The class is still in its early stages, but she doesn't feel that the critique is as complete as it might be.

A book review that one member wrote for another member's recently published historical novel is read aloud. A photocopy of another review is passed around. An announcement is made that author Leonard Bishop (whose novel-writing class at the University of California was the impetus for this group) will be in town sometime in May. Some sort of reception will be planned, but not now, not tonight. It's now 10:00 and time to wrap it up.

Quick tidbits of conversation take place as smaller groups pause in the doorway, on the front steps, and on the sidewalk. Literary gossip, deals with agents, and interactions with publishers and editors are shared as members walk to their parked cars. The evening was focused, thorough, productive, and satisfying.

On the drive back to San Francisco, I assess the dynamics and focus of this group. It was formed to help writers with their novels, and everything it asks of its members drives them from reading the initial rough draft through the various stages of rewrite necessary to get the novel ready for publication. It doesn't make any difference whether the member is a successful author honing yet another work into final form or a first-time author still struggling with the early stages of rewrite. This is a working writers group. While adhering to some basic practices, it changes to fill the current and immediate needs of the group members.

Sometime in the mid-sixties, this group was conceived by Leonard Bishop. A few of his students at the University of California at Berkeley suggested that he do some private teaching because they were not getting what they needed from academe. He agreed and began what became known as Bishop's Monday Night Creative Writing Class. It met fifty-two weeks a year for almost twenty years in the homes of different students. Group members started, finished, and published books. When Bishop had to leave the San Francisco Bay Area and move to Kansas, he left some basic instructions.

One was to set a day and time and stick to it. If the meeting will be Monday night from 7:00 P.M. to 10:00 P.M., keep it in that slot. Don't make exceptions because of holidays or vacations; it gets too confusing. Take no breaks. Meet every week, or don't meet at all.

Even now, this group's attendance is excellent. Members take leaves of absence from time to time when they can foresee great difficulties in regular attendance. Even though everyone is expected to be writing and sharing their works-in-progress, some let their own writing simmer for a while as they put their energy into helping others. Consequently, even those who aren't reading from their own work hold the same high level of responsibility toward attendance. Everyone calls ahead to explain an anticipated absence. Everyone has made the commitment, and that's what writing a novel is all about—commitment. It's like going to an important job.

Meetings always start at 7:30 P.M. and last as long as the work is being read and discussed. Of course, exceptionally long works are often submitted ahead of time. The goal is to be there on the prescribed night. "You'd think it couldn't be done," says a working single mother, "but it can and we do. Every week can be a tough grind. It's rough producing regularly and getting immediate feedback." They all agree that a writer's discipline is ultimately self-imposed.

Bishop also insisted that the group impose a financial commitment, too. It doesn't have to be much, but the idea of paying dues seems to hold the members together. It's interesting because as one member told me, when people fall behind two or three months in their dues, you know that they are ready to drop out of the group.

Aside from these basic logistics, the primary standard that Bishop emphasized was honesty. Give the most honest criticism that you can to help the writer. When receiving criticism, remember that it is your manuscript, not you, that is being examined and pulled apart, even though it may seem much too personal to bear. No one's estimation of you or your work should ever be so important that it affects your self-esteem. Eventually, you are going to receive rejections from agents and editors and publishers who, in Bishop's words, "wouldn't know a piece of fine writing if it stepped on their eyeballs." The group is there to help each individual develop a sense of self-worth.

Adhering to these basics, the group has continued through divisions and reattachments. Once their books were published, some members dropped out, only to return when starting another. Some took time out to attend to their health or to family matters. Some got what they needed from the group and left to teach workshops and classes elsewhere; now they refer their students back to the group for ongoing support. Throughout, a steadfast core has remained.

Joe Capello, a charter member of the group, which calls itself The Writers' Bloc, remembers his beginnings. He had once taken a course at a college in San Francisco where the instructor was so caustic that it stopped him from writing anything more for almost ten years. He had just about given up on himself as a writer when he saw a description of Leonard Bishop's writing class in a college catalog. He laughs as he recalls his first impression. There was Bishop sitting at the head of a very long table in a narrow, rectangular classroom, looking like anything but what Capello had expected of a successful author. Students were sitting at the table, beyond it, and around the walls and were standing in the hallway. Suddenly, Bishop said, "Here are my credentials," and he opened his briefcase and began throwing out one book after another, all of them his. This was no ivory-tower academic spouting dreary, condescending platitudes; this was an aggressive, intense, hand-waving writer who walked his talk.

Capello had to wrench up his courage to submit a chapter of his work.

Bishop brought it back to class with a critique attached. He then read sections aloud to the class. At the break, he told Capello, "I want to talk to you." Putting his arm around Capello's shoulder, he said that it was a great piece of work. His wife had read it and announced that this was the kind of book she enjoyed reading. Bishop then invited Capello to join the private group.

It wasn't all rose-scented praise, however. There was one chapter that Capello felt particularly good about—perhaps too confident. When it came back with a five-page critique, there was very little, if any, praise. He was devastated. When he left the class and got into his car, he looked at it one more time. In essence, Bishop had told him that his talent was an added tribute, but he still needed to learn more skills. Capello threw the manuscript and critique down on the passenger seat. It remained there for a week. He didn't care that Bishop had said that any harshness he might encounter in the group would be trivial compared to the viciousness possible in the industry. He didn't care that Bishop had said that you are accountable for what you do and say and provoke in your writing. He sympathized at an intimate level with all those students who had appeared in Bishop's class once or twice and never returned. He was hurt and angry. Finally, he was able to separate his self from his work, and sitting at his kitchen table one foggy morning, he reread the instructor's critique. Then he amazed himself by exclaiming aloud to no one in particular, "That son of a gun was right!"

This kind of experience is not rare in a good writers workshop. As a matter of fact, everyone in The Writers' Bloc feels that if you truly care about helping another writer, you will always offer an honest opinion. It is most unkind to watch silently as someone makes the same mistake over and over again; it is almost cruel to let the writer think that all is well when, in fact, improvements could and should be made. Writers who are well versed in craft and grammar, plot and character development, should help writers who are not as adept. Of course, for a successful experience, there must be a willingness to learn.

Marilyn Haiches is a perfect example of someone who was willing to learn. She had originally been in a group that she felt was more into stroking than critical analysis. Then a friend told her about The Writers' Bloc. She sent a letter and submitted a sample of her manuscript. "The marvelous thing about writing," she says, "is that age and gender and physical appearance and social status make no difference. The work is all that matters—and the work that goes into the work."

Haiches clearly understood the group's caution toward accepting rank beginners. She knew that editing skills come from years of expertise and practice and that it takes a great deal of energy to get someone new up to speed. She also appreciated that during this transition, group members might not get the quality and quantity of critique they require. Haiches chewed her cuticles and waited.

Then the group welcomed her. Members told her later that they saw that the work needed more structure but that they also saw the real writer speaking in it. They were delighted to have her join them.

She walked into an atmosphere of rigorous standards, exactly what she wanted, and it practically scared her to death. "Holy cow," she remembers thinking, "I'm like a complete freshman at the first day of school." It didn't matter that she had a successful background in producing advertising, writing radio spots, and working in documentary film. Everyone in the group was committed to putting in valuable time with an eye on getting published. They were not sweet, nor were they bullies, but they were undoubtedly focused on the craft of writing. Things she might have known intuitively, they articulated. She felt intimidated as she realized that the groups she had known previously were tea parties compared to this one, but she also felt very lucky to be a member.

Eventually, Haiches conquered the steep learning curve by total and intense listening. She gobbled up all the literary terms being tossed about regarding omniscient points of view and first-person narrations. She incorporated what she learned.

When it was her night to present a chapter of her first draft, she found it daunting. Someone else read it aloud, and she kept thinking, "Oh, how could I have written that!" She listened carefully as group members told her how the first draft gets the whole story out. "This is where you spew more than you'll ever use, and it is important not to self-edit too much at this point," she explains. "You find out where the story really is going in the next draft." She listened and learned because everyone else had already done what she was in the process of doing.

At her most recent reading, she tried something experimental at the end, something that would either kill the piece or make it more powerful. When she realized how the group grasped her intent and appreciated her efforts, it was the best feeling. "The quality of the group is really, really high," she says, "and I think that maybe three or four books are now ready to be published. Whether or not they are marketable, they are certainly finely crafted and well written."

Nancy Cossitt won the Alabama Writers' Conclave Award and came to the San Francisco Bay Area from Alabama to study novel writing under Wallace Stegner. Even with this writing background, Cossitt appreciates The Writers' Bloc. "I am receiving superlative editorial help in the final polishing," she says. "Without this writing group, my novels would not have been written."

Another writer who credits the group as the impetus behind the work is Lee Serrels. "I've completed one book and am three-quarters through another. The group sharpened my wit and kept me on a forward track," Serrels explains. "No one is unkind, but they are all honest, and if you can't handle the honesty, everyone is sorry that you have to leave, but goodbye. Believe me, without these special friends I might have had that novel in my head, but never would have actually written it."

Another writer who would never have tackled a novel without group support is Gloria Suffin. She lives very comfortably with the fact that the book is taking a long time. "I live a very vital life!" she says, and looks to the group to point out where she has blind spots. "In the process of writing, a writer has what is in the head, but it doesn't always come out directly on the page, and in a sense, that is the purpose of the group," she explains. Whenever the group finds little things in each scene that she had not made clear, Suffin is grateful. It prevents her from swimming around in murky writing and losing time.

Now on the fourth rewrite of her 600-page novel, Suffin claims, "Revision is what it is all about." Recently retired as an English teacher, she explains that most teachers don't assign rewrites in the classroom. "You get a grade and a paper marked with mistakes, but teachers don't teach creative writing, and they don't help you with alterations. Groups do. There's nothing like a group for working through revisions and rewrites, especially on long works."

"If I hadn't joined the group, I would have only written short stories," says Donna Gillespie, author of *The Light Bearer*, which is climbing the best-seller list in Germany and England. It was a major transition for her, going from the story to the novel-length conflict. The group insisted that her short stories were not long enough for what she was trying to do.

"There is something wonderful about knowing that there will be meetings and they are waiting for the next chapter," she says. "It helps you through those trying, fainthearted periods. At the beginning of a book it can easily disintegrate. You can disconnect and reconnect a lot. It's a very fragile process. The group gives you an outside discipline and keeps you from being swallowed up by your own demons."

She continues, "Writing a novel is so complex. Scenes grow out of scenes and characters put pressure on other characters. You really need the group as a sounding board when you read aloud your chapters. You want to get down what is real and most true, and you call on your fellow group members to keep you honest. You watch how differently or similarly each person responds, and it's very compelling when you hear the same critique from everyone.

"The biggest enemy when you write is yourself. This is why there's no reason for competition in a good writers group. There's always room for one more good work. The group serves as a kind of family, each wanting the best for each other. You can't get this experience from a correspondence class. I remember how proud I was when Donna Levin published; it was amazing, I was in such awe at her book signing."

Donna Levin is another of the group's successfully published authors. Four and a half years after joining Bishop's original group, she sold her first novel. Since then, she has published two more novels and has just finished another. She says that the group lifted her out of that limbo of wanting to write but not knowing how and being afraid to try.

The group helped Donal Brown in the same way. A high school English and journalism teacher for more than thirty-two years, Brown says that group participation has helped to reinvigorate him. Not only has he learned a lot, hands-on, about writing processes and techniques that he can carry over when teaching writing and literature to younger students, but he has become better able to "understand my attitudes towards writing, the mind-sets that I need to actually finish the confounded thing."

The group helped adjust the attitude of Karen Caronna, who has written three novels within the context of her group experience. "There were times when the group dynamics absolutely saved me. When I thought my writing, which of course is an extension of my self, was absolutely worthless, the group was present to buoy me up and encourage me."

And so it goes. Those who speak here echo many other writers who thrive and grow in the company of others like themselves.

I've discovered that all over the country there is a vast variety of groups for writers. Some are similar to the one described here, and some are very different. Nevertheless, in numbers impossible to count, they remain steadfast in the spirited services they provide. When you find the right group, the results will be an extraordinarily more effective writer. I celebrate the diversity and uniqueness of all gatherings of writers.

Part One

1

Why Writers Connect

At a recent writers conference in San Francisco, the entire day's discussions boiled down to one basic recommendation: Join a writers group. Do whatever it takes to get together with writers who critique one another's work.

One speaker flipped back the covers on a variety of books quoting authors who gratefully acknowledged their writer's groups and workshops. She then went on to tell a story about Nobel Prize winner Toni Morrison, whose novels changed the world for millions of readers. Stifled in her marriage and miserable as an English instructor, Morrison first began writing fiction in her spare time. Privately, she searched for and found a writers group. The members encouraged her to bring a sample of her fiction to a meeting. She hurriedly jotted down a quick short story that eventually became the initial manuscript of her first novel, *The Bluest Eye*.

The speaker went on to say that Amy Tan credited a writers group for helping her with *The Joy Luck Club* and that science fantasy author Karen Joy Fowler still meets with her group regularly in Davis, California. Even Molly Giles, the author of *Rough Translations* and a Pulitzer Prize nominee endorses and supports writers groups, even though she believes that writing cannot be taught.

In the flurry of questions and answers that followed, it was evident that a good many of the writers present at the conference had never worked in a writers group and were eager to know more about them. Although many had positive experiences with a semester or two of creative writing classes, they wanted something more intimate and ongoing.

Those who had been in writers groups spoke about the satisfaction that comes when writers band together against the isolation of their craft. They wanted to find and join other writers like themselves so that they could obtain regular evaluation of their work and some form of recognition for their efforts.

Hands shot up everywhere. Questions were fired at the panel. How do I find a group that's already established? How do I form a new one? What makes a group good? What do I have to do or be in order to join a group? What should I expect from the group? What will the group want from me? The panel was overwhelmed. The writers wanted to know what school didn't teach them, but the conference came to an end with many of those questions still unanswered.

1.1   *You Are Not a Private Peculiarity*

I went home and investigated, beginning in the library. Articles geared to specific groups or workshops appear from time to time in writers periodicals, and listings of conferences and seminars are available here and there, but no one had gathered both articles and listings in one guide. In my research, I interviewed hundreds of writers. I queried my creative-writing students, I consulted fellow writers and colleagues, and I questioned strangers at conferences. The message remained constant. I learned that the majority of writers who are pleased with their writing output are currently participating in a group. Others who outgrew their groups or left when they disbanded are in the process of looking for new ones to serve their specific needs. Most writers produce more and write best when their efforts are nurtured and validated by other writers.

Writers today live in a transient society. Families are scattered across the country, and good friends who help us nurture our good feelings about ourselves sometimes move far away. The encouragement of others who care about what we are doing is vital to writers, who find themselves creating in isolation with scanty rewards for their effort.

We struggle with the absence of a support matrix as we look for validation. Self-help books and correspondence classes notwithstanding, when it comes to sharing our creative attempts, we don't want any more dealings with impersonal, bureaucratic enterprises. We want personal. We want small.

Writers groups are nothing new. Since the Renaissance, writers have banded together. They have sought out salonlike cultural and artistic forms. They depended on such sophisticated gatherings to present their latest poems or chapters, to meet other writers, patrons, and influential folk, and even to do some freestyle scintillation.

Many writers today—less glamorous perhaps, though not necessarily less talented—meet regularly in steadfast groups, or they move from one group to another, seeking out the one that serves them best. This can be quite a task because there are thousands of groups scattered about and isolated. The specific needs of writers change. A group that was once perfect may now be inappropriate. Group criteria evolve. As new members join and old members leave, the group dynamics adjust to accommodate the differences. There are various coalitions of writers who initially got together to put on events and work on cultural issues but ended up more like therapy sessions. There are other groups that adhere strictly to critiquing manuscripts in progress. This is why they formed, and this is what they do.

Judging by the general needs of everyone in our society as well as by the particular needs of writers, it appears that writers groups will continue to prosper. Almost everyone in this complicated, changing, and most uncertain world is reaching out for a sense of personal, individual identity, and creative people are finding one another. Writers don't have to be private peculiarities. They can become interdependent parts of unique, supportive communities.

1.2   Interdependence Is Not Dependence

Interdependence with other writers will not make you a writer, but it will spur you forward in a positive direction. Once you realize that no writers group can make you create, you will begin to develop interdependent relationships.

In a writers group, no one will force you to do anything. However, the opportunities for acknowledgment and validation abound. You get to decide how best to use the benefits of the group. Then you will not waste valuable energy in maintaining your independence, as you may have to do in other areas of your life. Nor will you tire yourself out trying not to give away your power and become dependent, as you may feel pressured to do elsewhere.

Interdependence is a choice that can only be made by independent people. It means that you recognize the resources and potentials of others in your group and work just as hard accessing these resources as you do sharing your own. It is through such interdependent participation that you receive the support and sense of belonging that participation in a writers group offers.

1.3   Joining Reinforces

If your purpose is to write right now, the support system of a writers group can get you started and keep you going. If you have set specific writing goals for yourself, the experience and knowledge of fellow group members can help you stay on track. Most important of all, if all you know is that you want to write, belonging to a group reinforces your decision.

Having the opportunity to meet regularly with people who reaffirm that your writing is worthwhile gives you consistent bolstering. When you join forces with other writers who want to make similar things happen, you improve your own chances of success remarkably. Tips and techniques are shared, marketing suggestions are meted out, and solutions to difficult writing problems are bandied. Inclusion and acceptance by other writers give you a stronger sense of yourself as a writer within a community of writers.

1.4 Dreams and Needs

All writers have dreams. All writers believe deep down that they have a unique gift, one that can make a difference. Yet for many writers, these dreams become shrouded in the frustrations and routines of daily life. Even those who have written for years and view their writing as a commercial venture, something to feed the family as well as ambition, can use the stimulation of other writers to keep them in touch with their deepest writing aspirations. Personal writing goals are often resurrected in writing groups. Dreams and special writing desires are brought to light and honored. Writers' needs are examined.

If you are just beginning to write, you are probably wrestling with beginnings. If you are pulling together a book, it's likely that you are getting deadlocked at certain stages along the way. If you are trying to get an article published, you are probably dealing with rejection. No matter what your level of development, it's likely that you are experiencing frustration and need help to figure out a way around your problem. Whether you are a gentle dabbler or muscled pro, it's vital to your growth that you understand your needs as a writer and be with others who understand them, too.

1.5 Renewed Creativity

Rushing about, struggling to pull your unique gifts together can make you very, very tired. It's quite common for writers to lose their focus and, consequently, their energy. When your creative energy wanes, you need to renew the tired animus. The best way is to place yourself among other writers who can help you not only weather the creative storm, but recover. How much you have written, are writing, or intend to write is irrelevant.

Maybe you've written nothing much, but now want to get serious. Perhaps you've been dabbling with a writing project most of your life, and now you'd like to wrap it up. You may want to write simply to express yourself and make sense of it all. If you have had to delay your writing, keeping it as a secondary interest seldom tapped until now, you may be keenly aware of how weak your imaginative faculty has become through inaction.

Know this. It can be renewed. Just as a damaged lizard grows new limbs, you can regenerate your imagination. The process involves touching your creative energy with other creative energy. There are all kinds of active and fertile minds out there that can help you. The force that revives imagination is incredibly contagious. When you are around people who are busy manipulating language to express their own evolving thoughts and ideas, you almost automatically become motivated to get your own ideas out there, too.

1.6   Reassurance

The cold criticism that accompanies some rejections, not to mention the social cynicism that grates on nonpublishing writers, can scrape off a bit of your skin now and then, making you raw. At these times, you can use your group to insulate yourself against the skepticism of so-called friends and the ridicule of nonfriends.

The writing life can take some tough twists and turns. Other writers will appreciate how hard you tried to win a writing competition or how long it took to get a piece published. They will comfort you when you get a cranky rejection letter or an unfair evaluation. They understand. They feel with you.

We can all use a laugh now and then, not to mention a few undisguised blessings. Whether in a creative crisis or overflowing with ideas, you'll think you died and went to heaven when you get the right words of encouragement from your group. If you need nothing else, you'll need a friendly talking to from time to time. There are times when the lack of verbal encouragement can take a toll on the creative spirit. It needs occasional reassurance, and it needs a forum.

It is important for you to talk about writing with your peers, to have dialogues instead of silence or form letters. Rejection slips are not wildly informative. Teachers are overworked and inundated with paperwork. Editors are too busy and too tired. Friends and relatives who would be happy to read over what you've written are probably unqualified to discuss it.

1.7   Feedback

The best feedback available to writers comes from fellow writers. Even if you have been sharing what you write with a friend or family member and have every intention of continuing, if it is without excitement, gusto, or spirit, then you are ready for group critique. Other writers can appreciate your sensitivities and concerns. Tossing about opinions regarding what they admire and what needs to be improved can promote invigorating new ways of thinking and the confidence to pursue them. In such forums, the musings and reflections of one writer are magnified and clarified. Meaningful conversation, the blood of life, takes place.

The group is there to speak and listen to the individual. In especially effective groups, you are pushed to converse, to share your feelings and ideas. Even if usually you prefer to sit quietly in the background, when you participate in a writers group and share your work, you can't avoid eventually sticking in your big toe. Someone won't understand something, and you will find yourself speaking up to share what you know. You may disagree with the consensus and feel compelled to say what you believe. The more you do it, the easier it gets. Matters are tested and formulations questioned, but no one's feelings get hurt.

As everyone becomes more comfortable with delving into the conversation, they might discover that what was thought to be the issue wasn't. It wasn't what was written, it was the way it was written. Is it a good story? Did the poem work? Is this piece cultural criticism? Is it autobiographical? Does it intersect personal life and politics?

New perspectives are revealed. New ways of seeing current patterns emerge on the large loom of technical virtuosity. In fact, the dispersal of information inspired through fresh ways of interpretation and delivery is a basic function of writers groups. Questions to which there are no single answers expose you to a broad range of strategies and styles. They can introduce new facts, open your mind to new associations, and lead to new viewpoints on familiar issues.

Confident writing is rarely easy, even for the pros. However, the more options you have to choose from and the more you understand the reasons for your choices and their effects on readers, the more poised a writer you will become. This assurance is shown as improvement.

You begin to value your own opinion, a sufficient reason all by itself for joining a writers group. Ours is a culture and a time as rich in trash as in treasures, and sometimes it's a little hard to tell the difference. Listening to other discussions, pondering new information, and asking questions help you become more selective. You learn how to glean pertinent information and understand enough to formulate personal opinions and preferences. You can get enough data under your belt to draw confident and lively conclusions. You are pushed to think.

1.8   Healthy Mental Exercise

Mental health equates with mental exercise. Writers are fortunate in this respect. Aside from the fact that for some, writing is as restorative a form of venting as it is a tool for healing and problem solving, it is appreciated by most writers for the healthy mental exercise it provides. The whole process of writing is beneficial to ongoing brain fitness. If you are going to write, you have to think.

To say that a nerve cell creates thoughts may be true, but it is just as true to say that thinking creates nerve cells. In the case of new dendrites, it is the habit of thinking, remembering, and such mental activity that creates the new tissues. Writing with a purpose and then talking about your intentions in a group can be rejuvenating, especially if the discussion becomes animated and vigorous.

Sharing your written work also encourages you to present your thoughts in fresh, new ways, especially when other writers around you acknowledge your cleverness. Someone notices when you stop thinking linearly and start addressing concepts. You are applauded. You feel good. This prompts you to think things through more actively, which of course incites you to think more.

To rest is to rust (not my line, but it suits my message). Stimulating writers groups can keep your thinking processes from getting dull and sluggish. With your active attention to putting thoughts into spoken as well as written words, you not only learn new things, but you learn better how to better learn.

1.9   Learning Better How to Better Learn

In the fourth century B.C., Aristotle wrote a book called *The Rhetoric* in which he described the speech making of the great orators of Athens. Since then, generations of teachers have studied and tried to teach the findings of Aristotle without much success. This is because the act of learning how to do something is best learned by doing it. The best way to learn how to give speeches is to give them. The best way to learn how to write is to write.

Simply studying the craft of writing does not confer skill in writing. As a matter of fact, pedagogical studies have revealed that it is possible to act effectively without knowing the theory behind the action. It is possible to write beautifully without being able to explain the theory and technical skills utilized. It is through practice that you cultivate skill, and it is through feedback on how you apply your skills that you obtain a deeper understanding of the whole process. Feedback helps you learn better how to better learn.

Skills need to be shaped and sharpened. The various interactions of your group will train you to do this. For instance, you will alternate between a purposeful performer and an attentive listener. You will execute your work in clear and confident presentations, and you will listen in ways that help you differentiate between the marvel and the mud. Because everyone else does it matter-of-factly, you will get over being self-conscious about reading and discussing what you have written. You will develop a healthy attitude toward sharing your work, recognizing its value as a learning experience. Those who offer and those who receive constructive feedback all benefit by the process. You'll come to terms with the fact that it is not selfish or vainglorious to want to talk about what you are writing. Even if you sometimes feel a little guilty about all of the attention you are getting, you'll know that the feeling will pass.

When you challenge and are challenged by other writers, you continue and expand your education on a very personal level. Participation in a keen writers group not only broadens your horizons, but provides opportunities for new interests and intellectual growth. With every sentence you write, every use of feeling and imagination and intelligence, you learn something. Sharing the exercise with others who are doing the same thing only amplifies the learning experience.

1.10   Keeping Current

In fact, peer feedback may be just the thing you need to free yourself from sticky attachments to archaic language and old-fashioned styles. Working groups won't let you get mired down in what was once good enough. At least one of the members will challenge your rhyming *life* with *strife* or your poorly disguised rewrite of *Gone With the Wind*. Imitation, if not emulation or downright plagiarism, is confronted, as is doing what has already been done by the good old boys of bygone years.

You learn what you need to know today. You must keep up-to-date because the temper of the group discussions pushes you to stay informed on what is going on in the world. Exacting groups call for fresh-voiced manuscripts that reflect not only the current, but the future. What is ahead of its time? What is postmodern?

You'll find yourself reading more contemporary literature as well as current articles on the craft of writing and on publishing. You'll at least skim the surface of a few of the thousands of literary journals that illustrate what is being written today. Chances are that you'll read more than one how-to book and even tackle a writer primer or two. If you do explore these resources, it's more than likely that you'll eventually feel stranded in a blizzard of information.

This is where groups are invaluable. When writers pool their research data and share what they've gleaned from various publications, they can begin to sort and select the information. Suggestions and caveats regarding book clubs, subscriptions, and the various correspondence services offered to writers are deliberated. After hearing the experiences of others, you can opt for what seems will suit you best. You can also get the inside scoop on local creative-writing teachers and workshops and literature courses that may be of interest.

Writers groups are also a good place to find out more about typing or word processing. The group members who are familiar with today's technology will encourage you to join the twentieth century and use today's affordable tools. You can find out whatever you need to know (or find out where you might go for information) about computers, dedicated word processors, electronic typewriters, facsimile and photocopying machines, and other available technology.

Even groups with older members who are set in their ways will eventually succumb to the inevitable and bring in speakers to address such matters. Sidney Sheldon might dictate his books to his secretary, but the rest of us don't have such luxuries. We need all the help we can get.

Personal computers are coming down in price, increasing in memory and computing power, and more able to do complicated tasks than ever before. Why spend all morning rubbing two sticks together to make fire when automatic lighters are readily available?

The world is changing. Technology, once viewed as disempowering, has a new face—the face of a brilliant, energetic, and capable ally. An astute group can help reveal it to you. All kinds of resources are available within a writers group to help you further develop your craft.

1.11 Beginning to Write Irregularly, Regularly

To be a writer, you must write. When other writers are expecting to hear at the next meeting what you've written that week, you've got a compelling reason to get down to work. This is one of the most practical reasons for joining a group. Being accountable to other writers who are also accountable to you will keep you going. One of the most difficult things about writing is prioritizing the time for it. The key is motivation. When you are more ashamed of showing up empty-handed than you are of reading a rough draft, you are sufficiently motivated to belly up to your desk and write.

This is not to confuse writing a lot with writing well. It is to emphasize the need for impetus and your absolute cooperation and participation with it.

Creative souls that we are, we can conjure up incredibly legitimate reasons for not writing. We use all kinds of excuses—the ones that begin with "If only . . ." and "If it weren't for . . ." and "As soon as . . ."

If the other writers in your group haven't as yet been around the block, chances are that they've at least been nearby. They've heard it all. Only a death in the family, and it being yours, is a legitimate excuse for not writing. That is the subliminal message they'll give you.

One of the most gratifying side effects of being exposed to such attitudes is that you will find yourself writing not only when you feel inspired and inclined, but at other times, too. You may push yourself to write something down now for use at some future date. You might find that your ideas seem to wax and wane. Consequently, when you are on a roll, you should go with it so that later, when you lack even a shadow of an original thought, you can tap into these scribblings.

As rewarding as it may be when the ideas are gushing up and pouring all over the page all on their own accord, you can and should have some sort of control over the force of your creative flow. This dominion comes with practice.

Whatever the reason, you'll begin to experience the satisfaction that comes from spitting on your hands and getting busy. You'll learn to bring in stories and poems that are in progress.

Being stuck in a writer's block is a luxury only for those who plan to live a long, long time. The expectations of your writers group will help you get going. You will set priorities, simplify other tasks, and reorganize your time and energy to get more done. You'll do whatever it takes to create.

In your group, you'll share stories about what worked for other writers. For example, Willa Cather insisted on reading a passage from the Bible before sitting down to write. W. Somerset Maugham reread *Candide*. Thomas Wolfe and Johann Goethe enjoyed a long walk before writing, and Ernest Hemingway sharpened dozens of pencils before he sat down. Lev Tolstoy, Richard Wagner, and Henrik Ibsen discovered that they were most productive in sunny spring weather. Honoré de Balzac wrote on an early morning schedule because he wanted to take advantage of the fact that "my brain works while I sleep." Emily Dickinson worked at night in the dark when others in the house were in bed.

A member of your group might meditate first, another might exercise, and still another might need a hot bath. Find out what works for you. It might be immediate pen-to-paper scribbling.

Such freewriting, or stream-of-consciousness scrawling, works very well for many writers. Eventually, some of your words or phrases will start reaching out for new words. As you let it happen, one word will simply flow right into another. When you find yourself in a state of concentration that amounts to absolute absorption, keep going. Time seems to stand still when you are operating at peak performance. You might be expressing fragments, stanzas, paragraphs, or even chapters, but you will definitely be expressing. You started and kept going, all by yourself.

There are many ways to obtain this kind of flow in your writing. Knowing that you committed yourself to bring something in to the group on Tuesday will get you going. Once you've experienced a good flow, you will start looking for ways to grab it and hold it again. Like other writers who've discovered what best gets them started and keeps them going, you'll find yourself writing irregularly, regularly. When the circumstances are right for flow, whether you have an assigned deadline or not, you will find yourself using what works best for you to full advantage. Of course, this can happen without the influence of a writer's group, but it is easiest when your efforts are coaxed.

2

The Variety of Writers Gatherings

Participants in writers groups sometimes refer to their gatherings as salons or circles, sometimes as workshops. Some graded, accredited classes may refer to themselves as creative writing workshops. Seminars can refer to themselves as literary courses, which have been known to call themselves workshops. Workshops can refer to themselves as writers groups, and some of these call themselves clubs.

Are you getting a pattern here? Impossible to neatly compartmentalize, gatherings of writers call themselves whatever suits them. Interpretations of the terms applied to gatherings of writers can be and usually are stretched and compressed indefinitely. There are associations that also call themselves societies, leagues, or unions. There are guilds that are also fellowships, and alliances that are also confederations. Differentiating is as difficult as defining, especially between coalitions and conclaves and so on.

Among the larger congregations, there are international clubs and organizations that are jointly supported. They meet periodically, sometimes in conjunction with veteran organizations that refer to themselves as national societies of professional writers. There are also general organizations that dispense information and advocacy to writers. They serve writers in many different fields and at all stages of their careers, from beginners to seasoned professionals. Special-interest groups provide assistance and, in some cases, advocacy for a particular group of writers or for writers who share a specific interest. In addition, there are regional literary groups that focus their efforts on servicing writers in certain geographic areas. They may often be local branches of larger organizations. Sometimes, they gather in centers that provide information as well as conferences, workshops, seminars, readings, announcements, and resource-referral networking facilities.

On the smaller side, we find local clubs and groups of writers that meet informally to critique one another's work. Some are open to new members, and others are very selective, recruiting as they go. These groups can call themselves anything they please, and they do. How, then, do you know what is what? Let's begin with an overview of what you can observe.

2.1 Conferences

Also called conventions, conclaves, festivals, and forums, conferences are busy, highly energetic hives of activity, consisting of meetings that usually run from two to seven days. Some may be as brief as a single day, and others as long as four consecutive weeks. Workshops at conferences can range from full-day comprehensives to half-day and shorter intensives. The proceedings can include panel discussions with agents and publishers and editors as well as readings by published writers. Book fairs and literary exhibits are sometimes held along with signings and sales by participating authors.

Generally, there are ongoing lectures, which are often referred to as workshops. They can range in topic from craft to trends in manuscript publishing. Some put on excellent panel discussions among professionals who offer fresh insights, and questions from the auditorium floor can reveal new markets. Often, conferences invite potential attendees to enter competitions, awarding scholarships or discounted fees as prizes.

At some conferences, you can schedule a professional manuscript critique with an experienced, highly qualified writer or editor. There is often a charge for these private evaluations. Manuscripts are prescreened, and arrangements are made in advance. Many conferences offer workshop formats in which you work in small groups with a well-known writer or editor. Chances to meet with the guest writers as well as publishing professionals are often provided. They may be at group receptions or individual appointment sign-ups. Opportunities are also available at meal times or before and after in the lounge areas.

Most conferences offer double-occupancy rooms only and have no allowances for single quarters. If you don't already have a roommate, they may select one for you. Don't dismay. You might end up with a professional author or a workshop facilitator who will become one of the most important people in your life.

Quite often, writers who attend conferences go in groups of four to a room. This keeps the extemporaneous ambience up and the costs down.

You can spend less than $50 for a short session conference or more than $1,000 for a longer conference, plus room and board and travel expenses. The most expensive conference is not necessarily the best. Generally, the more you spend, the more personal attention you should expect, although this is not always the case. You may be paying high fees to compensate for expensive speakers who don't hang around once they've made their presentations. You may be paying for a luxurious location or lodging amenities. Then again, you may splurge, pay lots of money, stay in a tropical paradise, and interact socially and positively with the crème de la crème of the literary world. Make inquiries. Most conferences operate during the summer months, and details are available at no charge by requesting information from the sponsoring organization. Always do this.

It is a good idea to review the schedule carefully ahead of time. Some conferences have workshops that run one at a time, allowing you to go from one to another without missing anything. Others have two or more workshops going on simultaneously. You need to decide which workshops you really want to attend and which ones you feel you can miss this time around.

It helps to set some goals beforehand. Write them out in the notebook you will be taking with you. Concentrate on what matters most, and scribble yourself some questions in case you have the opportunity to ask firsthand. Carry this notebook with you everywhere, even to meals. You'll be coming up with so many new ideas and getting so much information that you'll forget half of it. Write everything down then and there. You can also have others write their names and addresses in your notebook for you.

The marvelous thing about conferences is that you don't really bother an editor or author. They are there for you, as are agents and publishers and teachers. It's a concentration of writing contacts. People are there to receive your ideas and give you immediate reactions and responses. It's not a bad idea to have cards to hand out as you connect with other writers, consultants, and miscellaneous freelancers in your field.

2.2   Writers Retreats

If making contacts isn't very important to you right now and getting down to the business of writing is, you might want to consider a writers retreat.

There are organizations that offer sites for writers who need to get away and do some dedicated writing without interference or distraction. Most are located out in the country, typically on the estate of a benefactor. Quite a few of them are receptive to unpublished or beginning writers. Such escapes are for writers who think they'll never get that book finished until they can have a rustic cabin in the quiet country with meals delivered on a tray. A jug of wine, a loaf of bread, and thou is replaced with a typewriter and a stack of paper and no phones, no television, and no interruptions.

Also called colonies, camps, and sanctuaries, these shelters may allow writers to participate in a residency or fellowship or to stay as a paying guest. Throughout the United States, writers colonies present unique writing environments that can range from mansions with formal gardens to commune-type camps and cabins. Some encourage interaction among the residents; others encourage quiet and solace.

Retreats are a standard fantasy of aspiring writers. Everyone deserves at least one shot at writing full-time in a setting that is conducive to great works, but be forewarned. Some writers must have a certain amount of communication and stimulation. Some need access to libraries. Some need to write from the life and color of a city. Beaches blow sand into disk drives. Woods teem with bugs that bite. Foreign surroundings can distract. Academic settings can homogenize raw expressions. Studies crammed with beautiful books and mementos can promote idleness and daydreaming.

Perhaps the best place for you to write is where you spend most of your time. "Going to sea is my salvation," said author Alex Haley, winner of a Pulitzer Prize special award for *Roots*. He taught himself to write during his twenty years at sea in the Coast Guard. "I become ravenous to get at this work, this writing I love so much."

Not everyone can put out to sea. Edmond Rostand, the author of *Cyrano de Bergerac*, claimed that he was reduced to writing in his bathtub because his social calendar kept him from his work. Raymond Carver took to his car to avoid interruptions.

Some people find it easier to concentrate when they have to block out other sounds. They play the radio or listen to the taped sounds of babbling brooks or ocean surf. Ernest Hemingway and William Saroyan did much of their earlier writing in restaurants in Paris and San Francisco, respectively. More than a few authors have been known to scribble down incredible ideas while riding subways or airplanes.

You probably have access to a college or public library, which is traditionally kept as quiet as traffic will permit. Most of the time, though, writers prefer a work space where they live. They may go out to connect with other writers, but they write at home, alone.

2.3   *Centers and Foundations*

For writers who cannot, or who have decided that they will not, take off for parts unknown, there are urban centers and foundations. These institutions, subsidized by government grants and donations from the private sector, provide networking and resource guidance for writers. They often operate as resource centers. If they do not provide what you are looking for, they can refer you to an organization that does or, at the very least, point you in the right direction. It is normally possible to become a member of any writers center for a small annual fee, but in some cases you need not be a member to make use of the center's services or to attend its programs and functions. These services might include the following:

- Newsletters (issued regularly, containing up-to-date market news and information as well as listings of literary events)

- Literary publications

- Book press

- Legal services (advocacy/grievance procedures to put the pressure on editors and publishers who aren't treating members properly; professional advice on contract negotiation, copyrights, etc.)

- Directory of members

- Referrals to
  —literary agents, attorneys, accountants, etc.
  —others seeking to hire writers or solicit manuscripts
  —editors, publishers
  —additional resource materials
  —other organizations and other writers

- Lectures, talks, classes, panels, seminars, workshops, conferences, classes

- Grants, fellowships

- Contests, ongoing literary competitions, annual awards

- Health, dental, life, and disability insurance plans

- Emergency loans for writers

- Open readings (published as well as unpublished authors reading from their works)

- Discounts on publications, office supplies, copy services, and computer rental/purchases

- Correspondence courses

- Savings plans

- Complete publishing services (including design, illustration, typesetting, printing, and binding)

- Pension plans
- Job listings for freelance writers, editors, researchers, and others in writing-related fields
- Income tax filing and consultation at reduced rates
- Credit unions
- College loan guarantees for members and their children
- Travel services
- Computerized record-keeping services
- Telephone information lines for business-related questions
- Support groups for manuscript criticism
- Libraries
- Reading rooms
- Sites for meetings
- Banquets, lunches, parties

Generally, centers provide requested information to any writer at no charge; however, some services will have fees. These services may be discounted or free to members and charged to the general public.

In addition to providing services, foundations represent a source of funding for writers. There are more than 3,000 foundations in the United States that fund writers in various fields and at various levels of accomplishment. They offer grants, honoraria, writer-in-residence fellowships, and colony residencies. The process is extremely competitive. Authors who apply for grants often have a work-in-progress or have been published in the past. A successful application requires planning, researching, writing proposals, filling out forms, and persevering.

2.4   Classes and Workshops

Writing classes and workshops are always available in the public and private sectors. It just takes a bit of looking around. They may be offered through private, academic, or public libraries, art centers, community groups, senior citizens organizations and centers, high schools, YMCAs and YWCAs, bookstores, literary cafes and bars, women's centers, and religious community centers. Classes and workshops are also offered by local published authors.

A huge variety of workshops, including graded and accredited classes of special interest to writers, is taught by community colleges and universities. Writing classes are most likely to be found in the English, creative writing, journalism, rhetoric, and composition departments, but they may also be found in other departments. For example, there may be a course in medical writing in the college of health, a course in technical writing in the school of engineering, or a course in script writing in the broadcast communications department. Private institutions also offer writing classes and seminars, as do alternative schools.

Most colleges and universities also offer noncredit classes through programs with umbrella names like adult education, community education and services, adventures in learning, lifelong learning, continuing education, adult enrichment, new college, elderhostel, and so on.

These sessions usually follow the academic calendar and meet according to prescribed class schedules. If you take a class, you will usually be assigned papers to turn in by a deadline. You may be graded and awarded college credits or earn a pass/fail or credit/no credit evaluation. You may have to buy books, read assigned texts, and demonstrate that you have done so. You will be expected to toe the line with regard to attendance and promptness. Writers gatherings are a little more formal in a classroom setting than huddled around someone's kitchen table, but they're still exciting if done right.

Even basic writing classes can be energetic if the instructor is so inclined. Real beginners may need to do a few exercises in composition classes just to get squared away on the differences between self-indulgent venting and expository prose. These classes are also great places for nonbeginners to brush up on punctuation and basic grammar rules. A good instructor will help you rid your work of clichés, run-on sentences, and overwritten paragraphs. It may not, though, occur to the instructor to discuss the commercial value of your work. Things like slants that aid in the reselling of a researched paper, editorial length requirements, and gearing your work toward specific readerships will be ignored. The primary goal in basic writing classes is to write it first and write it well. They will not emphasize marketing, but they will force you to write.

Adult courses in writing usually pay a little more attention to the business side of the profession, especially if the word *publication* is included in the course title. Practical as well as theoretical evaluations of work written elsewhere will take place. Everyone gets involved; no one is anonymous. Teachers do not read aloud bad or good examples of your work to make their point (as they may do in composition classes). Often, copies are made for each class member, and the instructor collects, corrects, and returns your original copy. The assignments require adherence to specified margins, format, length, and sometimes subject matter. Such classes also encourage you to rewrite what you have written. A main principle in many classes is that fine writing is almost always a result of rewriting—frequently many weary times.

Experiential creative writing workshops get students writing immediately in class. You do lots of exercises that encourage instantaneous and off-the-cuff thoughts and ideas. You bring your pen and notebook to class, and write like crazy. These techniques are designed to quell the inner critic. You may practice such exercises as clustering, a nonlinear brainstorming process; recurrence, a means of discovering a pattern in the clusters; creative tension, an exercise in learning how to connect opposite images to generate writing vitality; and revisioning, a selection process designed to sharpen your work.

Some experiential workshops issue no assignments, no research, and no required reading, and no one sees what you've written. You read aloud from the work you have just written. No papers are collected or returned, and you don't get to review red-inked corrections and suggestions from the instructor. Other experiential workshops include works brought in from home. Overall, experiential workshops appear under many descriptions that reflect the persuasions of the leader. They can be conservatively creative, engaging in freewriting, stream-of-consciousness exercises. Incorporating responses to suggestions, they get you to concentrate on capturing fleeting thoughts as they arise and to commit them immediately to paper. Usually, when we try to clutch fleeting and elusive ideas with the clumsy forceps of our mind, we crush them. Writing exercises that call for immediate written reactions enable this process. They are practice sessions. The writer discovers which mental muscles enable and which disable. In other words, lots of experimentation takes place.

If you have the funds, the ambition, and the academic preparation, university graduate programs offer marvelously sustained courses of study for writers. If you don't, you can still take advantage of nondegree programs and brief seminars. Many writers want a certified, accredited teacher. They like the feeling of being enrolled in academia. They work well under the extra pressure that the smell of chalk and pencil shavings evokes. They perform at their best when they feel that they must.

Classroom settings are not for everyone, however. Some writers associate school with stifling teachers and punishments. They inhale one whiff of chalk dust and sneeze it out like an allergic reaction to conformity. They rebel by never quite finishing the homework assignments, being habitually late, or consistently misunderstanding. Every request from the instructor falls as a death threat to their creativity. Instead of institutional instruction, they need their very own writers group, the kind that is right for them.

2.5 Writing-for-Publication Groups

The only thing more difficult than being a happy, contented writer is being a happy, contented, published writer. The road to publishing has high hills and deep valleys, and the efforts called for in this travel will at times be taxing. However, it will also empower you because you will be active, taking chances and putting yourself at risk. When you choose to publish, you are taking charge because the process of publishing is generated by the actions you yourself take.

To publish, you must develop productive habits. You must send out manuscripts. You should write more because you want to submit more and increase your chances. Getting published, like everything else in life, is more than timing and coincidence. It is usually the reward for working very hard, writing a lot, and submitting often.

Writers groups that focus on publishing insist that you become professional. Gone are the days when the joy of discovery for editors included wading through handwritten scratches on any available writing surfaces, coffee stains and cigarette burns included. There are recommended guidelines and formats for preparing a manuscript. The clean visual presentation of your work is vital.

You will learn how to keep track of your submissions. You will get used to reevaluating what you've written after it has been rejected. You will discern when and where to rewrite and when to stand by what you've written and leave it just as it is.

There is nothing wrong with receiving compensation for work provided, and you should surround yourself with writers who share this attitude. You don't want to be discouraged by those who have tried and failed and insist that there is a major conspiracy to keep the likes of you out of print. Nor do you need to hear how, even if you do get published, there are no guarantees that many people will ever read what you wrote. When you rebut this claim, you don't want to be accused of egotism. It is not vainglorious to want dearly to see your name in print. It is appropriate.

When you are ready to get published, don't deprive yourself of the support of other writers who also want to get published. Find a group whose main objective is to see every member's work in print.

2.6   Freelance Groups

If you are submitting what you write to publishers, magazines, or other publications, you are a freelance writer. This doesn't mean that you write for free. The term *freelancing* dates from the Crusades of the twelfth century when warrior knights who lost alliances with landed lords offered themselves as mercenaries—a lance for hire.

When you decide to stop giving your work away, you begin to freelance. You no longer donate the product of your skills because you know much too clearly that writing for free takes just as much effort and time as writing for pay. Like other professional writers, you are ready, willing, and able to accept any and all payments due you.

Jack London once said that he wrote for no other purpose than to "add to the beauty that now belongs to me." In other words, each book he wrote enabled him to add three or four hundred acres to his magnificent estate. As a matter of fact, he even wrote to Winston Churchill, H. G. Wells, and George Bernard Shaw asking how much they were paid for "their stuff."

Effective freelance groups assemble to help members with works-in-progress and marketing ideas. Manuscripts are read and critiqued, with an emphasis on their marketability. Members offer suggestions on matching your manuscript to the appropriate publication. Freelance groups often invite editors, publishers, and authors to luncheon meetings, and they organize car pools to book signings, conferences, and a variety of writing events. They not only help members prepare professional manuscripts, but they also offer personal tips on which publishers are buying what types of manuscripts. They pool their experiences and information.

Freelancers get lots of close calls; they are often among the top ten finalists in editorial screenings. They are also the recipients of lots of printed rejection forms. They sometimes need guidance in figuring out where to submit their work. Even published writers need help from time to time, especially if they get stuck submitting to the same publications over and over. No one is immune to rejection.

Freelancers love to share anecdotes about well-known writers. For instance, Ray Bradbury had stories rejected by *Weird Tales*. He turned around and sold them to *Harper's*. He had stories rejected by *Planet Stories* that he sold to *Mademoiselle*. It was a matter of progressing until the manuscript was placed.

Freelancers also like to recount success stories that show that persistence pays off. You might hear that Donn Pearce's novel *Cool Hand Luke* was turned down by almost fifty editors or that Irving Stone's *Lust for Life* was also rejected. Stone is virtually the inventor of the biographical novel. The reader's report for his book, buried in the files at Doubleday, reads a "long, dull novel about an artist."

It was in freelance groups that I learned how James Joyce's *Dubliners* was rejected twenty-two times; J. P. Donleavy's novel *The Ginger Man* was turned down thirty-six times; F. Scott Fitzgerald got more than 120 rejection slips for *This Side of Paradise*, Elmore Leonard's *The Big Bounce* was rejected eighty-four times before it was sold as a Gold Medal original and Warner Brothers made the film.

Groups that write for publication are usually quite familiar with the surprising number of markets hidden behind the visible big-name magazines. These include the little magazines of limited circulation, usually on literary or political subject matters. They also include alternative magazines directed toward individuals whose lifestyles or political or literary values differ from current establishment values. These noncommercial journals are underfinanced, often short-lived, and pay the writer in contributor copies only, but they give the amateur a chance. Their editorial staff actually reads what you submit and responds. These publications can range from crudely printed and stapled two-page fanzines to offset-printed, illustrated, and expensively bound volumes. Some are the result of writers groups that formed for the specific purpose of producing a small publication. Quite a few poetry journals are exceptionally beautiful in their presentation, both in layout and substance. Groups that focus on publishing will applaud your successful efforts, no matter how unorthodox or experimental the publication.

Freelance groups operate on the premise that the more often its members are published, the more successful the group and its individual members become.

Writers who want to get paid for what they write do more than their share of research. They work at maintaining a sense of what is appropriate for specific markets. They read *Publishers Weekly* and reports by the Book Industry Study Group. One group told me how they found statistics that tell how one in five Americans buys at least one book a week and studies that reveal that people eighteen to thirty-four buy 2.6 books a week and read them.

These writers keep up on trends because they intend to be part of the next wave of successful authors. They read publications that reflect what is current in our fast-paced society. What was "in" last year at this time may be "out" this year.

They study magazines. Which editors are giving which works to which readers? They examine specific markets for subjects, themes, treatments, lengths, and such. Which magazine editors want seasonal manuscripts five or six months in advance? What are readers reading now? Which are the most likely places to market your wares?

To keep their names out there and increase their list of published works, freelancers often write potboilers—works intended to keep the pot boiling while the writer works on bigger projects. Freelancers use group feedback to produce works written expressly for the purpose of making money right away. Some may be sold to large magazines, but most are submitted to smaller publications that pay minimally. Though such markets don't make them rich or get them nominated for Pulitzers, they do provide a forum for critical and editorial attention. The pay received for these fillers, short how-to articles, or seasonal pieces helps cover the expense of stamps and paper and printer ribbons.

Such publishing, if used properly, can parlay into a more than adequately successful writing career. Freelance income is irregular and uncertain. Major magazines, referred to as slicks because of their silky, slippery pages, do pay their writers quite well but don't buy an awful lot from freelancers.

2.7 Multiple-Service Writers Groups

Quite often, to bring in steadier income, freelance writers may offer multiple services, such as copywriting, technical writing, editing, proofreading, indexing, and so on. Such multiple-service writers often gather in groups to compare notes on marketing and job opportunities. Downsizing and mergers may cut staffs at businesses, publishing houses, and magazines, but as workloads increase, more employers look to freelancers to handle written communications. These writers often achieve enormous satisfaction in combining imagination with skill to produce written works that inform, sell, and entertain. Working freelancers live by the pen, rather than impale their hopes and dreams on it. They are writing specialists who apply their skills to meet the literary demands of our ever-changing world. Frequently a copywriter or public-relations specialist steps into literature. Because writers pursue other fields to augment their income doesn't mean that the novel will not eventually be written or the poems published. At a recent conference, I learned that Edna O'Brien was a licensed pharmacist who learned to write prescriptions. Cynthia Ozick was an advertising copywriter. Kurt Vonnegut wrote press releases. Wallace Stevens was an insurance executive who wrote business memos. Amy Tan wrote horoscopes. Joseph Heller wrote advertising copy. Danielle Steel and Judith Krantz wrote public-relations pieces. These examples all serve to show how freelancing can vary in its jumping-off points.

2.8   Poetry Groups

There are more poetry groups than any other kind of writers group. This is because the poetry of today represents a revolution in the expansion of language use. Today, poetry is the most controversial of all types of creative writing. You can expect anything and everything from the myriad poetry-writing groups out there.

For this reason, most poetry groups make room for all kinds of forms. Because many avant-garde and postmodern poets still enjoy the challenge of creating a tercet or ballade, it's not unusual to find poets gathering into groups within groups in poetry workshops.

Poetry groups usually give some consideration to getting published. After all, if you write poems, having them accepted helps convince you that you are right to believe in yourself. Just being published once in a while or winning an honorable mention in a contest from time to time can be incredibly encouraging.

A few major national magazines still feature poetry, but the competition is intense. The poets of today compete for space not only with their peers, but with the giants of the ages, as well. The couple of thousand smaller markets that do publish poetry are swamped with more than their staffs can comfortably read. Even if your poem is selected for publication, it may not be widely read, and chances are you won't receive any money, either. Nevertheless, having your work appear in a publication that also contains the work of a poet you admire is like finding money in the street. So are the congratulations your fellow group members will send your way.

Poetry groups are often the easiest to find and form; hundreds of people want to be poets. In fact, I believe that America is full of excellent poets who receive little if any notice. Luckily for the sake of our national poetry, through the staunch support of poetry groups, they persist.

2.9   Fiction Groups

There are many molds for fiction, many genres and styles and forms. The trick is finding a group that will support your way of telling a story.

There are probably as many ways of telling a story as there are reasons for telling them. We write stories to prove a point, teach a lesson, test an idea, solve a mystery, illustrate an idea, reveal a moral, tie or untie a knot, explain a puzzle, put to test an emotion or concept or instinct, and show how it alters under pressure. We write to show how we change or grow or learn or get lost or see the light or run away or stop wanting or die. We relate events in sequences. We want the way we tell our stories to be determined by the effects we want to leave with our readers.

Mainstream fiction uses conventional storytelling devices and is usually found on the best-seller lists. Experimental fiction shows more concern with form and structure and composition and literary style. Although essentially a work of the imagination, lots of fiction today incorporates large amounts of factual material. One can certainly understand why fiction writers so often divide into smaller groups when they meet. They may also divide into sub-groups of writers of mystery, romance, science fiction, Gothic, children's, fantasy, western, young adult, horror, historical, and confessional literature and so on.

These groups like to limit what goes on at the meeting by sticking to one category of fiction. They gather with their own because they are not interested in critiquing other kinds of writing.

Be clear about what fiction groups really are and what they are not. For instance, groups that focus on writing for children are not sweet little nannies hopping about like Mary Poppins. They are serious writers who are greatly concerned with the needs of their readers. In the bunny-eat-bunny world of children's books, the competition is fierce, and these groups spend a great deal of time examining appropriate formats for specific age groups. They study contemporary best-selling children's books and often bring in children's librarians and booksellers as guest speakers. These writers can be ruthlessly critical, especially if you bring in a story told to you by your mother and illustrated by your grandchild, expecting rave reviews. These world-weary writers have grown a bit impatient with attempt after attempt to jazz up Dr. Seuss or to see through the eyes of a wee mouse in the stable at Bethlehem.

Then again, there are groups of grandmothers and great-grandmothers who gather to share remembered stories and simply enjoy the nostalgia. Publishing is not a priority, pleasure is. The point is that categorizing a group in a specific way doesn't mean that it fits only that way.

Fiction-writing groups may include novel writers who share a chapter at a time from a book in progress or short-story writers. Storytellers may share one story at a time, either as it stands alone or as one from a collection of related stories. Amy Tan shared her best-selling *Joy Luck Club* in her writer's group as a series of short stories. It was later received by the reading public as a totally integrated novel.

When you gather with other fiction writers, you become very comfortable with other genres and methods of storytelling. You'll find yourself reading authors you ordinarily might have ignored, and you'll become especially familiar with what is being published today. From this, you can decide what you consider to be high-quality literature and what you consider to be rubbish. Some storytellers write in traditional styles; others tell stories in a contemporary style. There are also storytellers who find it difficult to get their arms around big stories. They feel more comfortable with sketches and slices-of-life and vignettes and short-short stories.

Within fiction groups, you can get a fairly clear notion as to the kinds of stories being written for today's publications and for the markets of the future. You get to expose yourself and everyone else in the group to what you believe to be fine storytelling. Then, of course, you chuck it all and write what you intended to write in the first place, and everyone else helps you pull it forth.

2.10 Nonfiction Groups

Most people equate writing groups with poems, stories, and novels, but there are also groups out there that zero in on expository writing. Their members include freelancers of magazine articles and authors of how-to books, essayists and biographers, and writers of creative nonfiction works in which real events are written in fiction form. Some members may be working on full-length books in the style of Norman Mailer or Hunter Thompson or developing a syndicated column of their own.

Adair Lara, columnist for the *San Francisco Chronicle*, facilitates her own exceptionally hardworking and effective writers workshop. I know this because she has used her ongoing column to share her group experience with her readers.

Exceptional nonfiction groups often have at least one columnist. Considering that the newspaper market is shrinking, columnists of today must be outstanding. If syndicated, they are committed, generally, for five years and need to sustain a long-term energy to bring to a 700-word weekly column. These writers will provide the sharpest, best-thought-through critique. It is in these groups that the demands for creative excellence remain steadfast.

Generally, nonfiction writers pull together essays. Some publications run essays as their usual cover story or lead feature. Most others run occasional essays on topics that are central to the publication's basic format. Many carry at least one essay as a regular feature, and most newspapers carry essays on their editorial and op-ed pages. Most magazine columns are regularly appearing essays of roughly the same length focused on the same range of subjects and topics that appear under the same title and author.

Some manuscripts are really personal essays, even though the writers may refer to them as stories. They may be anecdotes about fascinating, even horrifying, events, such as the death of a parent or child, drug abuse, cruelty, and so on. Because these stories are bound by the facts and do not allow for invention, it would serve these writers to share them in nonfiction critique groups.

Writers of the nonfiction that appears in magazines or newspapers are the bread-and-butter freelancers. These are the hardworking reporters who focus on research and getting the facts straight. They want clean, clear, concise language and have no time for poetic flourishes or purple prose. They depict how it really happened or how to do it, or they explain, warn, or advise. Typically, a question is asked and answered. Although they may express opinions freely, they do not invent.

Nonfiction groups are the most difficult to locate because writers of nonfiction are frequently hesitant about joining or forming groups, especially if they are publishing. They know when they are on track because their stuff is selling. When it isn't, they know they need to improve. Almost inherently astute and assured, they make fine group facilitators and teachers. They are also fascinating people.

2.11   On-line Writers Groups

Because being computer literate will probably be as important in the next decade or so as learning how to read, it's important that writers be familiar with the way writer's clubs are forming on the information superhighway. Not only are electronic magazines accepting e-mailed manuscripts, but information about book signings, readings, and conferences is readily accessible.

2.11.1 The Internet

All you need is a computer and a modem to connect to the Internet. This massive computer network allows you to share information with writers all over the world. As of this writing, the Internet has more than 30 million users and is growing at a rate of well over a million users per month.

The Internet is relatively easy to visit. Even if you are not fortunate enough to have Internet access through your business or school, there is a range of providers and many large user-friendly on-line services that can provide access for a fee.

Perhaps the most compelling reason for writers to enter the Internet is the opportunity to join writers groups that know no geographical boundaries. Frequenting one or more forums on a regular basis helps you get to know other writers, and before long a sense of community develops, which is why these electronic groups are called virtual communities.

There are countless books on navigating the Internet, but for our purposes, here's just a thumbnail sketch introducing you to areas that you might find it worth your time to explore.

A newsgroup is a place where a writer can go to exchange messages with other writers who use the Internet. With roughly 5,000 different newsgroups of interest to the public, it may take you a while to locate the particular literary forums that mesh with your personal writing needs. In a live conference, participating writers converse "live" as a group (through their keyboards) or ask questions of a special guest, such as an author, editor, agent, or publisher. There are rarely any extra charges for joining a writers group on-line. You can get to know some of the forums and their participants by reading their message boards. On most services, each forum also has libraries of computer files related to the topic of the forum. You can browse through summaries of those files and download to your own computer the ones that interest you.

Open communities of writers already abound on local bulletin-board services as well as on international commercial ones. Writers feel free to post questions in public with the hope that another member has an answer. They also air their complaints and cautions and post recommendations and suggestions for other writers to consider in their literary dealings.

Electronic mail (e-mail) sent to another person on the Internet is an alternative to posting messages in newsgroups if what you want to post is semiprivate. It's faster than "snailmail" (the U.S. Postal Service) and cheaper than a phone call, but it sometimes involves delayed connections.

2.11.2 America Online and CompuServe

There are countless commercial services to take you from your keyboard to the writers and their offerings on the Internet. You'll need to do a little research to find the one that is the most appropriate for you; however, you can use the results of my own investigation as a starting point.

As of this writing, two of the larger on-line services provide easy, extremely user-friendly access to their own writers clubs, as well as providing access to the Internet. America Online has a large community of writers who range from amateurs who are just starting out to authors on the *New York*

Times Bestseller List, and the club hosts and moderators are bringing in various publishers, editors, agents, and magazines as they expand further. America Online currently offers thirty-four writing-related workshops and chats, each with a completely different format. Some critique work, some have open topics, some have guest speakers, some have specific topics, and some have a combination of those. They provide feedback, information, motivation, and the thing that a lot of writers crave: the knowledge that they're not alone in a sometimes solitary occupation.

America Online also has more than twelve message boards that writers use for networking, conversation, and sharing information, and nine libraries, each with thousands of files, especially how-to resources, information about legal issues, and information from writer's unions and organizations. The Business of Writing area contains copyright information; the Genre Information area contains information on various genres and even has a mentor program. The reference area contains an extensive listing of Internet World Wide Web sites for writers (publishers, magazines, book resources). America Online also has a Meet the Writers area where writers can upload biographies and pictures of themselves. In This Month in the Writers Club, different authors are interviewed.

Another large on-line service, CompuServe, has an area for writers that is composed of three forums. The Literary Forum is primarily geared toward reading and the discussion of reading. The Writers Forum is for both experienced, established writers and hopefuls who are still learning their craft. This forum hosts several workshops that cover everything from poetry to film to short fiction to novels. They also have Art of Writing and Criticism sections for the in-depth examination of what writing is all about. Every genre is represented. For instance, a horror special may be going on one month, featured mystery writers may be available in both the Writers Forum and the Literary Forum, and a romance writer may be featured in the Book Preview Forum. Even workshops in business writing are offered. Special features on such things as freedom of speech, where hosting authors with special expertise on the limits of the First Amendment as well as PEN representatives are hosted. Crossover forums are offered. For example, Book Preview and New Age worked together to do a conference on Deepak Chopra.

The Book Preview Forum is intended to help writers and publishers get out the word about new and forthcoming books. All three forums feature several writers.

This overview of the two major on-line services is not an exhausting compilation, but should serve as an example of what the on-line world has to offer writers.

If you've read this far, checking out on-line writers clubs will probably not be daunting for you. Go ahead and use the Internet or on-line services to tap into the thoughts and ideas of countless other writers in exciting new ways. You will hardly be disconnecting from the world; you will be reconnecting with it.

3

Group Expectations of You

When Dorothy Parker sat at the Algonquin Round Table with the most sophisticated literati of New York City, there were unwritten though well-heeded group expectations, just as there were when Jack London and his buddies discussed writing at the First and Last Chance Saloon on the Oakland, California, waterfront. Later, when Jack Kerouac, Lawrence Ferlinghetti, and Allen Ginsberg gathered with other Beat writers in their North Beach, San Francisco, hangouts, subtle guidelines were adhered to and implied rules were followed.

These writers united to share information, to challenge one another, to correct their work, and to bond. In keeping with the traditions and courtesies of the salons, they abided with regulations that served to elevate the level of discourse among the participants. They knew what they were getting into, and they agreed to venture onward. You should, too.

3.1   Standards

When you enter a group of writers, you also enter a group of standards. As long as they don't hinder your healthy motivation, you will actually find that recognized peripheries are extremely advantageous to work within. A certain amount of structure serves as a hedge against the bedlam that can occur in groups that are too open-ended in their free-fall sessions.

Some behaviors are in order, and some are not. It all depends on the group's standards. Classes are usually fairly quick and clear about setting guidelines. The instructor uses the first class to explain what is desired of each student and what is going to happen during the sessions. A syllabus or handout is often given to each student. Everyone knows what is expected.

Large writers gatherings, though informally conducted, often establish ground rules with a written set of bylaws. These keep the club or association on track, set its mode of operation, define its goals, and establish its calendar.

3.2   Bylaws

The bylaws of some groups call for screening prospective members to determine their dedication to writing and voting on their admittance. Others state their aims—that is, to develop new writers or enhance the careers of experienced ones. Some ask that checklists and commentary guidelines be given to members who will be evaluating the manuscripts of others. Some bylaws call for mandatory attendance of at least 75 percent of the meetings each year. Even smoking restrictions and coffee-break limitations are implemented in some bylaws. From laid-back to uptight, each group encourages some behaviors and discourages others to reinforce a solid foundation for legitimate group principles.

Some bylaws are written down and passed around. They may establish an orderly process for members to read their works. They may limit the page length of manuscripts and sometimes even the amount of time to be spent on each person. Some ask for the prior distribution of photocopies or plot summaries. Some groups feel that these procedures save time and allow for more detailed and precise feedback. Others find that making copies and passing out papers is too much bother. They work at listening and look toward instinctive and instantaneous responses. Readers may be asked to read their work twice or repeat certain passages, but that is how the group prefers the process. When it comes to critique, some groups require verbal comments, and others written. Some tolerate excited outbursts and interruptions over interruptions. Others want members calmly to take a turn and raise a hand to be acknowledged before speaking.

Most small groups are very flexible and prefer not to feel straitjacketed by such documented agreements. They do not operate according to *Robert's Rules of Order*. No sergeant at arms controls rowdy or disorganized outbursts, no secretary takes minutes, and no esteemed chairperson controls the discussions. Nevertheless, agreements do exist, even if through some kind of telepathic groupthink. A practical format is applied, and it is one that generates the kind of result that the group has agreed to work toward. Some person or some thing is directing traffic.

3.3 Agreements

Whether they are stated orally, written as handouts, or mystically drifting about like dust on sunbeams, agreements exist in every group. Any visitor can quickly pick up on unwritten rules and regulations through observing the behavior of the group members. To figure out precisely what rules your group follows, you can ask questions. You can verify what you strongly suspect, and you can draw conclusions.

It's up to you to know what consensus you are entering. It's also up to you to enter only into contracts that you plan to keep.

Any agreement you enter into with your group is really made within yourself. You include other people. You give your word, one of the most precious things you own. Don't give it lightly. Work at keeping it, too. You are accountable for your actions. Avoid statements like "I didn't know" or "No one told me." These are lame excuses. Don't waste everyone's time trying to talk yourself out of what your behavior has gotten you into. Worse, don't try to shift blame if you get an assignment wrong or forget to check on something you told the group you would. Everyone knows that you, like them, are creatively driven, especially when it comes to inventing reasons for not keeping your word. Don't "bend" the rules of the agreement. You know what it is you agreed to; keep your word.

Joining a group means that you agree to be there. Your presence, the physical placing of your body within the realm of the group, goes without saying, but staying there when the ride gets bumpy is part of the agreement, too.

Leaving early because the group is not going as you wished, or not showing up because someone said something you didn't like last time or because no one said anything that you did like, is reneging on your promise. Just because everything isn't going the way you would prefer, don't get up and leave. This is running away from any possible resolution. If you do leave in a dither, don't expect anyone to come after you. The correct thing for your fellow writers to do is to allow you time to think things over so that you can return when you are ready.

The main purpose of group agreements is to sustain all of the opportunities for optimum creativity. They address rational approaches to civility, consideration, and clear communication.

Agreements are not meant as an inflexible system of rules that insist on strict adherence. Based on common sense, they are merely ground rules to ensure harmony in group logistics.

3.4   Commonsense Courtesies

The unwritten bylaws of successful writers groups include attitudes and actions that manifest themselves as well-mannered behavior. Remember that we communicate through our behavior as well as through language.

Everyone not only appreciates being treated with courtesy, but is entitled to it. Even though energy runs like wildfire within the confines of a writers group, graciousness refreshes. Little splashes of "please" and "thanks" and "excuse me" are like sprinkles of monastic rose water.

A more important courteous practice is your consistent presence and punctuality. Try to schedule travel and special events around your meetings. When you miss more than one or two meetings, many significant interchanges can occur in your absence. It may be impossible to clue you in adequately when you return. In effect, when you reenter, it may be like joining a new group.

If you know ahead of time that you are going to be absent or late or will have to leave early, let the group leader or someone in the group know. You can explain the reason for your absence or just say, "Something has come up."

Punctuality is also critical. A member's late entry is extremely disruptive to the flow of the group process. It's especially unsettling to have someone stroll in late jabbering excuses with a thermos of coffee and something scribbled frantically that morning. Courtesy dictates that if you must be late, enter quietly and don't let the door slam behind you. Finally, it offends others who have invested time and care in editing and rewriting their work to have someone else expect the same attention for something hastily thrown together.

3.5   Communicate

The fact that you bring your physical presence to the group indicates that you agree to communicate your thoughts with its members. You know that you are not much good to yourself if all you do is sit like a toad on a log. You are not much good to others, nor will they send much goodness your way, if the only time you participate is when the discussion focuses on your work. Good group communication involves giving and receiving. This means talking as well as listening.

Researchers have concluded that human beings communicate with one another for three reasons: to meet existence needs, to fulfill relatedness needs, and to achieve growth needs. As a writer communicating with other writers in your group, you are doing so for the same reasons. Communication validates your existence as a writer, fulfills your need to relate to other writers, and helps your creativity grow.

Effective group communication requires industrious discourse, not lazy gossip or repeated drivel. There is no room for such jabber and babble in writers groups. All too often, the very people who annoy the group most this way haven't a clue that they are being rude. Be sure that you aren't among the guilty ones in your group. You are expected to watch yourself that you don't babble without thinking. A red flag should go up if you find yourself always having something, anything, even if irrelevant, to say or to tack on each time someone else finishes. Such self-referential digressions might be prefaced with "That reminds me of the time when . . ." or "I'll never forget when . . ."

References to movies or media entertainment, unless directly related to the discussion or a book of group interest, should be kept to a minimum. This is a writing group. The written word is the focus. Save vacation photographs and gossip about Liz Taylor's new husband for break time. If someone else wants to know if anyone caught so and so doing such and such last night on the boob tube, politely avoid contributing to the discussion.

3.6   Always Speak to the Group as a Whole

Any form of whispering in a group is rude. Resist all temptations to converse privately with the person sitting next to you. Actively participating in a writers group means communicating with the group as a whole at all times.

Talking behind your hand, rolling your eyes in a "here we go again" expression, passing notes, sighing heavily, or falling in sudden dramatic slumps when someone aggravates you doesn't serve anyone. Furthermore, it makes you appear not only out of control, but bad mannered. A comment that draws the attention back to the task at hand is not only polite, but always appropriate. You are expected not only to communicate, but also to help ensure the communication flow within your group. This means speaking up when the talk is unclear or seems convoluted and you are tempted to nudge the person next to you to repeat or explain what was just said.

If you don't understand something being discussed, wait until there is a pause, then be sure to ask your question. Don't jump the gun, though. Remember, listeners listen faster than talkers can talk. Too often, as a person is in the process of explaining something, he or she is interrupted by someone who isn't paying full attention. The question asked is the precise question that is being addressed.

3.7   Focus on the Work

When you join a writers group, you agree to discuss writing and matters that pertain to writing. This is where it gets difficult. Being the social beings that we are, someone will inevitably have a stand to take or a premise to share regarding what was proclaimed or insinuated in someone's written work. Try very hard not to be sucked into this kind of vortex.

Don't get caught up in the energy of rhetorical questions. These are comments spoken in a question format to which the speaker already knows the answer. Rhetorical questions are often used to reroute the discussion or to include verbal exclamation points. Although sometimes effective, when overdone, such blatant manipulation becomes maddening. It cheats the group out of precious time.

Comment not on how you feel about what was written, but instead about the manner and style and voice used in the writing. Otherwise, those mischievous elves of religion, politics, and sex will tease up quarrels that are of no help at all to the writer.

Keep in mind that you are all there to focus on the work being done, not on what is yet to come. Asking the group for opinions about what you are thinking about doing is a waste of time. Write it first, then ask the group to deliberate about what you have written. It's been proved that talking about future projects deenergizes the impetus. It depletes the energy needed to sustain the effort.

Focus on the work calls for greater considerations than casual speaking elsewhere. During a critique, train yourself to take in what someone else has to say without protecting your position or surrendering your opinion. Listen without worrying about what you are going to say when your turn comes. Listen without being preoccupied with devising a rebuttal or formulating a correction. Pay attention to what is being said about the work-in-progress.

Apply prudence when it comes to speaking about your own work. Don't jump right in to defend it. If you feel that others weren't listening carefully enough, pause before you accuse them of missing the point. Consider the possibility that if your group did, in fact, miss the point, then it wasn't made well enough in the first place.

3.8   Self-disclose

Sometimes, a few words to the group about your state of mind is not only appropriate, but necessary. Learning something new about you can help your fellow writers bring added dimension to their feedback.

When you disclose personal things about yourself to the group, be brief, but also be candid. This is where aimless rambling gets cut, and honest statements are formed. There are times when you should confess, especially if you are vacillating.

For instance, being emotionally off-kilter can make you mentally tired. These are times when it takes extraordinary effort simply to drag yourself to the group meeting. You are there physically, but not spiritually. Perhaps your personal life is in crisis and you didn't bring any writing to share, but you feel that you need to get out and be with the group anyway. You simply want to be there to get away momentarily from the chaos in your life. Tell the group.

Tell it once, and tell it succinctly. Don't dwell on it. Allow the group to carry on. Not only will they value your honesty, but they will recognize the fine compliment they've just been paid. They will also appreciate the valuable time that could have been wasted in second-guessing your reluctance to participate.

You may sometimes want to stay away from a meeting because you haven't yet completed the assignment. You may feel that your latest attempt will not measure up. You may be a bit gun-shy because last time the criticism got a little rough. Understand that although your unwillingness to experience discomfort is perfectly normal, you should work through it. Bring your incomplete work or, better yet, what you wrote in your struggle to write it. Bring what you feel insecure about. Ask the group to listen carefully to your dialogue or rhyme scheme or whatever is giving you trouble. If you want it, ask for advice regarding technique or style. If you feel deeply about a piece in progress and don't want it dissected just yet, say so. Sooner or later, because what you wrote cost you emotionally, lumps will catch in your throat as you read. Go with it. Let your voice tremble, let the tears run down your face as they come. It's normal and nothing to be ashamed of. Don't let it get in the way of your reading. Keep going. Tell the group that you prefer to let it stand for now as it is. Claim that right. Remember that although it may sometimes not seem that way, you are gathering with writers, not mind readers.

3.9 Present Your Work

Even the most informal of groups expect a minimum amount of presentation. Bring plenty of pens and pencils and plenty of paper to scribble notes on if you are the note-taking kind. Bring your glasses if you wear them and a hearing aid if you use one and tissues if you have a cold. If you are supposed to bring your folder to each meeting, bring it. If you are supposed to have enough copies of your work to distribute, have them neatly sorted and fastened together if necessary. If the group asks for typed papers, type yours. It doesn't matter that Jackie Collins, after twenty years and twelve books, still writes her stuff in longhand. Nor does it make any difference that John Steinbeck used round pencils that were sent him by his editor because hexagonal pencils cut his fingers after a long day. They are not in your group. In fact, even if handwritten work is accepted, do try to type it anyway, especially if you find yourself stumbling over your own handwriting.

Control how your work looks on the page. Last-minute editing is okay, but don't pass out your work with a mess of type-overs and smeared corrections and globs of correction fluid. Don't get cutesy with calligraphy or colored stationery or decorating your work with drawings or stickers. These are most distracting. Be professional. When readers have a clean copy of your words in their hands, they are more inclined to give you detailed and precise responses. Finally, don't put that little copyright circle on your pages. It only shows how little you understand of the copyright process, and it suggests a suspicion that everyone is out to steal your manuscript.

Do whatever it takes to get the most out of your turn. Heed the sound of your own voice as you read your work aloud. The silent scanning of the written page does not allow you to pick up the much-too-long, overly complex sentences. Reading aloud will cause you to run out of breath if your punctuation needs some work. You will also hear the choppy sound of incomplete sentences and staccato phrases. Another key element brought out by reading your own work aloud is dialogue. If you find yourself stumbling over the way one of your characters is speaking, you'll know there is something stilted and unnatural to be smoothed out. What I have always found fascinating is that when I falter at a certain spot when reading aloud to the group, the group is usually having a difficult time with that section, also. It's as though the voice rejects what the speaker inherently knows is clumsy.

When it's your turn to read, jump right in and read. Prefacing your work with excuses or apologies just takes up precious time that could and should be used in getting valuable reactions. For example, telling everyone else what terrific writers they are and what an awful one you are doesn't serve anyone. Asking in advance for mercy and compassion may seem appealing and cute, but it doesn't fool the other writers, who know what is going on. No one wants to hear dissertations beforehand. The fact that you don't think your work is any good or that you've had out-of-town guests all week is not pertinent. Simply said, if your work is not ready to be read, don't read it. If it is ready, then get right to it.

Trust in the premise that every group member is there to work on manuscripts that aren't perfect yet. The perfect paper to share with your group is one that you know is imperfect.

Once you begin to read, continue until you get to the end. Attend to the tone and pitch of your voice. Don't stop at some point to clarify something for the listeners. This is an indication that you are allowing yourself to tell only the shadows of what you really mean to say. It means that you are leaving out the substance. Although it's quite acceptable to pause or chuckle or even sigh, it's never okay to cut in on your own work. If it needs to be said, then it should have been written into the piece in the first place. Remember the advice of industrialist Henry J. Kaiser: "When your work speaks for itself, don't interrupt."

Don't be long-winded, trying to take more time or get more attention by prefacing your work with lengthy explanations or adding on definitions or elaborations at the end. When you've finished, put down the manuscript, and wait patiently and silently for responses. Sit still and look up calmly.

Don't correct yourself or explain what you really meant to say or ask the group if they "got it." If anything is to be "got," it's you getting what you came for. Open up, and don't hinder the process.

The way that you present your work will be the way that it is received.

3.10 Pay Attention to Other Works

If you are like everyone else in the group, you anxiously await your turn to receive a critique of your work. There will be times when another person seems to go on and on. Other times, it seems that everyone is thoughtlessly discussing what seems to be totally inconsequential. Someone who just doesn't get what is being said is arguing with someone who's got it all wrong in the first place, and you find yourself internally heaving and sighing. Why don't they just get on with it, you wonder. Why don't they cut the drivel and get on to you, you ask yourself.

Although perfectly understandable, giving in to such impatience stops you from listening. A most profound discipline learned in writers groups is the art of actively listening to others. If you pay attention only to what is directed specifically at you, you are only getting a fraction of what the group has to offer. One of the chief ways to develop insights into your own work is to see what does and doesn't work in other people's writing. You can learn to recognize subtle and insidious flaws with which you, too, have been struggling. In fact, sometimes the criticism being offered to someone else will hold the solution to something you've been grappling with on your own. You obtain valuable insights into your own works by hearing what does and doesn't work in the writing of others. Explanations and examples will teach you more thoroughly than any textbook or lecture.

You will need to discipline yourself and ignore all of that superficial mental chatter that is competing for your attention.

You should be able to listen without displaying complaint, resentment, or resistance. You should be able to listen attentively while also looking around and observing the reactions of others. This is called "listening by eye."

Distinguish between various body languages. You will spot behavior that reveals more than it conceals in its subtleties. This is important because when you read your work aloud, you should be able to identify interest as well as boredom in your listeners. Notice how group members position themselves when listening to a piece that is much too long or has become redundant. Learn how to read their reactions so that one day, should it happen while you are reading, you will know to stop. Are listeners doodling or fiddling with pens or rearranging paperwork or reorganizing folders? Is someone nodding off? How many are staring at the floor or out the window? Observe and discern so that you can spot such signs when your turn comes.

Sit quietly, like a guest, as you pay attention. Active listening involves patience, openness, and the desire to understand what is going on. As you listen to another human being express his or her ideas, what you are hearing is part matter and part spirit; part thing and part thought. When you realize this, you can more fully appreciate the difficulty and importance of the task.

3.11   Brush Up on Basics

There are general principles of writing and specific difficulties that writers encounter. You must understand the conventional rules of our written language, even if you want to write in unconventional ways.

Your group will expect you to have developed a certain familiarity with basic writing skills, even though not one of them is likely to exclaim that you punctuate like an angel. Neither will you be singled out for special praise because you always know where apostrophes should go. However, if you don't know that periods and commas go inside the quotation marks, you can sabotage an entire sentence. Even worse, you can produce such a distracting paper that is so fraught with mixed metaphor or inconsistent tense jumps that what you are saying gets lost in the chaos.

If your writers group is efficient, the members will help you concentrate on these matters. They will deal with universal writing problems, pointing out mistakes that are commonly made by novices and issuing tips on how experienced writers avoid them. Group discussions will call attention to language usage, the rules of grammar, accepted Standard English, and the exceptions to these rules. You will find yourself looking things up or calling others in the group to be sure about the placement of this or the insertion of that.

Don't expect your group to be a remedial English class, though. It's up to you to master certain basic rules. If you need to brush up, you can take a composition class as a refresher or even browse through an English primer from time to time.

The more adept you become with craft-related skills, the more astute a reader and listener you will become. Your opinions will be requested and appreciated as you find yourself recognizing and identifying the weaknesses and strengths in the works of others.

Of course, as you experiment with writing about familiar things in new ways, you will inevitably discover that somehow, somewhere along the line you've developed some very bad habits of your own. Consequently, you will find yourself checking your own work much more carefully than you did before. You will also find yourself questioning someone else's suggestion or correction of your work. Your confidence will be sharpened, and you won't be as afraid as you once were to declare your opinion. Like others in the group, you will examine and argue and shake your head and become quite comfortable with being uncomfortable as you assure one another that there is no fixed, perfect, all-occasion model for writing.

Give yourself time to reach this point. If you haven't been paying attention to the basic rules of Standard English for some time, your writing may be a bit amateurish at the beginning. However, as you proceed, if you work at it, you will become quite adept. It's a matter of practice. You learn as you go. When writers gather to improve their work, they are always on the alert for misunderstandings over words, definitions, and rules. They frequently redefine key or controversial terms. You can ask for help with transitions, flashbacks, viewpoint, characterization, motivation, beginnings and endings, and any terminology that you don't understand. Almost through osmosis, listening to others discuss such matters will help you identify certain usages.

3.12 Your Expectations of the Group

What you expect from your group should be in harmony with what the group expects from you. Expectation is a puzzling phenomenon; it can both enlarge and diminish your experience of the group and vice versa. A writers group cannot give you something now that can only be yours in the future. It can, however, help you see what is available to you today. It cannot give you talent, but it can help you recognize your hidden gifts.

Don't expect what is, in itself, conflicted. One of the most destructive beliefs that writers sometimes bring to a writers group is the myth that you can have it all.

You cannot have it all. You cannot be at home writing while you are listening to someone else in the group. You cannot be physically in two places at once. You cannot go back and attend that workshop you now feel would have been most beneficial. You cannot reverse time.

You can only write the best that you can in the time you have to do it. Some days are better than others. The group will not teach you how to produce a masterpiece every time you write. The group will not make you a successful author. You cannot expect the group to make you into something you have not decided you will be. You cannot have it all.

You can have what matters, though. Before you enter a group, you should understand clearly what you want to gain from the group experience. What matters to you? Unless you seriously attempt to identify your own goals, your chances of gaining significantly from the group are diminished.

3.13   Different Group Synergies

What you want to see in a writers group, no matter the size or defining label, is evidence that group members are working together. You want to see synchronized energy, otherwise known as synergy.

The thing that manifests when the group interacts is the synergy, the persona of the group. Synergy is what makes groups what they are. You will hear some writers speak of their group support with what is akin to religious fervor, whereas others refer to group criticism as though it were a medieval torture. This is why some writers belong to more than one group. They attend whatever gathering fills the particular need of the moment and often alternate between very small, personal gatherings and larger, professionally conducted workshops.

Simply defined, *synergy* means that the whole is greater than the sum of its parts. The relationship that the parts have to each other is a part in and of itself. It is not only a part, but the most catalytic, the most empowering, the most unifying, the most exciting part—the part that may provide that one last push or shove you need.

There are aggressive and passive synergies. Those driven to creation (task-oriented) may meet next door to those being driven to recreation (social). Tough evaluations are given by groups that look for rapid improvement. Gentle treatments take place in groups that look for slow, sure growth.

There are groups rooted in traditional theories and beliefs. Some delve into consciousness-raising and are deeply guided by esoteric and spiritual modalities. Idealistic groups are often exceedingly serious. They operate on the premise that writers have responsibilities to share their talents in ways that enrich, enhance, and heal. Such groups often regard writing as therapy. They usually include a fair number of people who have suffered through the divorce mills, endured wretched childhoods, or survived horrible tragedies. Such groups provide vast amounts of sympathy and understanding.

Intense, high-impact groups usually form to experiment and try new techniques. They apply their craft energetically as they apply their zeal for reflecting the surrounding countercultures and subcultures. You'll find lots of poets here as well as activist prose writers. Sometimes, the energy ping-pongs so crazily that one wonders how anything at all gets done, but it does.

Writers groups that invite every genre of writer and validate every attempt based on its intent are the most adventurous, most electrifying groups. Anything goes, as long as it's related to writing and participants are encouraged to experiment with untried disciplines.

These are the ideal places to try out new forms that you've never dared to try before. Sharing original attempts with your group forces you to use different creative muscles, as does listening to the experiential efforts of your colleagues. Such exercises round you out as a writer and prevent your craft from becoming stale.

If your experience with your group encourages you to write in ways that make you feel good, it's probable that the group synergy is working with you. If you feel generally unproductive, the group synergy might be working against you. You need to find a group synergy that is harmonious with your creative temperament.

3.14 Small versus Large Groups

Large gatherings are the easiest to locate. They are visible and accessible conferences, workshops, one-day seminars, and the like. Through sponsored events that are open to the public, writers have the best chances to meet and chat with other writers. It is usually here that kindred spirits find one another, perhaps over a cup of coffee at the break or by sharing a table at lunch.

In ongoing workshops, larger groups can offer a sense of safety. Sitting in the last row of a church or synagogue hall or on a far bench in a park, you can get a feel for what is going on without having to become actively involved. Even large academic classes let you off the hook. If you are in a course with unlimited enrollment, you will probably never be called on to speak unless you raise your hand. If there are too many readers, there won't be much time for discussing anyone's work at any great length. At times, it may be difficult to see and hear everyone. This can get quite distressing. However, the buffering of bodies around you lets you hide if you want to. Larger groups have to focus on the work as it is, not on its potential. Due to time constraints alone, they must concentrate on the matter at hand and the writer who comes forth with it. If you are not yet ready to share, you can blend in as you venture slowly and shyly. When you want more, you'll know.

On the other hand, less is more. You'll get more individual attention in a smaller group. The smaller and more informal the group, the better it can help you improve. Smaller groups are not always easy to find, though, because so many of them gather in living rooms and kitchens in dozens of homes at any given time. Interestingly enough, most smaller groups are discovered through contacts with writers at gatherings of large groups. Here is where you can find out about the more intimate groups, where they are, and which ones are open to new members or, at least, will allow a visitor.

Some groups are closed to new members either because of sheer numbers or because participants have settled into a compatible mix. If your advances are spurned, don't take the group's disinterest in your interest as a personal rejection. It isn't. Some groups have been around for what seems like forever and allow new members to enter only when an old member exits. Accept their need to stay cloistered and look elsewhere.

It is also important to note, though, that so-called open groups that screen new members are not really open. They often require manuscripts to review, or they want to know where you've been published and what prizes or awards you've earned. Some will only allow new members to join if they are personally sponsored by a current group member. Others actually vote someone in or out. They have a definite membership and purpose.

Some groups don't know what they are about. They get together at random times, and although they will accept anyone, talk is the competitive activity. Stories are told, rather than presented as written works, and not much constructive criticism takes place. Such groups usually dwindle down to two or three members. Invariably, for each group that you find forming, another will be folding.

3.15   Group Tasks and Projects

Some groups work together to complete a group project. Whether the group formed for the performance of a single task or whether the project evolved as a sideline, the goal is the focus. For instance, some groups publish newsletters and rotate the duties. Members take turns at being editor, columnist, distributor, contributor, and so on. Everyone understands from hands-on experience the duties and responsibilities involved with each position.

There are even groups that form to publish an anthology to showcase the work of the members. The publication is a group effort. All expenses are shared, and care is taken so that all receive equal exposure. The major roles of anthology editor, publisher, layout artist, illustrator, and so on, are selected at the beginning of the project, and deadlines are firm.

Marketing-oriented groups compile and collect writers guidelines from various literary journals. They also collect sample magazines and copies of queries and cover letters that produced positive results.

Some groups share photocopying and fax machine privileges. They cooperate with other clubs and groups and work out reciprocal agreements where they join forces to obtain discounts at local print shops and office suppliers.

The most securely focused groups are those in which every individual member works toward the smooth functioning of the group as a whole. For instance, some groups conduct writing contests in which individual members learn how to initiate, coordinate, screen, judge, and award prizes. Experiencing the ins and outs of writing competitions firsthand makes members more confident and secure about entering other contests. They see how they can better fit into the larger writing scene.

3.16   Take a Chance

Once you have exacted what you want from your group experience, give that expectation a good shake. Open up to serendipity.

Get ready to expect the unexpected. Put yourself in a frame of mind to anticipate it. Actively court chance. Know that what you make of what happens to you in the group is precisely what you make of the random chances that arise within it.

Be prepared to change your mind. Don't get locked in. Nothing you decide should be carved in the proverbial granite. Your goals may change and revert and expand and shrink, but as long as you have them, your direction will be forward. Even if you are not sure about what you want, as long as you keep considering the options, a goal will eventually catch up with you.

In the interim, enjoy the camaraderie of other writers. This satisfaction alone is a commendable thing to want.

4

Receiving Criticism

The moment you share what you have written, you exhibit your ability to know and purvey what is interesting and what is not. It is possible to expose yourself as a fascinating thinker or total bore, or as Edna St. Vincent Millay so cleverly put it, "A person who publishes a book willfully appears before the populace with his pants down."

Writing calls on more than the ability to create words and ideas. It also requires the ability to decide which words and ideas to use and which to discard and how to shape what is left into something strong.

Most writers don't have the benefit of editors and agents to read their work regularly. Many either cannot afford or choose not to pay the substantial reading fees that qualified critics require, and all agree that form-letter rejection slips say nothing of worth. Even when comments are handwritten on the returned manuscript, too often they are accompanied with confessions of preconceived editorial preferences and whims. It's frustrating flying in the dark, especially when you know that one well-placed suggestion or opinion can turn on all the lights.

4.1   Group Manuscript Evaluation

Manuscript evaluation is one of the greatest services that a writers group can provide. It is through appraising and assessing works that breakthroughs occur. Whether from critics, colleagues, or readers in general, you will require appraisal from other people as long as you write. You can always use sincere and constructive assessment; otherwise, you will never cultivate an honesty about your work.

Unless you are exceptionally objective, you will never become ruthless enough to find all of the defects in your writing, and if you don't train yourself to receive critique in the spirit in which it is given, you will be deflecting incredible gifts shining in your direction. What you once called criticisms are truly gifts, if you choose to see them that way.

How do you fix something if you can't see where it's broken? How do you resolve a problem if you think there is none? There are times when it helps to have areas needing improvement pointed out to us.

If you are like most writers, you can't proofread your own work. You tend to see what you intended to be there, not what is actually there. For example, when you write the word *and* twice, you may see it written only once on the page.

The feedback of other writers can be the best tool you have for honing your work. You want this service and owe it to yourself to obtain it. Once you find a group of writers that suits you, try to become very comfortable with not only facing up to, but encouraging, commentary. Soon, you will be working very hard at ways to get critique and keep it coming.

The benefits of hardheaded consistency are reconsidered. Examples are pointed out. Sections are questioned. The criticism of others is sometimes enlightening, and it is almost always necessary.

4.2   Mistakes Are Not Failures

Making mistakes is not the same as failing. Writers make mistakes all the time. That is why there are editors and proofreaders. If you are going to share your creative attempts with fellow writers, you are going to discover what may seem like errors in judgment and in application. You are going to confront phrases that simply don't make sense to anyone but you. It's unavoidable.

Don't grieve over blunders, but don't deny them either. When someone points out a mistake of yours, be sure to thank him or her. Say, "Thank you for pointing that out to me." That's all. There's no need to "mea culpa" all over the place. Remind yourself that mistakes are things that you do, not what you are. They are messages. Mistakes resulting from poor judgment are arrows that clearly point you toward what needs improving. Motivator Anthony Robbins points out in his seminars, "Good judgment is the result of experience, and experience is often the result of bad judgment."

The lessons you learn from making mistakes bring power—when you act on them. This approach is very different from the one taken by our educational system, which punishes mistakes, marking them as wrong. The shame of it all is that we've been programmed by most of our teachers and guides and counselors to be ashamed of making mistakes. This does not encourage creativity, but discourages it.

Inventors make mistakes all the time, even when they're intuitively sure that they're right. A reporter once asked Thomas Edison how he felt about failing a thousand times before he successfully developed the light bulb. Edison replied that he did not, in fact, fail. The lightbulb was an invention that took 1,001 steps.

It's awfully hard to be creative and not make what are called mistakes. The avoidance of any attempt that may result in criticism is a dreadful mistake.

4.3   Attitudes

Writers need to form a positive attitude toward criticism. Unfortunately, the word itself is defined in many dictionaries as faultfinding and disapproval. This is not appropriate for writers symposia, which should define *criticism* as constructively pointing out, distinguishing, evaluating, or analyzing the written work with knowledge and propriety.

There may be certain kinds of writing that don't lend themselves to your particular talents. You will be better at some things and not so good at others. Although you know this, constructive evaluation can stir up varying levels of uncomfortableness.

Some writers and some writings elicit stronger, more extreme responses than others. However, no matter what is said about your work, only what you actually hear and understand is of any use to you. We sometimes erect protective barriers that serve as mufflers and get in the way of our hearing important comments.

Resistance is to be expected. Having someone else size up your work can hurt, especially when it feels as if the critique were being delivered impatiently or gruffly. However, most critique is well intentioned and generously informative. It inspires just as much as it bothers. Honest self-appraisal is needed to discover why some forms of criticism are much more difficult to accept than others. The striving toward such realizations can bring you from contention to appreciation.

Even when a comment sounds mean spirited and nit-picking, it is not necessary to waste precious time justifying your anger at the speaker for hurting you. Look within yourself and disengage the internal triggers that set off your anger.

Stored in everyone's mind are unconscious images of many painful and even life-threatening past events. You may be carrying memories of the teacher who called you stupid or the sixth-graders who laughed at you when you gave the wrong answer. You may have been told by a school counselor that you did not quite measure up. You don't think you remember all these things, but your unconscious never forgets. It reminds you every time it is necessary to prevent your reliving such incidents. You remember how they hurt, and you don't want to open yourself up to that kind of pain again. These protective mechanisms are your fixed points of view. Like walls, they will repel and ricochet everything that is coming at you without regard to the value or possibilities inherent therein. As understandable as protection is, it can work as a hindrance to your growth and improvement.

If you don't develop a positive attitude toward criticism, you will end up getting in your own way and being your own worst enemy when it comes to improving your writing skills.

4.4   Avoidance Techniques

Like all other humans, you are capable of putting up barricades when criticism comes your way. You will discover that there are things you can do to ward off objections: clever little behaviors as well as some not-so-subtle actions that you can put up as blocks.

Accepting criticism is the optimum training experience. Because they haven't been exposed to such a concept, some writers allow themselves to feel victimized and helpless when constructive criticism comes their way. They become angry and resentful toward those who try to help them—the very people they actively drew to themselves in order to learn.

4.4.1   Scare It Off

Some writers learn how to scare off criticism. I was in a group with a man who used to throw down his paper after his final sentence and look around with a fist of a face. His body language dared a challenge. When some brave soul did attempt a bit of feedback, he would attack, his best defense being a tough offense. Eventually, we all sat silent. It took a few meetings, but when he realized that he wasn't there to be ignored, he changed his tactics. He has since stopped scaring off criticism, and he is now the first one to step in and work with another writer who is caught in that same self-defeating behavior. He quotes the old Hindu saying: "It takes a thorn to remove a thorn."

4.4.2 Beg It Off

Some writers beg off criticism by making it clear to everyone by a very dramatic disregard that they simply can't bear any disapproval. I once had a student who would make no eye contact after she finished reading a piece. She would drop her shoulders and grind her face down to the desk. Then she would go on to display manic attention to doodling all over a piece of scratch paper. She so obviously didn't want any criticism that her fellow classmates obliged her.

4.4.3 Be Precious

Another avoidance technique that some writers use is making sure that everyone is aware of the mystery and preciousness of their own personal drama. They give the impression that you had better not say anything because you don't understand the depth of it all.

These writers sometimes present only pseudoconfessional works that titillate and take advantage of the listener's compassion. These works hint at off-limit thoughts and feelings, concealing much more than they reveal. Quite often, they don't make a great deal of sense and come across as confusing babble. When inquiries are made, the reader insinuates that the topic is simply too painful to discuss and doesn't need further explanation. It's deeply personal and private. Any suggestion, then, that perhaps it shouldn't have been shared with the group usually gets a rebuttal.

4.4.4 The True Story

Some writers stop suggestions from coming their way by convincing everyone that what they are reading is a factual story, told honestly and accurately. Announcing that what you have just read is a true story provides no special dispensations. Too many new group members say this as if expecting the entire room to gasp in awe. It really doesn't make any difference in the long run whether the story is true, and any insistence that it is can work against you. Group members get weary of offering well-thought-through criticism to deflectors like "But that's the way it really happened" or "I have to write it the way it was." The group didn't form to be an audience for such defensive ploys. When we retell incidents that are ragged edged (and they all are), they come out that way. The purpose of proficient writing is to present a piece that is coherent enough that readers can understand what is underlying what really happened.

4.4.5 Mumbling

School children are very good at racing through stuff they have to read aloud. Some of them will whisper or swallow back their phrases. It's as if they are afraid of mispronouncing a word or are painfully embarrassed at being singled out. What they don't realize is that all they accomplish is to draw more attention to themselves. Don't believe for a moment that if you read rapidly or softly, no one will catch your less-than-perfect areas. Mumbling and muttering with no regard to the people trying to listen to you is an avoidance technique. When you entered into the unwritten agreement to share your work with your group, you agreed to read so that everyone could hear and understand you. This means that you will not hide your mouth behind your paper or rest your chin or cheek in your open hand. Such acts smother articulation.

If you recognize these as your habits, correct them. Rise and read. Standing helps the softest voice to project. You don't want your listeners to get frustrated and stop listening. Appreciate it if group members interrupt to tell you that they cannot hear you and ask you to start again. This is a good group. You are being pushed forward.

4.5   *Expand Your Comfort Zone*

Centuries ago, when mapmakers ran out of known world before they ran out of parchment, they would sketch dragons at the edge of the scroll. No one was quite sure of what unknown territories lay out there, so symbols were posted to warn and caution adventurers.

It boggles the mind to imagine what our world would be like today if no one ventured beyond the limits. One wonders how, if monsters and unknown edges were taken literally, new worlds could have been discovered.

Have you placed dragons beyond your protected area where you look fairly good to yourself and others?

Your comfort zone, as it is called, describes your standard operating procedure and defines the boundaries you are not likely to risk traversing. It is held together on the premise that life is much easier when you don't push yourself to the edge. The wonder of it all is that you wouldn't even have approached the idea of joining a writers group if you weren't, to some extent, willing to push the perimeters of your comfort zone.

Be grateful when your critics speak up because you are carelessly omitting vital punctuation or lazily repeating yourself. Be glad when they intervene because they see your creative spirit becoming frightfully sterile and dry because you continue to write something you were once told you write well. Appreciate their nudges to get you to push yourself. You won't fall off the edge—there is no edge.

Don't get mad, get busy.

4.6 Harness Anxiety

If you are going to put your work out there, you will have to handle the rough stuff. The attitudes and adventures involved in being a writer will sooner or later bring about anxiety.

Anxiety does not necessarily emerge because of what you can and can't do. It arises from what you do not realize you must experience if you are going to write well. You need to accept all of the developmental stages involved in becoming and being a writer—that is, impulses to abandon, to retrench, to do something safe instead of new, to quit. To get the most that you can from criticism, you need to consider and inspect each evaluation. Don't ignore critiques that may sound totally off the wall. Even if you feel that members of your group are missing the point or focusing where they shouldn't, don't dismiss anything. Considering everything coming your way at once can be very stressful unless you receive it reasonably.

This means using your gray matter and thinking with your intelligence and not your feelings. It means training yourself to behave in ways that mold anxiety like the spiritual clay that it is. You can harness anxiety and transform it into a force that works for you instead of against you.

Instead of wasting energy playing the victim, throwing up your hands, being passive, pleading for mercy, or slumping into a beaten-down position, you could be taking control and learning. You could and should purposefully take complete charge of how you react and respond.

4.7 Don't Underestimate Details

Group critique is marvelous when it comes to pointing out little discrepancies, apparent minor flaws, and trivial technicalities. As annoying as these corrections may be, be thankful when they come your way because such careful attention to detail could take your piece from possibly publishable to prizewinning. Let's say the focus of your story is on how the cancer of a child affects the emotional stability of his mother. If somewhere in the background you have an orchard of curry trees in full blossom, the attention of the group may be diverted. Anyone who knows that curry is a powder of more than one spice will point this out.

Errors like this will ruin an otherwise well-researched piece of work. What is going on at the top level of your story is just as important as your deeper message because you use the details to pull the reader in. Once an editor or reader discovers that you've presented misinformation, you lose credibility. No more attention will be paid to those layers you carefully developed. The seemingly inconsequential inaccuracy in your top story or surface happening will cause all further messages to be lost.

Show your appreciation to your group for helping point out such errors. Display your flexibility and adaptability. Let them see you marking the correction.

4.8   Take Notes

Capture as much as you can during the group's critique of your work. Be sure to write down all of the comments that offer some kind of substance for you to work from later. You need to digest such remarks. Scribble down as many key words and phrases as you can so that later you can review your notes.

Some will make sense. Some won't. How much did you really catch of what group members said? Sometimes, an offhand remark or a quick reference is the very thing you need to help you decide about keeping or cutting a particular phrase. Everything falls into place suddenly with only a hint. Sometimes, you need to hear things repeatedly.

Most people hear what they think is being said, not what is actually spoken. They tend to listen selectively, and it isn't until much later when they reread and reconsider their notes that this becomes evident. The plausibility of more than a few of the previously ignored suggestions becomes brilliantly clear. That is why it is so important to keep all of your marked and highlighted work together in a binder or folder. Date everything.

Many of my students tell me that when they review their first draft, the work seems pretentious. Their stories did not get to the heart of things. Their poems were, on the surface, very much involved in showing off fancy poetics.

The students knew pretty well how to do things, but they didn't know how to pull up the best of the raw material. Any deep emotional or psychological experience was cloaked or changed until it became unrecognizable.

Other students told me how unfair they thought the criticism was when they first received it. Time passed. Life went on. Then, perhaps one rainy afternoon or while cleaning out some files, they reread an early piece, and lo and behold, the thing was absolutely terrible. No question about it, it was awful.

It's a great idea to take notes often. It's an even greater idea to write all over your manuscript. Cross things out in pencil; you might want to put them back in later. Insert notes in purple or green ink. Even if you will be handing your work in to an instructor, your corrections allow the instructor to see what you heard. Circle words that you want to change later; underline questionable phrases; scribble comments and any new ideas you may be considering in the margin. Listen carefully, and insert proofreader's marks or your own symbols wherever you think you might want to check for proper grammar or punctuation. Go over all of your notes later at a comfortable time and space for you to review them. Try the suggestions, and see what happens. If possible, report back on the outcome. Group members who tried to help you will be delighted, and you may find that even the people who did not intentionally try to help also helped you enormously.

4.9   Speak Up

Generally, the best way to receive criticism is to listen respectfully to each person. Afterward, let each critic know that you heard and understood what he or she had to say. You can nod, or you can echo the critic's exact words to indicate that you're listening. Accurately restating the comments in your own words shows beyond any doubt that you fully understood. Be sure to thank everyone for their remarks.

Being receptive to critique does not necessarily mean that you lay yourself down like a doormat. If you don't like the way something you wrote is being evaluated, address your feelings immediately. Speak up if you feel that someone is picking on you. It is absolutely in order to say, "I feel overwhelmed right now" or "I'm having a hard time with your criticism today." It helps others to help you. When group members understand what is going on for you during the session, they can gear their feedback more appropriately.

4.9.1 Ask for Clarification

If you are not sure that you understand what someone is telling you in a group critique, be sure to ask for clarification. Responses to your work can come loaded with unfamiliar terms or five-syllable words that mean absolutely nothing to you. They might also sound ambiguous or redundant (as they may well be) or be worded in a kind of verbal shorthand that group members have developed among themselves.

If you don't really understand what is being said, say so. Don't be intimidated into thinking that you are hearing something brilliant. "I'm not sure I understand what you're saying," is usually enough. If, after another explanation, you still don't have a clue, ask if you can speak to the critiquer later. This shows great respect for the time of the class as a whole and validates the importance of what the other person is saying. Sometimes, a quick conversation at break or after the session will clear up your confusion. If not, don't worry about it. It'll come to you when and if you need it. The message wasn't lost, simply deferred.

4.9.2 Ask for Suggestions

Ask for suggestions on what to edit out and what to save and perhaps condense. You are not writing for a deadlined, word-counted column for the city paper; you are in a working writers group. Learn how to reach out with your variety of thinking capabilities. Elicit the kind of feedback that can help you consider more than one option at a time. Shape the structure of the responses. Go with the discussion that pushes you to hold more than a singular thought. One person may say that your character is acting out of character. Another might say that it is, in fact, this unexpected behavior that makes the character so interesting. Yet another might insist that, of course, you knew this all along and purposefully constructed the story to go as it did. Another might call the entire piece poor character development. Work with such feedback. Think it through. It requires you to float many points of view in your mind simultaneously. Thinking like this is marvelously mobilizing, even if the thoughts are objectionable.

For instance, let's say that you write a story about a homeless veteran who finds a job and an apartment through the efforts of a beautiful social worker who used to be a nun. It's an upbeat ending, and you intend it as a spark of hope. One of your critiques says that your dialogue does not reflect the way real street people talk. Another says that the cute former nun-social worker concept has been done to death in B movies. Yet another says that your story is implausible. It's disheartening to find out that your characters or settings are not believable. It's worse to be told that your plot is not at all convincing. In fact, the whole thing stinks. It cuts to the quick and causes you to reexamine your very opinion of yourself and your talent.

Go ahead. Do it.

Tell everyone exactly what you are feeling, and ask for specifics about what you might do to make this story better. Push for options and alternatives. Take advantage of the special, customized attention coming your way. Use it to spur yourself on to writing more realistically. Turn it into a chance to feed your craft exactly what it needs. There is a possibility that you might not like what you hear. Make the choice to hear it anyway.

4.9.3 Interrupt Name-droppers

Don't be unnerved by people who use your critique session to tell interesting anecdotes that display their scholarly knowledge, especially if it's regarding something or someone with whom you're unfamiliar. Don't be put off when they go on about how the piece you just shared evokes this or that literary style.

Don't be intimidated by name-dropping. Tell anyone who makes a habit of doing this on your time that you'd love to hear that story or more about that writer or work later, but right now you need to focus on your piece. This is your allotted time, and you value every second of it.

An interesting phenomenon in writers groups is the amount of quoting and paraphrasing that gets tossed about. Many writers are avid readers and have committed certain lines to memory. In responding to something you have written, they may suggest that you might be interested to know that a Nobel Prize–winning poet or an editor at Random House feels such and such. They might also let you know that a Pulitzer Prize–winning author always used such and such technique. Some people have developed the ability to hide behind quotations. Instead of revealing themselves in what they say, they spout a biblical phrase or a bit of Shakespeare or a profundity issued by a great philosopher. At first, such communication devices impress the listener, but eventually it becomes clear that the speaker never commits himself. Exactly how he truly feels is never revealed. By all means, enjoy these quotes as the entertaining tidbits that they are. Ultimately, though, you should accept or reject what is said on its own merits, not because of who was supposed to have said it.

This applies to consensus, too. "They" might say and "everyone" might know and the "whole English-speaking world" might agree, but you are the one who decides whether to follow or disregard a bit of advice. Immediately treat with suspicion any suggestion that is presented as universal—that is, any sentence that includes the word *all*, for example, "All stories must . . ." or "All characters should . . ." Consider how appropriate the "rule" is to your work, which may be an exception, an experiment, or an intentional and blatant flaunting of tradition.

4.10 Distinguish

Sometimes, the best thing to do when you feel a bit confused about the group's reaction to your work is simply to listen. Don't always be quick with a retort.

Just because the group applauds one thing you do doesn't mean that everything else you do will be applauded. Even when you use a successful device or technique a second time, your fellow writers can still go from flattery to criticism in nanoseconds. This might seem a bit inconsistent, and you might be tempted to point out how they all loved it when you did it before, but after the fact you might see how what you thought was the same, wasn't.

If you are to ever trust your own instincts, you need to train yourself to consider and reconsider. You want to help yourself realize that there are as many different views as there are different observers. Your creative success cannot be measured in terms of the group's praise and criticism. If you are to deal with professional editorial suggestions down the line, you absolutely must learn that you can distinguish valid criticism from inapplicable criticism.

This is why you should always review your critique and feedback later. A very astute observation may be worded clumsily, causing you to be so distracted that you do not hear the inner message. A useless suggestion may come your way dripping with brilliant academic rhetoric, so much so that you don't have a clue as to what is being said. Don't worry about it. Neither swallow nor reject what you hear during your critique. Appreciate the efforts and absorb. It doesn't make any difference who the criticism comes from or how authoritative it may sound. You can always sift the marvel from the mud later.

4.11   Recognize Personal Preferences

The group members who size up your work bring to their opinions and suggestions a complete system of beliefs. This consists of ideas, thoughts, and philosophies as well as a past life rich with events, human interactions, and messages—millions of messages. Everything you hear is coming from a personal place. Everyone who judges, evaluates, approves, or disapproves your work does so on the basis of his or her life experience.

You will never see what someone else sees. You will, however, be able to get a feeling, a perspective, of how another person is experiencing your work. From this, you can decide how you feel about such responses and reactions.

If some members like what you wrote and some don't, where does this leave you? It leaves you with an idea of their collective personal preferences and opinions. Nothing more, nothing less.

Sometimes, the evaluation you receive has nothing to do with your work. It has more to do with what is out there, what is in vogue, and what is selling today. All major publishing houses and literary agencies have stories about major works that they overlooked or missed entirely. There have even been several hoaxes involving the submission of established "classics" with the author's name removed. According to Norman Cousins, a friend of his mailed out the first two chapters and a synopsis of *War and Peace* to ten publishers in the fifties. Only four publishers spotted the material for what it was; the others returned it with a basic letter of rejection.

Improving your own work is an acquired skill that comes with lots and lots of group work, coupled with lots and lots of afterthought and followed by lots and lots of rewriting.

4.12   Share the Rewrites

Whether you feel that your piece needs only a few punctuation corrections or should be filed away for a while so you can give it a rest and approach it anew later, after rethinking the group critique you will probably discover that in some areas the result you first produced did not match your original vision. You will need to alter some areas, and you will need to rewrite others.

Sharing rewrites with your group is incredibly helpful because members are familiar with your early effort and have a feel for what you want to get across to the reader. They will be patient and persevering with you because they too rewrite, and they understand how it often takes many attempts to get the intended final result.

All writers rewrite. Raymond Carver routinely wrote twenty to thirty drafts of a story and forty or fifty drafts of a poem. Gore Vidal never reread the manuscript on which he was working until he had completed the first draft. Truman Capote reviewed what he had written in longhand at the end of every productive day and made his changes on the spot.

Not only do all writers rewrite, but many save for another piece a great deal of what they cut from the original.

4.13   Save the Good Stuff

Groups are delighted when they recognize something that you cut from one piece because it didn't work and used in another piece where it worked wonderfully. It's much easier for writers to condense if they save everything that is cut for use in another piece. Then it is not lost, but available and retrievable.

So, after tackling a piece that you feel you have rewritten to death and is just not working, carefully go through it for the good stuff before you toss it into the wastepaper basket.

Pull out the opinions, the self-conscious references, the details, scenes, and bits of description that appeal to you. Pull them out as they come, all jumbled together like hunks of raw amethyst. Save these good parts—the pieces that you know can be used again someday, the fragments and paragraphs that are precious to you. Retype them on fresh paper, or use scissors and glue. Some of these pieces may be good in an eerie, almost dreamlike way. They are not stories and not character sketches and not poems, but it doesn't matter. What you will make them become is what matters, what you will do to polish and shape this raw material. Don't be afraid to seize whatever you have written and cut out words and phrases to use later.

I have a three-ring binder labeled "Fragments" that holds lots of bits and pieces teachers and other writers have especially liked. Whenever I'm stuck in my search for the perfect expression, I leaf through my binder. I might not find the language I'm looking for, but at least I'll find possibilities to modify.

For the Ballantine anthology *Literary Outtakes*, Larry Dark asked well-known writers to contribute work they never intended to publish. He asked for lines or passages that had been cut from works, ideas that were never used, false starts, missing chapters or verses, or anything else along those lines. Ninety-three writers contributed outtakes, ranging from a few words to more than twenty pages, that included failures in phrasing as well as altered endings. So, save those thoughts, lines, titles, or passages that you've cut from or couldn't squeeze into your finished work. You never know where they might end up one future day. They might even be appreciated.

4.14 Cultivate Your Own Voice and Style

Sometimes referred to as voice, your style is the characteristic language of your writing that sets it apart from the writing of others.

This personal way of writing is strongly affected by the way you draw from the language spoken by your parents, the dialects of your neighborhood, and the nuances and pronunciations of people in your life. If you are blessed with bilingual or multilingual capacities, your voice is richly enhanced. You can probably twist and transpose words and phrases beautifully.

Every writer displays an individual style that involves personal presentation and expression methods. Every writer possesses style, and it can be good, bad, or a combination of both. Part of your style reflects your personality and will probably echo the speech you heard as a child.

Style can be cultivated, too. This means that to develop your natural style, you will sometimes attempt new forms, and the best place to try them out is in your writers group. At first, you may sound alien and strange to group members as well as to yourself. You may be told, "That doesn't sound like you at all" or "You've never written like that before." Be pleased. Ask for elaboration. Discover what may be emerging. Listen to fellow writers who recognize your own very special way of writing. Pay attention when they offer feedback that helps you build up the strong points in your own natural style systematically while eliminating the weak ones.

Criticism that persuades you to imitate or emulate other writers only encourages you to sound like a mimic. Ask yourself: Will this suggestion improve my own unique style, or does it ask that I try to sound like someone else? Don't be overwhelmed into presenting what you want to say in an artificial and overly trendy way. Don't spin your wheels actualizing another's idea of how you should write. Actualize your own ideas in your own voice.

5

Offering Criticism

Let's face it. It's much easier to pat someone on the back than to call attention to something that could be better. A compliment gets a smile; criticism doesn't. However, writers groups can't rely solely on what makes everyone feel good. Whenever valuable information is withheld, the writer is cheated out of honest evaluation.

In any good group, there is at least one person who seems to give the cleanest and clearest appraisals. Often, this is the leader or facilitator. This person somehow manages to say perfectly what everyone else in the group is struggling to articulate. If you have such a person in your group, you may want to use his expressed attitude and behavior as a guide. Listen to his choice of words and phrases as well as his tone of voice. Get a feel for his facial expressions and body language. Emulate these approaches, and ask for pointers in giving effective critique.

When offering criticism, there are some tried-and-true techniques that everyone can use. Begin by looking at what you hope to accomplish with your criticism. Do you want to impart knowledge? Do you want to share what you know enthusiastically and benevolently with other members of your group? Do you want your group to understand that your knowledge is based on your experience up to this point in your life—and only up to this point? Do you want the group to know what you consider a good piece of writing to be? Are you influenced by preconceived notions about style or subject matter?

Once you have decided not to censor yourself by saying what will be least likely to upset people, no misguided sense of decorum will stand in the way of your contributing to a good writing session. You'll be working on the best way to express what you mean and taking the necessary steps to ensure that you do so sincerely.

5.1   Understand and Be Understood

Always listen carefully. Seek first to understand and then to be understood.

Direct criticism is always in order. As long as you stay focused, your critique will be clear and concise. You will know you are off track when you find yourself talking too much or forgetting what you wanted to say. Vague or apologetic discourse can sometimes invalidate a very important criticism, causing it to lose its effect.

In constructive criticism, it is essential to identify a particular roughness and then offer a suggestion for making it better. Provide plenty of details. Try to pinpoint what bothered you in the piece you just listened to, and determine why it stood out. Did you find a passage jarring because of its broken rhythm or mixed metaphors? Did it sound clumsy or pretentious? If you are not sure precisely what it is that bothers you, say so. Withholding feedback because you fear that you will sound unsure facilitates nothing.

There is nothing wrong with acknowledging that you, too, are guilty of the same bad habit and that you understand how difficult it is to break. When two people tackle the same problem, it is often easier to identify solutions that otherwise might have remained hidden.

5.2   Use Concrete Language

Concrete language is especially important. Use words and phrases that are clearly understandable. Fancy words and phrases are no substitute for clear language. The use of elaborate phrases to express simple thoughts is both wasteful and annoying. Choose the words that best suit your critique.

If you use technical jargon, no matter how familiar a term may be to you, make sure that it does not resemble a foreign language to others. If you want to refer to a dangling participle, be sure that the writer knows what you mean. Define the term if you must.

At the same time, do not use more words than you need. Start with as few words as possible, weed out the excess, and stop when you are through.

5.3   Don't Repeat a Point That's Been Made

Don't tack on afterthoughts that only reiterate what you have already said. Once you've said your piece, drop it and move on. In other words, don't expect a signed confession after you've spoken. The reward for patiently listening to your criticism ought to be exoneration from having to hear the same crime discussed again. If what you wanted to say was already said by another group member, there's no need to say it again.

Make one complaint at a time, If you make more, you'll demoralize the other person and perhaps obscure your major point. Above all, don't nag, especially when you know what is right.

5.4 Remember That You Are Not There to Be Right

Sometimes, a member's continual pursuit of being right can become a real pain in the group's collective tush. There are times when it really isn't important whether the word is *lay* or *lie* or *laid* or *lain*. This is especially true when, for example, the reader is showing major improvement in her previously unsuccessful struggle with dialogue. Hush any competitive internal voices that repeat that you are right about the rule on this one and she is not. Go with the positive. Interrupting another person's special moment to show how right you are about a trivial matter can kill off the credibility you will need when offering future suggestions or ideas to the group. You become dead right, as they say.

5.5 Use Questions

The Socratic method of teaching, which dates back to ancient Greece, is based on questioning that directs the student's focus so that eventually the teacher's point emerges from the student's answer. Everyone in your group doesn't have to use this technique, but from time to time a sincere inquiry will elicit many realizations.

The Socratic method doesn't mean prefacing your critique with "Couldn't you have . . . ?" or "Why do you always . . . ?" These phrases ask for defensive answers. Questions that elicit thought are preferred. "I noticed that you did not describe your protagonist. Was that intentional?" is a well-phrased question. "How do you think it would work if you . . . ?" is another.

When you want to gently zero in on a specific weakness, put it in question form. This should eliminate the expressions that cause the hair at the back of the neck to bristle—expressions that begin "What you've got to do is . . ." or "You have to . . ." or "I hate to say this, but . . ." or "Gee, I hope this doesn't hurt your feelings, but . . ." Not only do such expressions dispose of reality by seeing people as objects to be ordered about rather than people to be contacted, but they predict doom.

You can also use the question format to address a mannerism that is driving you and the rest of the group to distraction. For example, you might say, "Sylvia, I've noticed that you've used the word *okay* at the end of everything you've said so far. Were you aware of that?" or "Bill, did you notice that you began most sentences in your piece with the word *she?*" These inquiries elicit thoughtful replies, not defensive retorts, and they make your point.

The more you comment in question form, the more you will find yourself avoiding words like *always* and *never*, which are exaggerations intended for emphasis. These expressions rob what you have to say of accuracy; there are more than a few cases in the world of writing where things are relative.

Another good thing about using the question format is that it gets you to take responsibility for what you say. You use the word *I* instead of *you.* "You must always put the period inside the quotes" is replaced with "I think the rule calls for the period inside the quotes, doesn't it?" The question gives the same information as the statement, but without the command.

Beware of using questions to compare the writing of one group member with the writing of another. Unless you are absolutely sure that you can avoid one being judged inferior or superior. Avoid implied comparisons, also. Such deliberations all too often get mired down in their own redundancies, and they predispose most group members not to listen. Should the group become involved in such a discussion, especially if there is an embarrassing lull or uncomfortable sticky moment, questions can lead the way out. They don't necessarily dissolve stalemates, but they do help to remove blocks in group work.

5.6   *Vive la Différence*

The cultural myth that all human beings have equal abilities is simply not true. Every member of your group is not equally capable. Every member does, however, deserve respect and dignity, regardless of his or her creative talents or development of craft. Every working level should be appreciated.

Incorporate a healthy allowance for individual choice. If someone wants to write only erotica or blood-and-guts murder and mayhem, accept that preference and go from there.

Even repetitive writing must sometimes be allowed. If the veteran needs to relive the fighting in everything he writes, then so be it. If a death is mourned over and over or an injustice proclaimed again and again, let it be. Writers need to write some things away, and this purging need not be critiqued. Attentive listening that allows for expression of the trauma and pain is in order, as are comments that appreciate such attempts.

5.7   Be Sensitive

Don't worry anyone's creative expression out of its dignity by picking at it heartlessly. Go easy. There is merit in almost any work, including that which you may judge to be totally unpublishable. Look for the good as well as that which needs improvement. If you can, begin your criticism with an appreciation for the work as a whole or for something specific within it.

Be kind. Kindness isn't something you carry around in a paper bag to take out for widows and orphans and put away when you enter your writers group. Consider the subject matter. If the writer is reading about the loss of a pet, back off. Don't jump in immediately afterward to point out split infinitives. Address the grief. Relate to it. This is not the time for hard-core corrections; this is the time for compassion.

However, don't start role-playing the rescuer, either. If the reader is evidently swallowing her sobs, don't jump up and rush over with hugs and "there-theres." Don't offer to read the work for her. Sit still. Allow the reader to work through the process to completion. Be sensitive.

Some writers are so afraid of writing a poor story that they can hardly summon the nerve to write a simple, honest sentence. Others have been brainwashed with rigid rules regarding construction, plot, unity, mass, and coherence. Somewhere along the line, they were rewarded for writing pretentiously, doing exactly what they were told. Situations like this call for lots of patience and encouragement. There will be plenty of opportunity later for fine honing.

Allow for exceptions. There will be times to offer criticism and times to graciously yield and simply listen.

5.8   Pay Tribute

If you are going to make the occasional objection, you have the obligation to pay the occasional compliment, too. From time to time, make it a point to acknowledge the talent and the improvements that others display. Don't let their hard work go unnoticed. Acknowledging improved performance is possibly the most overlooked and understated contribution that group members can make to each other, but it must be done forthrightly.

You know how wonderful you can feel when you receive a compliment given honestly. You also know how uncomfortable you can feel when the praise sent your way seems insincere. You might find yourself responding to an insincere compliment with something to invalidate it, or you might change the subject or even behave in a way that deflects the tribute away from yourself. You want acclaim that makes you feel good, not blarney that you doubt. Unctuous flattery rings just as much of deceit as does excess adulation.

Praise that is truthfully appreciative pays tribute. It acknowledges work well done and spurs the recipient onward. The language doesn't gush or patronize, it recognizes a specific praiseworthy aspect of the work. It is genuine flattery that focuses on the manifestations of talent, creativity, technical virtuosity, or style. Credit is given where credit is due—not just so the praise-giver will be liked.

Writers groups are not popularity contests. Group members who always have something nice to say because they want people to regard them well and respond favorably to them are looking to others to validate their niceness. The fact that they are trying to solicit support for their own writing eventually becomes evident, and everything they say becomes suspect.

Remember, you are not there to make friends, although some of the finest friendships have been formed in writers groups. You are not there to tell everyone how marvelous they are and have them return the compliment in kind, although such events do take place from time to time. You are there to serve your colleagues as you would have them serve you.

5.9   Use Praise as a Motivator

Let's say that you have a new group member who is bringing in trite, cliché-ridden, practically plagiarized stories. Asked about the similarity of his descriptions to those written by well-known authors, the new member announces that he doesn't read books, doesn't need to, and doesn't intend to. Don't get exasperated. Instead, each time he presents a new piece, listen very carefully for fresh expressions or suggestions of realistic feelings. Then praise these sections. Praise them to the sky. Don't mention the other stuff, the possible and probable bones of contention.

Focusing on the bad in this kind of situation doesn't get results, just frustration. Point out the good stuff each and every time you hear it. Don't look for pearls in eggshells. Don't expect what is not possible. Object only to writing faults that the other person can change. Try to offer suggestions that are viable. All of us are performing at certain levels, and we advance one level at a time. Listen for improvement, and acknowledge it when you hear it.

5.10   Don't Misuse Compliments

Some group members misuse praise by issuing it to avoid conflict. They apologize for their criticism with a halfhearted compliment, not realizing that this takes away the credibility of their earlier comments. Anyone who dishes out unmitigated, unqualified compliments to placate, appease, or pacify others is fooling no one. Eventually, everything that he or she says is disregarded as pacifist drivel.

Criticism given in good faith doesn't need ingratiation. This is not to say that praise cannot be used together with criticism. The "sandwich" approach continues to be most effective. This means that you say something nice as you begin your criticism, say something not so nice in the middle, then finish off with something nice again. This approach works as long as it isn't obviously done to prevent someone from getting angry.

To ensure that your praise is well received, double-check with yourself that you are not lauding your fellow writers to gain ground for yourself when your turn comes. Then be sure that what you say is specific. Telling someone that you liked what they wrote because it was very nice or it flowed or sounded good is lazy. When you put as much effort into your praise as you do into your criticism, you will be respected and greatly appreciated by your fellow writers.

5.11   Lighten Up

We have been convinced that our classrooms should be quiet and serious and orderly and somber. We call the disciplines of art and music and creative writing frills, and we banish them from our academically correct, basics-first schools. It looks too much like the students and teachers are having fun in these classes. We've been taught that if it's important, it's not fun.

Often, we try too hard. We wrestle and struggle too much. When we get frustrated, we make bull-headed, explosive attempts to force solutions. We expect difficulty. We believe the old saw, "No pain, no gain."

We've forgotten how much fun it is when we're doing what we love to do, how good the process feels. This is why the most effective groups I know laugh a lot. They use humor to cut the psychological negativity that groups can fall into. They use laughter to free their vitality, loosen their inhibitions, and renew their perspectives.

A robust laugh gives the muscles of the face, shoulders, diaphragm, and abdomen a vigorous workout. With convulsive or sidesplitting laughter, even the leg and arm muscles get involved. When you laugh, your whole body laughs with you.

You don't have to be miserable and starving and in psychic pain to create. Vincent van Gogh might have been psychotic, Paul Gauguin schizoid, Edgar Allan Poe an alcoholic, and Virginia Woolf seriously depressed, but this does not necessarily mean that their creativity was the product of their neuroses. You can be happy and creative concurrently.

Some people think that laughter is a frivolity. They suspect that a group of writers getting together and having a good time, laughing aloud and visibly relaxed, is nonproductive. Nothing could be further from the truth. Recent studies have shown that creative juices flow more readily when a sense of humor is in evidence.

Think about it. You don't run fast because of the swiftness with which you can contract our muscles, but the swiftness with which you can relax them. A relaxed muscle can be stretched to a greater length than a tense muscle. Up to a point, the more stretched it is, the more forceful its contraction. It is the ability to relax that enables small people to hit a golf ball great distances.

Participants in good writers groups have long recognized that when it comes to the group's performance and productivity, laughter is essential.

6

The People Connection

You've decided to take full advantage of every opportunity to meet, know, and really get involved with other writers. You've made up your mind to locate and join groups of people who can and will foster your writing skills without demands and expectations that hinder more than help. You feel that there is no longer a valid reason for you to operate without the support of other writers who truly understand when you need to burrow away like a meditative hermit. You are going to do more of what you love to do. You are going to commit more time and energy to writing.

It is at this point that you may find that your relationships with the people around you are changing. It's not them. It's you. You are the one causing disruption, especially if you are declining invitations or rescheduling visits because you want to finish your writing before the next group meeting. Whether you are newly involved in, more firmly entrenched in, or looking for a writers group, you are less available now than before. You are changing the priority you assign to writing in your life. If you feel that you are being overly sensitive to what seems to be coming at you as discouragement, you are probably right. You are not as free with your time as you used to be.

6.1   Your Time

How you divvy up the time you spend writing is up to you. No matter how much friends and acquaintances complain about the dwindling time you spend together, your need to take time to write must be respected and supported. The sooner everyone understands this, the easier your writing space will be to claim. Don't be subtle or even polite about the seriousness of your endeavor. If you have a schedule, announce it. You may need one. Some people work best on a strict routine.

For instance, when at home in Mill Valley, California, George Leonard, an urbane New York City editor-writer and a high-profile California human potential leader, maintains a disciplined work schedule. He writes each day from 9:00 A.M. until 1:00 P.M.

You may prefer to work only when on a roll. Anne Rice, the author of those sensuous vampire books, used to write at her desk in her bedroom. She usually wrote all day, from 10:00 A.M. to 5:00 P.M., and she sometimes wrote into the night. "When I'm rolling," she said, "I use every available minute. I can write till 1:00 A.M., then fall into bed."

Attack and retreat may be your mode. Danielle Steel claims that she has clacked away almost without stopping on her 1948 manual typewriter for twenty hours straight. Some days, she starts about 8:00 A.M., goes to her desk, and just sits there until she can't sit anymore. Someone brings her food every three or four hours, and she works late into the night. She may stop about 3:00 or 4:00 A.M., sometimes as late as 6:00 A.M., and sink into a hot bath.

Regardless of whether you follow a schedule, you will need to be left alone more often as you become more serious about your writing. Some people who like to spend time with you will feel threatened when you decline invitations because of your new priorities. They won't understand it, and they may react in ways that hurt you.

6.2   The Demands of Others

Insinuations, though perhaps not intended as such, will be directed your way. "Who do you think you are? You are not a real writer. It's just a passing fancy. You'll never get anything published. Who are you kidding?"

You may find yourself running into difficulties with others who until now have supported you. They may suddenly begin to interrupt your writing time with phone calls or visits. They may also display various forms of frustration when you refuse invitations because you want to write.

Unfortunately, such conflicts sometimes cause writers to sabotage their chances of becoming better writers and possibly being published. They allow the wishes of others to undermine their own, and they settle back into a lifestyle of weary repression.

There are people whose downs are stronger than your ups. Addicted to negative thinking, they refuse to recognize what a downright drag they are on those around them. People like this can immobilize you just when you need to be energized. Avoid them. Instead, populate your life with those who applaud each positive action you take. It is your responsibility to seek out positive, achieving people and remove yourself from the influence of those who stifle you.

This is when a good writers group can really do its stuff. Your fellow writers know what you are up against. They understand. They, too, deal with similar matters and can remind you that you don't have to be published to be respected for your involvement with writing. It doesn't matter how others measure the worth of your efforts. It is your choice that should be honored.

6.3   Recognition as a Writer . . .

Once those around you see that you mean business when it comes to your writing time, they will begin to accept you as a writer. You'll be accorded a certain amount of recognition.

Once they see that you are getting published or winning awards or even hanging out with those who do, you'll be regarded as semipro at least. They may cluck at your accomplishments or close vicinity to success and ask where you find the time. Even when you remind them that everyone gets the same twenty-four hours in each day, they will suspect that special dispensation has granted you more time than they have. Unfortunately, this presumption is usually followed by requests for more of your time. They may even come as demands.

Now that you are a "real" writer, people will want you to write for them. You'll be called on to be the official scribe. Any organization you join will expect you to be the secretary. Friends struggling with written applications or resumes will probably ask for your help. You'll be asked to contrive letters of recommendation, complaint, and political persuasion. Last-minute pleas will urge you to think up the wording for party invitations, anniversary poems, and eulogies. You will also be expected to be on top of all your correspondence. After all, you are the writer, aren't you?

People you hardly know will have suggestions for what you should write. You will discover how many people have what they think are great plots for blockbuster novels. Others have clever ideas for television scripts. The most persistent are those who believe you should write their life story. Whatever the premise, none of them have the time or the typewriter, and they are much too busy with everyday living to do it themselves. However, they will *allow you* to do the work. They can scribble it on yellow lined pads or talk it into a tape recorder or just chat it at you. The deal is, you write it, clean it up, market it, and sell it, and we'll split the profits fifty-fifty.

You will receive lots of offers like this—and even more requests to serve as a reader.

6.4   . . . And as a Reader

Being a writer who belongs to a writing group or takes writing classes seems to qualify you as a reader, quite often for people who themselves should be participating in a group or class. If you are not careful, you will become the local free-reader and be inundated with manuscripts.

It won't be just friends and relatives who will want you to read what they have written. Drafts of current writing and notes and outlines for future writing will be passed to you on the oddest occasions. Anyone and everyone will be bringing you what he or she or her husband or his daughter or Aunt Mary's niece wrote. You will be expected to read this material free of charge— and not take too long. Your friend presents you with a collection of her grandmother's journals. Your neighbor wants you to look over her boyfriend's book-length manuscript. Someone you don't even know calls you at the suggestion of your mutual dentist's receptionist. She's thrilled to inform you that in a day or two you will be receiving a few binders of poetry containing her life's collected works.

"Oh, just look it over," they say. "Take your time," they nod. "It's just a little something, a few scribbles, not very good, but you might enjoy it." "Let me know what you think," they say. "Tell the truth now. I want criticism. I want your honest opinions." "No big deal," they mutter. "Just read it."

You do know what they really want, don't you? They want what you and I and everyone wants. They want recognition and validation and appreciation. They want you to be absolutely blown away with the talent they exhibit in their writing. They want you to be rendered speechless with the beauty and power and magnificence of such written expressions. If you aren't, consider yourself warned here and now: Don't say so.

Years ago, I read some poetry written by my friend's boyfriend. I spent a whole day reading and rereading and carefully typing up my responses on different sheets of paper so as to not mark his poem pages. I was as honest as the day is long, and I pointed out specifically what I liked and what I felt could be improved.

He thanked me. "Thank you," he said properly and succinctly. "Thank you."

That was it. End of discussion. To this day, every time I am published, he can't wait to proofread what I wrote. His entire literary relationship with me is looking for mistakes I might make.

Thank you?

Another time I read the work of a friend's cousin. My written comments were very kind. I suggested very gently that he do away with so many clichés and not preach quite so much. He responded with a scathing five-page letter not only attacking my intelligence, but accusing me of performing unnatural sexual acts with close relatives.

Get the point?

People who haven't experienced the constructive criticism that is bandied about in industrious workshops don't understand how it could possibly be warranted in their case. They don't understand the kind of time or energy you put into reading their stuff. They can inadvertently wear you out.

So, if you are asked to read for someone who is outside the perimeters of a writers group, know the possible consequences. Believe me, it's much easier all the way around to keep your writing interactions limited to group members.

6.5   Writers as Friends

Years ago, I took a creative writing workshop at a local high school. It was an evening class offered through an adult-education program. It changed my life. I looked forward to going each week and missed it terribly over holiday periods. I felt totally alive and appreciated there. So did everyone else. We worked hard at reinforcing one another. We held diversification in high regard and respected each individual temperament. If we had met under different circumstances, there may have been personality clashes, but in this class we all genuinely liked one another. Deeper, more forgiving alliances formed around our central creative nucleus. Many of the writers who attended that workshop are still some of my closest friends. I thought this was because an exceptional group of people were brought together at the right time under the most perfect circumstances for their bonding. As it happens, this is not so rare.

6.6   Writers as Colleagues

Friendship with another writer, where there is mutual deference to each other's talent, can be a major factor in becoming a better writer and, as a result, being published more often. A friend who is also a writer whose opinion you value can bring invaluable information and stimulation to your writing life.

There is a myth that writers work in total isolation until the day their work is ready to be sent to the publisher. Most writers have at least one respected associate to whom they show their writing along the way. They often submit their work to criticism by other writers.

F. Scott Fitzgerald regularly showed his works-in-progress to his friends. As their letters made clear, he chose as critics friends like Ernest Hemingway who were quite willing to tell him if they did not like what they read.

Sylvia Plath took a class from Robert Lowell and sought the advice of Lowell and of Anne Sexton. Even Emily Dickinson, who resisted suggestions to publish her poems, shared drafts of her work in her letters to relatives, friends, and literary advisers. She considered her poetry to be "letters to the world." Though some may argue that the audience Dickinson wrote for was ultimately only herself, the undeniable fact remains that the language she chose was a public one.

Walt Whitman joyfully credited Ralph Waldo Emerson with getting *Leaves of Grass* noticed and accepted by the press and by the public. "I was simmering, simmering," wrote Whitman. "Emerson brought me to a boil."

Some colleagues even write things together. Hemingway and Faulkner collaborated indirectly with Sherwood Anderson, who gave both important inspiration and help in their literary careers. Ford Madox Ford and Joseph Conrad wrote three novels together. Conrad was subject to fits of exhaustion and despair about his writing that Ford helped him weather. Ford corrected proofs of Conrad's stories and suggested subjects for further work.

The best place to hook up with another writer as a colleague is within the confines of a working writers group. There, what is important always overrides the trite and petty.

6.7   *Dealing with Envy*

You must learn to handle envy because eventually you will find yourself becoming especially friendly with someone in your group who has managed to fulfill his or her writing dream. Even though you truly like this person and admire his or her writing skills, you probably won't be able to help feeling jealous. This is fine.

Everyone's experience with writing and publishing is unique. What works for one writer may fail for another. Some writers get lucky breaks, and others get unlucky ones. Circumstances beyond your control may play a significant part in your writing career. It is quite true that good work often goes unpublished and that some bad work gets into print. We've all, at one time or another, read a perfectly dreadful piece written by an author whose talent is evidently hanging out elsewhere to dry. However, it remains generally true that good writing gets published more often than bad writing. It also remains generally true that when someone else in your group gets published and you don't, more than a twinge of envy flutters in your gut.

There will always be achievers who pass you by, superachievers who pass the achievers by, and so on. You may even secretly disdain those people who know precisely what they want and not only go after it with a vengeance, but get it! Give such feelings a good five minutes, and then thank goodness that you have enough sense to let them spur you onward.

Don't compare yourself with your colleagues except to learn from them. You don't have to evaluate your situation with that of others around you. In the final analysis, you are not going to be judged according to what your fellow writers did or how you measured up against them. Everyone knows this, yet we still do the silliest comparisons in our feeble search for winners and losers.

Compete only with yourself. Maintain the highest standards of excellence with yourself. So what if Mary cranks out a true confession every week and sells it promptly. So what if Harry has won yet another poetry contest. They are themselves, doing what they have chosen to do. You are you, doing what you have chosen to do.

When a fellow writer gets a decent story published or wins a prize for a poem that you thought was good but not *that* good, go ahead and feel jealous. Let all of those mean-spirited and nasty thoughts flow through you. Acknowledge them as they pass, and then let them all go. Realize that you are in the best of company, hanging out with achievers. Be glad that you have opportunities to form friendships with such successful writers.

6.8   *Setting Boundaries*

No matter how wonderful your writer friends and colleagues are, if you are going to squeeze in adequate time for your own writing, you have to set up people boundaries. "Love your neighbor as yourself," Carl Sandburg cleverly stated, "but don't take down the fence."

The strain of being accessible to anyone and everyone just because they are writers, too, can cause you quite a bit of frustration. You are in charge of guarding your writing time. It's up to you to make sure that your group commitments work with you, not against you, in providing space for your craft. Any group member who expects you to put your writing aside for the pleasure of working on his or her manuscript is not being fair. Fellow writers sometimes do this. They are often completely unaware that your writing time is just as precious as theirs. Friends from your writers group may also try to tempt you away from your desk for social activities, especially if they can be justified as related, even distantly, to writing. Invitations to catch a movie about an author or browse a bookstore or tour a literary site can come at you hot and heavy. You may need to remind the others as much as yourself that in order to be a writer, you must write. Help your fellow writers enable, impel, and sustain you in your craft by setting examples with your own behavior.

6.9   Tormentors

The tormentors in a writing group offer remarkable learning opportunities for the others. Dealing with difficult behavior is part of the group training experience. Not only do the people who push your sensitive buttons provide some of the most interesting characters for you to use in future works, but they can provide some of the most interesting insights into your own behavior and attitudes, as well.

A good example of this was an incident that took place in one of my classes. Once, when Hilda was absent, Chet complained to the class that he was driven to distraction with the way she always strolled in late asking questions about what she had missed. He was totally amazed when the class gently reminded him that he always left early, letting the door slam after him, and never bothered to find out about collective decisions and determinations made in his absence.

Positive lessons are not always learned in positive ways. Before I understood them, I used to have a great deal of trouble with people I privately called exasperaters. These are the people who claim lots of valuable group time unnecessarily. They never quite hear or understand the idea behind a suggestion. They forget what was asked three seconds ago and interrupt to ask it again. The simplest rule gets contravened. They just don't get it. I did, finally.

I knew that I couldn't change one member of my group, but I could change my attitude toward her. This meant taking time out and honestly looking for those same traits in myself. At last, I recognized that nervous and scared part of me. I recalled times when I got very stressed and preoccupied and simply did not hear what was being said because I was so busy thinking about what to say next. These were horrible times for me. The more others displayed impatience and agitation, the worse I got. When I remembered my own distress, I was able to call on my patience and repeat and go slower. This served everyone.

Using the same technique, I've also discovered that overbearing members who talk too much aren't really so difficult. They simply have so much they want to say and share. An occasional reminder, presented clearly but with tact and firmness, about the collective rules usually does the trick. From time to time, however, the overbearing do need a special space or time to spill over, but it's allocated and time-framed.

6.10 Teachers Who Shouldn't Teach

I've dealt with group leaders and teachers who shouldn't have held these positions. Fresh out of high school, I enrolled in a poetry workshop at San Francisco State University. It consisted mainly of graduate-level poets who were accustomed to giving readings at bars and coffee houses. They had studied with the original Beat poets and wrote brutally beautiful poetry that was way ahead of its time in scope and style. I had just left an all-girls parochial academy of nuns and uniforms and imprimaturs. I was still rhyming in iambic pentameter about life and strife. Clearly, I was out of my element but very excited about being with such avant-garde poets. When I turned in my first batch of poetry, the professor told me to forget it. "Save yourself a lot of grief," he actually wrote.

In retrospect, I must admit, that my sonnets and dramatic monologues were pretentiously gaudy. They were also childish and dogmatic. However, instead of acknowledging that I needed to develop, that I was at a very low level of competence and needed to lift myself to the next level, that I should get all of the trite stuff out of my system so that I could move forward, the professor made a judgment call, banishing me to never write again.

I thought I believed him, but I kept writing anyway. Some inner drive compelled me, thank goodness.

As the years passed, I was blessed with educators who actually taught. These teachers helped me see where I was and how to get to where I wanted to be. Under their guidance, I went on to say what I meant and to mean what I said. I stopped trying to sound like someone else and gave up trying to dazzle. At last, I became decently published, earned a few awards, and felt a certain amount of confidence about my writing. I honed my craft and pursued and persevered. Writing became an essential and consistent part of my life. However, it wasn't until I, too, was in the position of teacher that I realized the invaluable lesson I learned from that professor years ago. It has had a direct impact on my own teaching methods.

That prominent and much-published professor wiped his dirty feet all over my fragile, early efforts. I experienced firsthand how seriously a teacher can abuse his or her influence. I was made to feel totally inadequate and advised to give up trying any further. I didn't give up, though, and I didn't ignore what happened either. I thought about it and finally understood the professor's arrogance for what it was. I recognized it in other teachers, too, whenever it opened its esteem-eating jaws. Years later, I went on to train myself to recognize potential and encourage growth. I was able to learn from this debilitating stomping of long ago. Because of it, I became a more discerning student and a more compassionate teacher.

6.11 Damaged Students

I still suffer with writers who have had teachers as bad as mine or worse. Instead of seeing any lesson in the experience, some writers unfortunately wallow in the unfairness and injustice of the past. They work very hard at being eternal masochists and insist on riding on the coattails of ruin. I've watched such people turn the happiest occasion into a disaster, change a compliment into an insult. They are very good at protesting how hard it is for them and how much easier all the rest of us have it. No matter how hard they try, no matter what they do, the world has made them victims, and it's not their fault. This is their chant.

I've suffered with them not because I've fallen for whatever racket they've been running, but because such people have great difficulty benefiting from any gathering of writers. Other members eventually get fed up listening to their endless litany, their life-denying script, and they stop responding. I work very hard to validate only their positive communications.

6.12 Saboteurs

Saboteurs often issue clues as to their mode of operation. I always note anyone who finds it necessary to go on and on about how trustworthy they are. All too often, the people who are most adamant about confidentiality are often the very ones who repeat some of the more personal and intimate conversations of the group to anyone who will listen. These poor souls don't know how to apply common sense; they cannot differentiate between what should be kept private and what can be discussed freely. Eventually, they make someone in the group very upset and angry because of something they told someone (who told someone else whose business it wasn't) about an incident that occurred within the privacy of the writers circle.

Others who disrupt the group are those who openly confront leaders, being very picky about minute, unimportant things. They go on to point out why this company of writers is not working properly and why it never will. They are usually the rumormongers. I've seen such people go so far as to sabotage any progressive movement. They are the ones who can't wait to add fuel to any little spark of discontent. Then, when the destruction begins to show itself, they threaten to leave.

Up to a point, a clear and firm reiteration of the purposes of the group usually tightens the reins a bit. When a member's discontent becomes a threat to leave, it's time to let go. I've blown kisses and said good-bye and meant it. As much as one can sympathize and empathize with the pain some members plunge themselves into, I feel very strongly that no one should be courted or coerced to stay with a group when they've expressed a desire to leave.

When a group member leaves the group in a huff, allow it. Do not stop the meeting to discuss the tantrum. This kind of behavior is done to disrupt the session, and if the group goes along with the high drama, it allows itself to be manipulated by a single member. This is not good.

Being afraid to do or say anything that might upset one person makes the entire group dysfunctional. The group's focus and energy goes into dealing with the disruptive person. It's a case of one spoiled child running an entire family. When anyone walks out on the group, the group must carry on. Anyone who chases after a person walking out becomes part of the problem, not the solution. This means that there should be no follow-up telephone calls, no notes, and no gossiping after the fact. It is a group matter. The entire group was walked out on, and the entire group should deal with it. The problem is that one group member wants his or her way and will communicate about it no further. The solution is to remain as a group, open to communication but not to manipulative behavior. Let the person walking out go. No exceptions!

6.13 Collaborators

Quite often, partnerships form within writers groups. Two people discover that they share similar ideas, and they pool their talents and energies to produce written works through joint effort. They collaborate.

If you think that you might like to have a writing partner, I suggest that you approach the collaboration on a small scale. Begin with a short piece. The finished manuscript must appear as though it were written by one person. This means that there should be no jarring or clumsy changes in style where one voice ends and another begins. It may take many tries. If, no matter how much you try, you can't blend your two voices, give it up. Call it quits.

If what you get is a seamless result and you feel attuned to each other, establishing a joint agreement at the very beginning should be uncomplicated. No matter how much you trust and like each other, an initial contract should be drawn. Clearly allocate specific responsibilities. Decide what each of you wants to do, hates doing, and would like to share doing. These things must be resolved at the beginning, no matter the extent of the mutual compatibility and respect. Whose name or what name will be shown as author? If both names are used, in what order will they appear? How will your earnings be divided? Who does the research? the typing? the marketing? What are the time frames? What about expenses? mailings? long-distance telephone calls and faxes? Who will keep the accounts?

Flexibility and freedom are essential in working partnerships. Even though you share similar motivations for the work, it is most important for both of you to understand that you don't have to collaborate on everything you write in the future. Each should be free to work alone or to collaborate with another writer on future projects.

Sometimes, a group member will pass around information regarding a nonwriter's request for a group member to serve as a ghostwriter or to write an "as-told-to" piece. Such works are based on the views and insights of another, and they involve collaboration of another kind.

However you choose to write in connection with a cowriter or subject, be sure that all expectations are clearly defined ahead of time. Have a long talk with yourself about coauthoring or ghosting and how easily you can accept anonymity. Be brutally honest, and if you decide that working with another is not for you, accept your decision. Don't feel compelled to do for money what you won't do for inner satisfaction. People who have—and for some of us, the only way to know what works for us is to do it—have sorely regretted it. No amount of money, they tell me, takes the place of what they had to give up.

If you are already or think you can become comfortably accustomed to working in tandem, collaborating may be right for you. For some people, half a share of something is better than a whole share of nothing. For others, haggling with someone else over details isn't worth the earnings, no matter what they are. Collaboration isn't for everyone, although it's uncommonly resourceful for some.

6.14 *Mentors*

This fast-paced, high-tech, impersonal era has also become the age of the counselor and the coach, the private trainer, and the specialty service. We rely on people who have more professional training and are more experienced than ourselves to serve as guides. Fortunately, within the context of the writers group, each participant has the opportunity to work with approachable, accessible mentors.

In decent-sized gatherings, such relationships develop and redevelop on a kind of round-robin basis. You may be coaching one writer who, in turn, is coaching another while someone else is coaching you. You may be part of a comentoring team. Often, while you are setting up another member as a potential mentor, someone else may be priming you for the same role. It's difficult to be an effective mentor if you've never experienced what it's like to have one. Quite often, a good mentor spawns a good mentor who spawns another good mentor, and so on. A positive learning cycle is set into motion. The more you experience of mentorship, the better you do it.

Good mentors push you to take risks that are emotionally hard. They also serve as buffers against life's blows. They lend emotional support, help you in getting rid of injurious attitudes that interfere with your fulfillment, interact with you, and, most important of all, set examples.

Facilitators

A productive writers group operates with direction. It has a facilitator who almost serves as a chauffeur, driving the vehicle of the group toward one destination at a time. It is through the sureness of this steering that each member travels forward.

7.1   Leading

Facilitators of good groups are responsible for directing each session effectively and efficiently. Even in cases in which different people take on facilitating roles at different times, group members rely on the acting leader to ensure that group rules are followed. One person at a time must have the final word that keeps the ground rules obeyed. The leader is responsible for ensuring group logistics in productive time frames. This leader starts and ends the meeting on schedule, keeps tab on who has read and when, and watches the clock so that the time spent on each manuscript is reasonable and equitable.

The group leader keeps all activities on track while safeguarding all elements of care and trust that are critical to the life of a good group. It is not an issue of control. Rather, it is a concern for each individual in the context of a healthy, functioning group. Don't fool with this one.

7.2   Communicating

Group facilitators must be aware communicators. It is up to them to ensure that all communication channels are kept open without any intruding, controlling, or forcing. Participation of the quieter writers should be encouraged through skillful drawing out and questioning. Helping members articulate must be done respectfully and gently without dominating or monopolizing the speaker.

The leader also takes charge of and diplomatically handles the person who talks too much. This should be done firmly enough to keep the chatterer from running the meetings. The group shouldn't have to listen to long, boring monologues, nor should the group be expected to politely tolerate someone who has something trite to say every few minutes. When listening is the point of order, these time wasters need to be quelled. It is the leader's responsibility to keep the discussion pertinent and moving forward. This means taking control when discussions drift off into side tangents. It also means putting an absolute halt to any talk that might degenerate into an aimless debate or, worse, the perpetuation of ongoing, redundant disagreements.

The leader also steers criticism away from becoming a knock-down-drag-out affair. Without chastising the critiquer, the leader soothes the hurt while gently showing the critiquer a better way of accomplishing the desired effect.

A good communicator should be able to enhance the overall vocalization of the group by propelling all of the loquacious group members in ways that utilize their rhetorical enthusiasm. In other words, what could be a communication disaster is turned into a communication asset.

7.3   Intervening

When it comes to group interaction, timing is everything, and a good leader works on yielding and pushing, each in its own time. It is up to the leader to nudge the group forward, to step in and pour oil when the waters get too troubled, to back off when the group is working through some vexation, and to keep the humor alive.

This is not to say that there won't be pitfalls, because there could and should be. Even if you are blessed with a particularly astute leader, there most certainly will be times of discomfort—lots of them. They are essential to the growth of the group. You really want a leader who neither avoids nor seeks such encounters.

The ideal leader dismisses no incident as insignificant but recognizes upsets when they arise and responds to them while they are still maneuverable. You don't want a leader who waits until power becomes an issue, but one who expertly intervenes on the spot, using firm communication skills to clarify conflicts and reestablish harmony.

Sometimes, personal attacks take place. If these come in your direction, leave a space for the leader to interject. A discreet silence in the face of an irresponsible tongue-lashing can be the most eloquent means of making others see the value of your position. Don't make any petty, personal counterattacks, no matter how on target you may be. This is the time for leader intervention. Your challenge is to remain steadfast, with a clear idea of purpose and goals, while remaining open to a variety of solutions. You can disagree tactfully and objectively, keeping your focus on the issue.

Accusations and win-lose arguments only degenerate, or worse, one person starts to rehash old conflicts, then another tries to initiate a new one, and before you know it the whole group is bellowing back and forth like rutting alligators. Leaders need to intervene in such situations. This is not to say that it is the responsibility of the leader to protect people from themselves; it is not. It is the responsibility of the leader to know when to advance or retreat, when to control or delegate control. If the intervention is truly effective, a form of teaching takes place.

7.4   *Teaching*

Teaching well is an ideal and a calling just as much as it is a performance art. It is not simply a trade or a living. Good teaching in writers groups and workshops is directly reflected in the results of the students.

Just because a writer is successfully published or esteemed for literary accomplishments, it doesn't mean that he or she will be effective as a workshop teacher. Many letters after a person's name is no indication of teaching ability, either. Just because a person has earned academic degrees doesn't guarantee that he or she can impart knowledge. Doing something well and teaching something well are separate functions, not necessarily paired. There are many talented and gifted writers who publish one literary masterpiece after another but cannot speak before a group of people in any understandable terms. Either they don't know how to reveal what they know in everyday language, or they find oral presentations so difficult that their struggle obscures their message.

Good teachers teach. This means that they explain theories and get across ideas in terms that everyone in the group can easily understand. They demystify what may seem impossibly mysterious. Suppositions and hypothetical questions flower in their classrooms. Important matters of expression aren't buried in academic or technical rhetoric. These instructors actually inform as they explain, reiterate, clarify, and simplify. They shed light on the dark corners in writers workshops.

7.4.1 Finding a Good Teacher

The best way to locate a good teacher is through referral by one of the teacher's students. However, if you are new to the area or don't know anyone to ask, it's up to you to decide whether a teacher is delivering the goods. Though there is a sense of adventure about connecting with a brand-new teacher, you may want a bit more information before committing yourself to the class. If you want to check your instructor's qualifications, ask for them. Contact the English department or the creative writing division or whatever office serves as the umbrella for the workshop. In the case of a private school, ask the workshop sponsor, if there is one; if the sponsor is the teacher, ask the teacher. Look for experience in writing or editing in conjunction with a reputation as a teacher with successful former or current students.

7.4.2 Teachers Who Showcase Themselves

Watch out for teachers who simply list their credits to establish their credentials. Sometimes, you are required to purchase all of their books to use in the class. Although this published work may be used to illustrate the progress of an idea from inception to publication, it could be replacing time that you dearly need to spend on your own works. Unfortunately, in a few creative writing workshops, the focus on the teacher's work can become so expansive that little attention is paid to individual students. You are not being served when a teacher discusses his or her own work at too great a length. The class was not intended as a sounding board for the teacher's work-in-progress. Updates are fine, as are anecdotes and informative tidbits, but that should do it.

I once received a telephone call from a woman who was interested in taking one of the workshops I was conducting. She asked a few questions about the logistics of the sessions and then, comfortable with what she heard, told me about her last experience. Jill wanted to focus on her novel in progress. She felt that she was close to her final draft and wanted lots of feedback. She enrolled in a novel-writing workshop conducted by a local author. It was a very expensive six-week course, and she looked forward to the intensive and extensive professional response promised in the course description. What actually took place was totally unexpected. At the first session, she was instructed to buy all four of the author's novels because all of the assignments would involve writing papers that examined his techniques. The workshop progressed into a tribute to the author-teacher. A portion of her work was discussed only once and briefly. She felt used by the instructor's ego and received nothing from the class to help her mature and develop her full creative potential.

7.4.3   Assignments

Getting involved with an instructor who gives minimum attention to student manuscripts can turn out to be a most frustrating experience. You learn to write by writing and by surveying what you have written. Unless the focus is strictly on works-in-progress, go with an instructor who will require you to write. Except for short exercises, writing should be done at home on a regular basis from assignments that arise from the needs and desires of the class. Instruction and homework assignments should progress logically from one lesson to the next so that sure and steady learning can take place.

You don't want an instructor who permits grunts and groans to interfere with the forward progression of the learning experience. Teaching is not a popularity contest. Student objections to certain assignments are to be expected, not appeased. Some exercises may seem almost ridiculous, but these are usually the ones that shed the most light on the creative process. For instance, it's advantageous for writers who claim to hate poetry to attempt to write a poem. It's useful for nonfiction writers to tackle a story. Anything a teacher does that gets the writer to use new creative muscles is beneficial.

7.4.4   Inflexible Instructors

You don't want a teacher to use his or her role to justify an "infallible" sort of approach. When the teacher is coercive and dominating and views himself or herself as holding the key to all of the writing secrets of the world, you will not build confidence. The onus will always be on the teacher not only to catch all mistakes, but to fix them, too.

If you're like the rest of us, most of your teachers insisted that you continue doing things the way you were told to do them: correctly! You don't need more of the same. You do not want someone who feeds you linear, restricted information and expects the same parroted back. You are not studying for a game of Jeopardy or Trivial Pursuit. You want to think for yourself. You want to create new things.

Watch out for teachers who have made up their minds and differentiate rigidly between what is good and what is not good in writing. An inflexible instructor who perceives only one kind of writing as valid is committed to such negative consistency. You need someone who is open to whatever natural and organic series of events evolve, someone who has little investment in a preconceived method of how to get there.

Especially watch out for taboos. Beware of someone who won't let you do realistic dialogue or stream of consciousness or test out new styles. Watch out for those who forbid the use of what they define as vulgar words or unacceptable ideas. Good teachers do not impose their own way of writing on their students. Instead, they help each individual understand who he or she is as a writer.

Life, after all, is an experience of the self. The hell of it is not knowing that or not giving yourself permission to act on it. The height of irresponsibility is to serve the yearnings and callings of another person's expectations. It is in trying to accomplish what you want for yourself that you open yourself up.

7.4.5 Motivators

How you are heartened and authenticated by teachers directly affects how much you learn. Experiments have proved this. For instance, several years ago, a teacher in New York was told that she had a class of gifted children when, in fact, she had a very normal, ordinary group. Because she believed what she was told, she went out of her way to develop what she was convinced were exceptional students. She spent lots of time preparing special lessons and staying after class. Her students, in turn, responded in a most positive way. They all scored higher than average on the same tests that had previously classified them as average. Because they were treated as gifted students, they performed as gifted students!

The influence of a fine teacher is possibly the most profound and moving event in one's life. An extraordinary teacher can crystallize your creative motivation. Charles Darwin, for example, was not considered particularly bright and didn't have the slightest idea that he possessed a talent for science. That was until he was a young man at Cambridge University and received powerful encouragement from his botany professor, John Henslow. Henslow successfully supported him as the candidate scientist for the voyage on the

Beagle, a voyage that Darwin likened to a rebirth. You, too, deserve someone who recognizes your far-reaching possibilities. Never underestimate the effects a motivating teacher can have on your creativity.

Do not settle for an instructor who reads the notes taken from lectures by a previous professor. Chances are the previous professor was reading notes taken from a prior professor, who took them from an earlier teacher, and so on back to when they were first scratched on a piece of slate.

All of us learn best by doing. Trying to write a sonnet or use a flashback episode teaches far more than memorizing any definition. Group discussions around particularly good and poor examples get the processes out in the open. Teachers who encourage spontaneous interactions provide fertile atmospheres in which to learn. They often use clever open questions to elicit ideas, and they present arguments to keep discussions moving.

Such classes become even more energizing when the teacher knows enough to call on students, especially the more reluctant ones, who may have a useful contribution to make. These fine teachers also seek out those who are levelheaded and can summarize or pinpoint ideas. They are not intimidated or threatened by clever and astute students. They draw from their brightness and guide it into the center of the discussion. Obviously, they enjoy their students.

7.4.6 Humor

A joyful countenance may be the biggest clue to an extraordinary teacher. You don't deserve one who is preoccupied with scowling and haggling over negotiable, moving clauses. Joy doesn't have much of a chance to flourish in an environment of "always" and "never." Nor do you need to be force-fed esoteric symbolism or psychospirituality as though it were some kind of metaphysical fast food. Sometimes a funny story about an elephant is simply that: a funny story about an elephant. A teacher who isn't afraid to laugh aloud when something is funny is a teacher who isn't afraid to delight in accepting some things at face value. Students learn best when they have one roaring good time doing it.

7.5 *Group Altercations*

Anytime you join a group of people, you set yourself up to agree with the opinions of some and disagree with those of others. Everyone does this.

Open disagreements should be encouraged because so much of one's creative development reveals itself through symptoms of apparent discord. If everyone agreed with everyone else, there would be no conflict, no tension, no energy. It is this struggle between opposite tendencies that produces creative energy in its finest sense and makes good groups into better ones. There are many creative ways for groups to disagree purposefully and with good intentions.

7.5.1 Change the Rules

You are not gathered together to blend and meld into a lukewarm general consensus. The intention of a writer's group is not to be bland and blank out all spirit with preconceived, homogenized, pasteurized definitions.

Nor is the collective intention to establish and conserve bylaws and general rules in a single-minded and rigid way, whatever the circumstances. "Because that's the way it's always been done" is an absolutely unacceptable attitude. Your group made rules based on reasons that made sense when the rules were made. You followed these rules. Time passed. Things changed. The original reasons for the generation of those rules may no longer exist. If there is a problem with the rules, they need to be reexamined and perhaps adapted, compared, reimagined, eliminated, reversed, parodied, connected, or incubated. Just because they are still in place is no reason to continue to follow them.

7.5.2 Reflect

One way to work things through is to set aside a limited amount of group time to address the problem. Each person presents the dilemma as he or she sees it. It is up to the leader to ensure that everyone speaks and that everyone is brief. Then the leader has everyone sit in silence and think. This detached process sometimes has miraculous results. Too much drama in the group clouds consciousness, just as too much talk overwhelms the senses. Continual input obscures genuine insight. This timed, silent reflection calms and stills. Then everyone writes down considerations and possible resolutions. After enough time has passed, everyone reads aloud what was written—and only what was written. No extemporaneous comments or asides are permitted. Usually a positive pattern emerges. If not, the entire procedure is repeated until a new path is uncovered.

There is a difference between this technique and reaching a decision through compromise. Compromise can leave some members of the group consciously or subconsciously resentful. Fresh troubles emerge out of every coerced solution, even when coercion was not intended. When a compromise has been reached in which each side grudgingly surrenders part of its real objectives, the solution is likely to prove to be temporary and unsatisfactory. When everyone participates in achieving a newly created clarification, then everyone feels part of a joint resolution. Productive activities originate when the group works together as a whole.

7.5.3   Brainstorm

Brainstorming is also a remarkably effective way to reach group resolutions. If it's done as it should be, which is completely democratically and relatively manic in style, much more emerges than was ever expected. A good brainstorming session is very difficult to lead properly and effectively. It sways far and wide in sense and nonsense. A typically successful session doesn't confine itself to too narrow a field by following preconceived rules. As a matter of fact, there is only one rule that everyone agrees on: Every rule you can think of can be broken except this one. When creative people get together to solve a problem, as many ideas as possible should be tossed around, built on, and brought eventually from a wild state to a practical one.

7.5.4   Freewriting through a Problem

Another technique for group resolution is to have everyone take some time to freewrite thoughts and ideas. This is done individually—no telephone calls, no huddles, no complaints to the person you think is at fault, no tattling to the leader. These are childish and spineless actions that skirt the issue at hand. Each person removes himself or herself from the group for a while to establish distance and perspective. Every thought is written: what is wrong, and what would make it right; what is hoped for, and what would be settled for; even random ideas. These writings will not necessarily be read aloud verbatim; they will serve as reminders so that everything, no matter how seemingly insignificant, is brought out and addressed.

Quicker on-the-spot resolutions can be initiated, too. If you are bringing up what you feel is a problematic situation, do it respectfully. Ask the group leader to give you five or ten minutes in which to speak about what is troubling you. You can also request suggestions and solutions, written or verbal, then or later.

7.6   Resistance

Writers who have been gathering for some time and are still going over the same stale works according to the same musty scripts are stuck. They are leaderless. Writers who gather only to reinforce initial preferences, with no regard to the discoveries of new information, are stuck, too. They are teacherless. Some groups have more difficulties than others and become mired in their problems. Some seem to flounder about and never quite get off the ground.

The problem is seldom a lack of leadership qualities or skills; too often it is the negative energy spread by group members who are resisting and contesting the facilitator. Instead of an "us" attitude, it's a "we-against-them" standoff. Infighting and battles for control only plug up the creative flow of the group.

Groups that maintain high levels of productivity and satisfaction support their facilitators, who, in turn, support the group members. These groups have mutual respect.

7.7   Mutual Respect

To tap into the resourcefulness of the teacher-student, member-leader polarity, mutual needs must be respected. This means acknowledging the premise that leaders need people to serve, and people need leaders to serve them.

When one person is entrusted with the responsibility of ensuring group logistics and guiding group energy back on track when it strays, others should cooperate with such efforts.

You must allow and support this flow as it waxes and wanes. When you do it generously, a kind of shared knowledge deepens to the point where there is no difference between learning and teaching. It all begins to blend into one totally integrated and balanced experience. If it doesn't, someone is preventing it.

I once had a student come up to me after a class with a smug and knowing smile to commend me on the way I "put down" another student during the session. Can you see why I struggled with that? First, I did not put down anyone, and second, to be thanked for doing something I abhor and discourage was disheartening. Such an attitude of going one better has no place, ever, in writers groups. Lauding what appeared to be unkind behavior reflected badly on the applauder. This was an abuse of role reversal.

7.8   *Fitting Role Reversals*

When you work with a teacher or leader in keeping the group's collective purpose in mind at all times, you exchange role responsibilities. In essence, the writing student becomes the writing teacher, and the teacher becomes the student.

When I began this book, I elicited the help of Jane, a student of mine whom I knew to be a prolific reader. She wrote succinctly and cleverly and was amazingly astute in class discussions. She became my first reader, going over my initial draft with a red pen (at her hesitancy and my request). She not only caught typos and grammatical errors, but she knew how I felt about writers groups and workshops and read my manuscript to ensure that all of the inherent messages clearly expressed my beliefs. In essence, she became the teacher, and I became the student.

This is how it should be: The participants become the group leaders, the unpublished become the published, the contestants become the judges. I see this happen again and again with writers. After I've left teaching assignments, core groups of students have sometimes formed to carry on the group synergy. Spin-off clubs have been organized by new leaders to work together on specific goals, such as putting together anthologies of their collective work or coordinating literary contests. Two writers who grew weary of being rejected by publications that accepted what they regarded as less-competent works went on to publish *Lines in the Sand*, their own successful small-press journal. More than a few of my students have gone on not only to judge local competitions, but to help other writers connect with local editors, publishers, and organizations that can help with grants and endowments.

Role reversal is not only appropriate in writers groups, but in some cases it is absolutely vital to the growth of the conclave. This is especially true when the group begins to explore new directions and is ready to reach extraordinary levels. These are the times when the group is propelling itself into what seems to be an undiscovered world. Neither the teacher nor the student knows for sure what is going to happen. This is when leaders and participants work together. They search together.

8

Starting Your Own Group

If you think you are ready for your own writers group but haven't as yet found one that fits your needs, then it's time to gear up to create one. If you've been in and out of groups but still haven't found the one that you think would serve you best, or even if you are in an operable group but somehow you still find yourself wanting, then you are ready to start up one of your own.

8.1 Signs of Trouble

Every group has its times of trouble. If every one disbanded each time difficulties arose, no group would survive its initial meeting. There are, however, some warning signs of irreconcilable problems that you should not ignore.

For example, if you write something good and your group members shrug it off as though they expected it, or you write something not so good and they go into a feeding frenzy of criticism, it's time to reevaluate.

Don't overreact at the first sign of trouble. Just mentally note certain incidents. The problem isn't in the isolated event; it's in the count and the amount. Everyone has off days. An occasional upset is to be expected, but when you find it happening more often than not, it's time to sit down and ask yourself some pertinent questions about the worth of it all.

You can use the following quiz as a guide. You'll get a feel for the aspects of your current group that you feel aren't up to par. Embellish and elaborate as you see fit.

Yes   No

( ) ( ) Most of the time, I am hesitant about asking for explanations or clarifications.

( ) ( ) My group is very impatient.

( ) ( ) When I am in the group, I worry about asking dumb questions, even though I know that no question is ever dumb.

( ) ( ) The writers in my group prefer seeing battles and rockets bursting in air rather than real, albeit sometimes plodding, progress.

( ) ( ) More often than not, when other group members laugh, I don't.

( ) ( ) I find many remarks to be offensive or annoying.

( ) ( ) I am becoming a nervous people-pleaser.

( ) ( ) I play it safe, never daring to assert any of my real convictions.

( ) ( ) Sooner or later, someone does something to irritate or aggravate me.

( ) ( ) Everything I write is to impress someone.

( ) ( ) I feel I am being force-fed by people who want me to think as they do.

( ) ( ) Whenever I try to talk about my own work, I feel that I am on the defensive.

( ) ( ) Whenever I excuse myself, I feel like the circus clown who keeps trying unsuccessfully to sweep up the spotlight.

( ) ( ) I am mostly bored listening to other people's work.

( ) ( ) Though I think the leader or teacher seems okay, I have a difficult time understanding him or her.

( ) ( ) No matter how many times I ask questions about craft and how many times it is reexplained, I still don't get it.

( ) ( ) I am writing more and more like an angry adolescent.

( ) ( ) I become very annoyed with those who insist that I write when I don't feel like it.

( ) ( ) I can't seem to help it, but I am becoming belligerent, throwing out things like "That's not what was said" or "You weren't supposed to do it that way" or "You can't do that."

( ) ( ) I know that I show off with foreign or technical words and references to obscure sources.

( ) ( ) I know that I flaunt last-minute works, scribbling as I walk in the door.

( ) ( ) I hate the assignments.

( ) ( ) There is one person in the group who sorely intimidates me.

( ) ( ) I hate the stupid written exercises we have to do.

( ) ( ) I feel much smarter than the rest of the group.

( ) ( ) I could run the group better than it is being run now.

( ) ( ) The general tone of the group is too superficial or too metaphysical or too academic.

( ) ( ) One or two mean members are infecting the others with their nastiness.

( ) ( ) These writers don't know the difference between honesty and brutality.

( ) ( ) I am always sticking up for someone else.

( ) ( ) I wish the group could be different.

( ) ( ) The group doesn't appreciate me.

( ) ( ) It is taking lots of extra effort to drag myself to meetings.

( ) ( ) I have fallen out of *like* for my group.

Did you get more yes answers than no answers? Interpret it as you will. This quiz will serve you only if you honestly think about what some of the questions mean to you.

You may discover that you are being rebellious, behaving in ways that disrupt the rest of the group. If this is the case, you may need to be challenged more. It's probably time for you to move onward and join a tougher, more rigorous group that will recognize your bad habits for what they are and not let you get away with them any longer.

Are you sensing communication problems? If you don't understand what is going on or feel that you are being misunderstood, there is a major glitch here that could be nearly impossible to work through. It's best to begin a search for another group in which communication channels are open and clear for you.

Are you afraid to speak up or hesitant to disagree? Assertive and aggressive groups sometimes seem to chew up and spit out shy and timid members. If you feel this is your situation, remove yourself from it. Find a group with a different temperament—one more compatible with yours, where you can build confidence.

8.2   Outgrowing and Embarking

If you feel as though you are not getting all that you want from your group experience, it could mean that you are sharing your works in a vacuum. You don't have to assign blame or fret over being too fussy or demanding. You need not reexamine yourself for hidden motives or chastise yourself for running away when you think that perhaps you should have stuck it out. Enough is enough.

No matter how hard you try, you won't come up with what went wrong. You will, of course, pull up countless logical and rational explanations. Like the fish that cannot see the water in which it swims, it's difficult to see what is going on around you while it is happening. In fact, it's not always readily apparent when a group has ceased to serve your needs. It's just as perplexing trying to determine when you have ceased to serve the needs of the group. It just happens.

8.3   Compatibility

The point is that you don't need suffering. Tribulation and confrontation may be great teachers, but every day you face quite enough adversity without any invitation on your part. You don't have to seek trouble; it will find you soon enough. You can and should remove yourself from a writers group that irritates you.

Similarly, you should remove yourself from a writers group that has become too comfortable. You know your group has become too comfortable if you feel bored most of the time. When you find yourself becoming creatively sluggish, it might be time to move to a higher, more rarefied atmosphere. Don't try to instigate radical change in an already established group. It would probably be better for everyone involved if you started fresh elsewhere.

If you feel impatient with the monotony, your current group might be too burrowed in for you. It's possible that you have already given what you were supposed to give and gotten what you were supposed to get. There is no sense in dragging the lesson on.

When you feel that no one else takes writing as seriously as you do, chances are you are right. Your fellow writers may be a wonderful bunch of people who like each other very much but are quickly losing ground to socializing. You may feel that they are more caught up with potlucks and barbecues than writing and critiquing and that the bulk of the meeting is spent planning outings. It may seem to you that the group has lost sight of its initial purpose. If group members really want a social club, you should let them have it.

You are dealing with a major reason why old groups fall apart and new groups reform. Deterioration begins when group members lose sight of their original goals. A kind of splitting takes place. Members who like the way the group has become stay. Those who don't like the way the group evolved simply relocate. There is no fault and no blame.

What you need is unanimity, not the perfect leader or the perfect group. You don't need to behave as though you were the perfect group member. You do want to search for the perfect match. It is within this third entity, the actual relationship between you and your group, that compacts develop.

8.4   Research

Research means "to search again." Why the repetition? Because in your search for a new writers group, you will first have to find one. Then you have to search again because once you are inside, you must look for what you need. You do research by visiting other groups.

Quite often, the most accessible groups are those that have been around for a long time and are still going strong every Wednesday night or on the first Monday of every month or some such magically appointed date. These groups are truly open, and they welcome the talents of newcomers. These capable groups can comfortably absorb the uneasy beginner as well as the fully developed professional. They will often let a potential new member sit in for a few meetings. If you are fortunate enough to receive such an invitation, grab it and graciously attend.

When checking out a new group, sit in and listen and observe. In most cases, visitors to the group hold no status, and others may view their excessive talk as presumptuous. Don't set yourself up for dismissal. It can be especially hard on your ego if a suggestion you made at the start of the meeting was rebuffed, only to be presented by someone else later and adopted. Don't take it personally. Understand that the group cannot afford to concede too much deference to a newcomer. Everyone else has paid some kind of dues, and as yet, you haven't.

Get a feel for the ambience. Pay attention to the way knowledge is imparted. Check the communication channels, and see if they are clear and working. Watch for idle gossip or silly social chatter. Good groups focused on obtaining information and putting it to use are too busy to waste time manufacturing small talk. They are ambitious.

Searching for a writers group will have you entering unknown territory for which there is no map. You may make many false starts. One group may seem promising until you check it out a few times, and then you may find that it isn't what it seemed. You will need to take off in another direction. All of those new doors opening, all of those opportunities for discovery, can cause you to flounder for a little bit.

Be discriminating. Be selective. Pay attention to what you know you require. Don't join just any old group in order to belong to something literary. You don't want to keep filling a niche; you want to fulfill your writing life. Don't allow yourself to be railroaded by a group because it appears to be prestigious or elite. If the group doesn't complement your current writing needs, you will be unbalanced, and your group experience will be without accord.

8.5   *Making Room for the New*

Start sorting things through. What were the ways of the old group that stopped working for you? Looking with new eyes and seeing new possibilities doesn't necessarily mean that you have to give up everything from the past. Instead, you must reevaluate. Keep from the past that which is still effective, and let go of that which no longer fits.

Make sure that you have plenty of opportunities to initiate new behaviors. Perhaps this time around you would like to listen more, or perhaps you would like to see what happens if you speak up more. You might want to be who you really are and say an honest "no" instead of putting up a front with a dishonest "yes."

You might be looking for a safe space where you don't have to continually worry whether you are disappointing or hurting someone else, or perhaps the opposite is true. You want a space where other people will stop and think before hurting you.

If, during your research, you don't find a group that offers the support and stimulation you are looking for, or if you find yourself wishing for the group you never had and even longing for it, then it is time for you to get busy.

8.6 Logistics

Making the group experience happen exactly as you think it should means fleshing in the details. It means making decisions that will guide the development of the group just the way you want it.

First, you will need to pull together a core group of a few writers who can work up the group expectations. You will need to consider the group's purposes and objectives as well as group activities that will help achieve them. Questions that ask "What if . . . ?" and "How . . . ?" will need to be answered. Likelihoods and limitations will have to be formulated. For example, will you review one another's already published articles to reslant them or revise them for other markets? Will you share books and magazines? Will you have a newsletter? Will you cosponsor events with other groups? Will you have contests, readings, or lunches? Will you help one another get publicity? Will you make available a directory of your members? Will you challenge one another with short writing assignments?

After you've gotten a fairly good idea of how you would like to operate, it's time to get practical and pay attention to the logistics of group size, time, and space. Though utilitarian and seemingly mundane, these elements do provide the table for the feast. Though group restrictions and stipulations may change and evolve, initially they need to be established.

8.6.1 Group Size

Groups can work as successfully with three participants as with thirty, but in groups that meet regularly, the size greatly affects the creative dynamics that emerge. Usually, when there are few participants, everyone plays multiple roles. For instance, if two members get into an argument, a third can become a neutral facilitator. Small groups may not have enough people to achieve the critical mass required for the best creative problem solving, but they are easier to manage, and their informality and flexibility can generate interesting energies.

Larger groups need more recognizable structure. They can easily get sidetracked, bogged down, or too emotionally charged for effectiveness. They require experienced leaders who know how to facilitate because such group dynamics become extremely complex. Even the task of making sure that everyone has a chance to be heard without being interrupted can become overwhelming. Subgroups and cliques form, and sometimes getting everyone pointed in the same direction can be time-consuming and frustrating.

Seven to fifteen people is the ideal size for a writers group. Attendance will not always be 100 percent, and although a core group will attend regularly, others will drop in and out. A group of this size will always have enough and never have too many, and participation will be effortless. Everyone will get to know and appreciate everyone else's writing intentions and goals. The group will be small enough to maintain informality and spontaneity but big enough to accept leadership. Sitting face to face with others in a group of this size allows for on-the-spot, effective communication. Each writer can react immediately to suggestions directed not only at him or her, but also at another writer. Issues that are clearly unnecessary can be omitted. Ideas that may not occur when individuals struggle alone can emerge.

8.6.2   Time

Two- to three-hour sessions with a five- to fifteen-minute break halfway through are the most effective. Depending on the schedules of the members, these sessions may be in the morning, the afternoon, or the evening of an appointed day of the week or month. They should begin promptly, and allowances should be made for late closings. Creative surges, someone's unexpected publication, and heated disagreements can all cause a meeting to last longer than anticipated. Generally, meetings should finish on time, but here and there they may run over.

8.6.3   Space

Where the writing group meets can affect how successfully the group works. In a room that is too big, the group may be intimidated by the huge surroundings and complain of cold drafts and echoes. In a room that is too small, writers will feel crowded and crushed, and the air will become hot and stuffy. Temperature, light, and noise may seem to be mundane problems, but they can interfere with the group's progress when they bother you and others around you.

A suitable temperature for working and saving energy is 68°F. Bodies give off heat, so rooms become warmer with people in them. Windows that open to let in fresh air are a plus. Lack of oxygen can drain the mind and the body.

Good, even lighting is essential. The lighting should not be too glaring or too dim and murky. Natural light is wonderful, but a combination of indirect incandescent and overhead fluorescent light can work at eliminating heavy shadows.

The room shouldn't be too noisy. Interruptions and distractions should be kept to a minimum: no phones, no puppies or kittens jumping on laps, no rustling bags of potato chips being passed about, and no background music. Note that I said "kept to a minimum" here. I've hosted and participated in many groups where we munched on cheese and crackers, drank wine, and at least one person held a purring cat. Once, we had someone practicing piano upstairs, and another time we sat around a splashing fountain in a member's foyer. Everything went wonderfully. The key word is *disruptive*. The workshops I conduct in my home always include tea and coffee, something to nibble on, and three Yorkshire terriers running about, yet we still accomplish great feats. Of course, we are seated at tables where everyone can clearly see and hear everyone else.

Whether your group sits in a living room on pillows or at tables in a meeting room, the seating pattern can make a tremendous difference. Although the closed form of a circle encourages a sense of warmth and togetherness, a semicircle is the best seating arrangement for writing groups. The facilitator (and a blackboard or equivalent if you have such) should be positioned in the front of the group. Full circles encourage intense, face-to-face exchanges. Semicircles allow the release of energy. Ideally, the semicircle should face away from the entrance so that people coming in or going out will not disrupt the flow. It is a reality that some people will arrive late, others must leave early, and still others will need a few quick visits to the bathroom. No one wants to feel like a prisoner.

If tables are available, narrow ones are preferred. They should be arranged in a splayed **U** shape with the participants sitting around the outside.

The way writers position themselves within the group reveals a lot about their interpersonal dynamics and levels of involvement. Certain people like to isolate themselves by leaving an empty seat next to them, which serves as an energy leak, a hole in the group. Others may disrupt the focus by sitting outside the semicircle. Consciously or not, this creates a position of power. The member can pretend to not be there and then suddenly toss out a cryptic contribution, causing everyone to swivel around in their seats.

Go for what feels best.

8.6.4   Focus

The entire group's focus should always be on the writer who is sharing his or her work at the moment. The group should provide a format for the suspension of individual opinions, beliefs, and judgments in order to be able to listen to each writer fully and completely. This also calls for sufficient sympathy and interest to understand the meaning of the other's position.

If these and other group purposes are stated clearly at the outset, it will rarely be necessary for the leader to reinforce them. As trust builds and the necessary spirit of goodwill and friendship develops, the urge to go deeper and explore new ground will bring new life to the circle.

All of these logistics should be worked through clearly so that everyone operates from a primary interest in empowering the others in an environment of openness and flexibility.

8.7   *Imposed Deadlines*

Groups that set impractical deadlines can hinder the creative growth of their members. Try not to impose unrealistic deadlines on yourself, and do not permit group pressures to establish them. Group leaders are too often unduly influenced by our hurry-up world. We are convinced that it's best to get rich quick, remove stains fast, cook instant foods, and obtain immediate results or our money back. We focus only on getting from point A to point B as quickly as possible.

What matters is what happens along the way. Your writers group is a living entity. It has a life. The life-journey of the group is what matters, the way it travels. It gets born, and it dies. What matters is what happens in between. You need to ensure that the between time is sufficient. You don't want to set up restrictions.

To form a group and put a time limit on what you expect from that group is to manufacture time pollution, which thickens into a time for giving up. The pressure of time, in whatever form it takes—internal or external deadlines of any kind—is an emotional catalyst par excellence for paralyzation.

I am not suggesting that when you form a collective, you reduce your own standard to unrealistically shoddy levels. What I'm saying is that impossibly high demands can prevent you and others in your group from acting on and attaining goals that are humanly possible and satisfying.

8.8   Levels and Limits

What is the range of expertise you would like covered in your group? Do you want only members who are currently writing or those who want to begin? Will you want manuscripts submitted first? Will there be prerequisites? Will the group be open to everyone, no matter what or how they write? Will it be limited to specifically defined writers? There are pros and cons to all of these group focuses.

When all of the writers are at a similar level of development and are working in the same general area of writing, group progression seems to flow with more ease and less resistance. Being regularly in the company of other people who are trying to do essentially the same thing as you and having the same sort of problems doing it can cut a large amount of slack. Frequently, the most ambitious writers operate within a group in which everyone is equally published or nonpublished and has been writing for a similar length of time.

Then again, members of varying levels of experience can bring inexperienced writers to the level of professional ones by offering much-needed distance and perspective. The challenge of reaching out to writers at different levels can be sheer motivation for some. Even simply listening to questions and suggestions can stimulate others to think in new ways because such symposia interpret and summarize lots of valuable information.

Whether you find your newly forming group attracting like minds or a mish-mash of thinkers, know that group members can set in motion some invaluable learning experiences. No matter that their very energy may call for alertness and quick thinking. No matter that they don't hesitate with their recommendations regarding your masterpieces. There are writers who would die to spend time in such a group, if it would have them.

8.9   Age Differences

A wide range of ages in a writers group is good. In fact, the wider, the better. Segregating writers according to age only tightens the time-experience boundaries of group discussions. Too many of these writers will have had the same experience of the same events. Views will begin to get moldy. When you have young and old writers mixing together, you've got an abundance of wonderful differences.

Youthful exuberance apart, many writers get better as they get older. Frances Parkinson Keyes might have published her first novel when she was thirty-four, but she published her first best-seller, *Honor Bright*, when she was fifty-one, and she achieved her greatest success at sixty-three with *Dinner at Antoines*.

Keep in mind that suggestions that may be important for one age may not be appropriate to another. Insights of the older writers should never be imposed on younger group members who do not want to hear them. By the same token, younger writers don't have to rule the collective opinion on what is current.

Group members need to be sensitive toward each individual's race, sex, and creed as well as age.

8.10   The Responsibilities of the Leader

Usually, the person who starts a new writers group leads it. This person may be a college professor, a published author, the organizer with the most energy, or the person with the biggest living room. Regardless of his or her background, the leader must assume a certain amount of responsibility for the power of the leadership role—and powerful it is! Although not expected to be a guru or a magician, the leader will need to serve as guide, peacemaker, enforcer of rules, generator of excitement, moderator of discussion and arguments, and unifier of group spirit.

It is the leader's responsibility to keep the group on track at all times. This does not mean scowling and halting. It means controlling discussions when they drift off into tangents. It means recognizing and diverting any talk that might degenerate into an aimless debate or, worse, personal opinions regarding sex, religion, or politics. This is where the leader must interject, pick up the pace, and move the group forward.

Overall, it is up to the leader to ensure that whatever feedback is being encouraged, it is understood clearly by everyone. The leader must know and understand what is being communicated in the group at all times. More specifically, the leader should be in a constant state of vigilance, keeping eyes and ears receptive to all kinds of subtle signals.

8.11   What about You as a Group Leader?

Perhaps you feel that you would like to be the group leader. What must you know? You must know yourself first of all.

Think about what matters to you. How much effort are you willing to expend to motivate people to perform at their highest levels? How much money or appreciation do you expect in return? How much praise will you want for fostering success in others? Will you gossip with other group members? How will you feel if they gossip about you, criticize you, or, worse, misunderstand you? How important is it to you to always be right? Can you admit to being wrong in front of others? Can you allow someone else to be wrong and let it slide?

These questions require honest answers. If you don't deal with them before you become a leader, you will have to do so later. There is no way to get beyond them, except by working them through. It's up to you to figure out the group's accountability as well as your own.

Do a little self-assessment. What are your communication strengths and weaknesses? What is the status of your human relations skills, your technical skills, and your organizational skills?

It's up to you to accept and acknowledge what you realistically can and cannot do, what you will and will not do, and what you might and might not do. Examine your sense of self. Know where you stand and what you stand for. If you don't do it beforehand, believe me, you'll find out soon enough once you start taking charge.

8.12   What If You Stumble?

No matter how carefully you study leadership techniques, no matter how diligently you apply expert theories, you will stumble. You will wonder at such times what in the world possessed you to involve yourself with such a lot of ungrateful, unappreciative people. You'll have moments when you will feel that no one is paying attention to what you say or, the flip side of the coin, that everyone blames everything on you. You may have to admit that you were wrong or made a mistake or forgot. You may have to deal with the fact that someone doesn't like you and is leaving the group because of you. Something in your personal life could be sapping you of all energy and health. You might sense mutiny in the air and cannot rise to meet it.

Whatever the challenge, it is this jumping-off point that you must reach before you can rise in your leadership. When you face the challenge, you'll develop a better understanding of group dynamics and of your own personal limitations. You'll find ways to better keep your egocentricity in check. This means not insisting that everything comes out a certain way. You'll know how to speak the words "I don't know" or "I could be wrong" with utmost confidence. You will have come to terms with the fact that you don't know everything and that you have much to learn—and you'll be grateful that you are in the perfect position to do so.

If you have the incredible privilege of leading, accept the challenge with gusto. Stretch yourself beyond the commonplace as you work to empower storytellers, poets, speakers, timid venturers, message bringers, sensitives, and singing rebels. Actively pursue the extraordinary. Be the best leader you can be, and you will value yourself as you never have before and you will learn how to allow others to value you, also.

8.13 Reaching Beyond the Group

Writers participate in a communal art. Though the craft of writing is accomplished in private, the work itself brings all of us together over centuries and national boundaries. It's just as natural for writers to want what they have written to be read as it is for writers to make their talents visible and accessible. There is nothing wrong with reaching out to others. In fact, there is an awful lot of good in sharing your creative talents.

One of the more generous acts a group leader or group members can do is to reach out to other writers beyond their inner circle. In any metropolitan area, small groups of writers can be found presenting open readings to their communities. They usually read their poetry, but excerpts from prose pieces are sometimes read, too. Open readings can take place at a variety of locations, from coffee houses to bars to rented halls. "Open" means that anyone may come and read: all ages, all levels of achievement, all writers willing to read aloud from their own works.

Some sort of donation is often requested at the door, but usually no one is turned away for lack of funds. Sometimes a hat or the equivalent is passed around for donations.

The reading usually opens with one or more scheduled guest readers; then the open-mike session begins. There is sometimes a sign-up sheet, and readers perform on a first-come, first-served basis. Some programs are spontaneous, and readers jump up whenever there is an opening. The time designated to each person varies according to the number of participants, but ten minutes per reader is usual.

Participating is much more energizing than simply observing the proceedings, although watchers and listeners are vital links in such reading chains. "To have great poetry," Walt Whitman wisely pointed out, "there must be great audiences, too."

Writers groups often attend the open readings of other writers groups in a show of support and validation and read from their own works at the open-mike session. It is an empowering experience for everyone involved.

Whether inclined to write or driven to write, ultimately your highest duty is to please and satisfy yourself. Eventually, however, the time comes when you produce something that others really ought to have a chance to see. You don't pretend anymore that it doesn't matter, because it does. Being creative and using your writing to express your creativity matters a whole lot. You've reached the point where you would love to share what you are doing with other writers, where you would love to read to an audience. When you reach this stage, you should read your work to others, and you should encourage your group to do so, too!

Today, we are seeing more writers groups organize open readings. They find and secure appropriate locations and handle any advertising in local and subculture newspapers. They often unite with academic sponsors or participate in bookstore events.

When your group is ready to put on its own reading, you will be called on to calm frazzled nerves if you are leading the group. It's difficult to get up in front of a group of people and perform your own work, so a few words of advice here may help you and your fellow readers.

The word *perform* is used here in conjunction with oral interpretation. You will want to practice beforehand so that you can perform audibly and understandably. You'll also need to get a feeling not only for the amount of time each piece requires to be read aloud, but also for the sound. You may need to speed up or slow down the pace.

Don't frustrate the listeners by mumbling under your breath as you shuffle through papers, not knowing what to read next. Have a decent idea beforehand of your presentation options. The mood of the room may be such that what you had intended to share would fall flat. You can sometimes sense the appropriateness of a particular piece of work just before your turn.

Be nervous, but don't be afraid. At these readings, the audience is on your side. They want you to do well and will applaud when you do. Relax as you read. Recounting an anecdote related to the piece you are about to read or mentioning the circumstances surrounding its creation is not only acceptable but most welcome. Remember that the audience is composed of fellow writers. They are there just as much for you as you are there for them. Enjoy!

8.14 Community

As a writer, it is fitting and altruistic that you offer your gifts to your community. There are many instances in which a small donation of your time will prove invaluable to a community effort.

You can help coordinate or judge local writing competitions. You can conduct workshops in the schools. You can represent writers on various boards and committees and lend a hand to agencies in your region that help artists and writers. You can participate in benefit readings and even master-plan letter-writing campaigns to representatives and senators to support and extend local programs. When you contribute your talents as a writer to your community, you begin to weave a network with others like you. Consequently, as you become more visible at these organized events and are identified as the writer that you are, the scope of your literary world will widen. You will meet not only other writers, but also people who can be of enormous help to you personally and to your group as a whole.

This is called making contacts, and like it or not, who-knows-who has an awful lot to do with what makes our world go around. However, contacts will rarely, if ever, make a success out of a bad writer.

Some writers feel that making such connections is somehow cheating, that talented writers should be able to make it based solely on the quality of their writing. If you are a writer who finds the whole game of making contacts repugnant, you are not alone. If you can't bear glad-handing and socializing or even making polite phone calls and are attracted to freelance writing because it allows you to avoid such things, don't despair. You can do all of your writing in a cavern and still get published. It is possible to make it on talent alone, but what is wrong with smoothing the way?

Unfortunately, the publishing world cannot be very easily accessed unless you go through the channels. Contacts can be enormously helpful. The right people can help put you a step or two ahead of the rest of the competition. They can make the difference between the reading or dismissal of a decently written manuscript. They can even affect the scope and size of your success. Eventually, at conferences and such, you will get to know publishers, agents, sales representatives, and publicity people. Don't underestimate the value of knowing people in writing and writing-related fields.

There is nothing wrong with acknowledging writers that you respect, especially if they live in your area. Sincere comments on works that you admire and questions about local writer's clubs, workshops, and classes may bring you some worthwhile advice and suggestions, not to mention unexpected invitations.

One of my students approached an author at a conference. They ended up chatting, one thing led to another, and she now participates in monthly one-day romance-writing workshops at the author's fabulous home. Along with a gourmet catered lunch, she receives editing and encouragement on the book she is working on. She is now circulating a book proposal to agents recommended by the group.

Another student, an exceptionally gifted young poet, wrote a letter thanking a local, established poet for an exceptional performance at a recent reading. A month later, he received a telephone call from the poet thanking him for his letter and inviting him to join a group he was forming at a local coffee shop. A small press publisher heard my student read his work and is now printing up a beautiful chapbook of his poems.

There are countless other stories I could tell. Suffice it to say that an unselfish acknowledgment of another writer's talent can sometimes be very rewarding.

Venture

Reward yourself. Tap into that wonderful world of writers. Use the rest of this book to help you connect. Browse through the following listings, and don't hesitate to make inquiries. Wherever possible, I've included phone numbers, fax numbers, and e-mail addresses, but remember that these are subject to change from time to time. Your best bet is to write; mailing addresses seem less apt to change as much. Don't forget that if you send away for information, it is a professional courtesy to include a stamped, self-addressed envelope (SASE) for the recipient's convenience in responding or sending you brochures and flyers.

I would love to hear your success stories as well as your suggestions for areas that you'd like to see addressed in future updates of this book. You know all you need now to get started and keep going. Good luck!

Part Two

9

Major Writers Organizations

Listed in this chapter are the major organizations that writers use to keep in touch with one another. A few may not be large in terms of membership, but they have developed giant reputations. The programs, individuals, and institutions that help writers connect with other writers fall into three basic categories:

1. National organizations of professional writers, usually restricted to one particular genre, which provide information to and advocacy for their members

2. Regional groups, often functioning as branches of larger national organizations, which focus their efforts on a particular geographic area

3. Writer's clubs, usually informal and local in membership, which provide places for writers to meet and talk, to hear speakers, and to read and critique one another's work

Some organizations are geared toward professional and financial advancement. Others, much less formal, are designed to get aspiring gentle dabblers chatting comfortably with tough-muscled published authors. Most organizations offer a newsletter filled with current market news; advocacy and grievance procedures to put pressure on editors and publishers who aren't treating members properly; professional advice; and a member directory. Some offer legal services, discounts, referral services, group insurance plans, and emergency loans to writers. Conferences, lectures, panels, classes, seminars, annual awards, grants and fellowships, banquets, wine tastings, cocktail parties, lunches, and presentation dinners are sometimes offered.

Some organizations provide information and services to all writers on request, often at no charge. Most, however, offer services and benefits only or primarily to their members. The cost of joining writers organizations varies greatly. Some charge annual dues as well as initiation fees.

If you find an organization that looks promising, request a brochure. Ask if there are branches or chapters in your area. Don't be intimidated about contacting these organizations. Remember that they all started out as smaller groups or clubs.

Academy of American Poets
177 East 87th Street
New York, NY 10128
(212) 645-2368

Membership 2,000. Publishes *Envoy*, *Poetry Pilot*, the Lamont Poetry Selection, and Walt Whitman Award books. Sponsors the Lavan Younger Poets Award, the Lamont Poetry Selection, the Walt Whitman Award, and the Harold Morton Landon Translation Award. Also sponsors more than 120 college and university prizes around the country and holds workshops for high school students. Awards fellowships to American poets for distinguished achievement.

Alabama Writers' Conclave
117 Hanover Road
Birmingham, AL 35209
(205) 871-6855

Membership 400. Publishes a newsletter quarterly and *The Alalitcom* annually. Membership is open to all and includes contests in poetry, fiction, and nonfiction. Annual conference held at the University of Montevallo campus features workshops on the writing specialties, lectures, discussions, and public poetry readings.

American Dialect Society (ADS)
MacMurray College
English Department
Jacksonville, IL 62650
(217) 479-7000

Membership includes 300 institutions and 550 individuals who study not only the English language in North America, but also languages that influence or are influenced by English. Provides research information to writers with questions about regionalisms. Publishes *American Speech* quarterly, *Publication of the American Dialect Society* occasionally, and *Newsletter of the American Dialect Society* three times a year.

American Film Institute (AFI)
Outreach Program
2021 North Western Avenue
Los Angeles, CA 90027
(800) 999-4234

Created by the National Endowment for the Arts. An independent nonprofit organization that provides the professional film and video community with a forum for screenwriters, independent artists, and the general public. Offers workshops, seminars, and weekend courses year-round, as well as seven-session beginning to advanced writing courses.

American Library Association
50 East Huron Street
Chicago, IL 60611
(312) 944-6780; Fax (312) 440-9374

Membership of 48,000 includes libraries, library trustees, individual librarians, and other individuals interested in promoting and improving library services. Publishes

Booklist semimonthly; *American Libraries* monthly; *Choice* monthly; and various pamphlets. Holds an annual convention.

American Literary Translators Association

University of Texas at Dallas
P.O. Box 830688
Richardson, TX 75083-0688
(214) 690-2093; Fax (214) 690-2989; E-mail: ert@UTDallas.edu

A tax-exempt organization founded to provide essential services to literary translators from all languages. Publishes *Translation Review* triquarterly. Provides a translation clearinghouse and library. Sponsors an annual conference that includes panels and talks, bilingual readings, and an exhibition of presses publishing translations.

American Medical Writers' Association (AMWA)

5272 River Road, Suite 370
Bethesda, MD 20816
(301) 493-0003; Fax (301) 493-6384

Offers an annual conference for professional medical communicators, with sixty workshops scheduled concurrently. Participants may specialize or take a multidisciplinary program. Workshops are designed to improve skills in the audiovisual, editing/writing, education, freelance, pharmaceutical, and public relations areas of biomedical communications.

American Society of Journalists and Authors (ASJA)

1501 Broadway, Suite 1907
New York, NY 10036
(212) 997-0947; Fax (212) 768-7414

Membership 800. Publishes *Annual Membership Directory; ASJA Newsletter; Code of Ethics and Fair Practices with Letter of Agreement;* and *ASJA Handbook: A Writer's Guide to Ethical and Economic Issues.* Offers lectures and meetings to provide an exchange of ideas and market and service information. Serves as a professional referral and First Amendment advocacy group. Sponsors an annual writer's conference.

American Translators Association (ATA)

3818 North Ridgeview Road
Arlington, VA 22207
(914) 941-1500

International membership of 2,300 includes active, associate, student, institutional, corporate, and sustaining members. Publishes *ATA Chronicle.* Sponsors the Alexander Gode Medal; the Lewis Galantiere Prize for literary translation; the Distinguished Service Plaque for outstanding and dedicated service; and the Academic Programs Fund for students. Convenes annually.

Appalachian Mountain Club (AMC)

Box 298S
Gorham, NH 03581
(603) 466-2727

Membership approximately 50,000. The nation's oldest recreation and conservation organization. Offers more than 150 workshops and programs on a broad range of topics, including writing, as well as two- to six-day seminars for those aspiring to staff editing positions and freelance contributing.

Appalachian Writers Association (AWA)
Box 6935
Radford University
Radford, VA 24142-6935
(703) 831-5269

Membership approximately 300. Open to anyone who identifies with the region, is a native, or writes about it. Sponsors an annual conference for all levels, offering readings, workshops, book sales, and conversation with prominent writers.

Arizona Authors' Association
3509 East Shea Boulevard, Suite 117
Phoenix, AZ 85028-3339
(602) 942-4240

Membership approximately 250. Publishes Authors' Newsletter bimonthly and Arizona Literary Magazine annually. Strives to provide members with information and counseling to achieve their writing objectives. Serves as a referral center for members. Sponsors workshops and seminars. Conducts an annual writers conference and literary contest and holds writers retreats. Offers membership for published writers or those who are working toward publication.

Arizona Christian Writers
Box 5168
Phoenix, AZ 85010
(602) 838-4919

Conducts an annual two-day seminar for 150 to 250 writers specializing in Christian writing, travel, children's writing, devotional, fiction, nonfiction, poetry, drama, and songwriting.

Associated Writing Programs (AWP)
Old Dominion University
Norfolk, VA 23529-0079
(804) 683-3839

Membership approximately 12,000. Publishes AWP Chronicle newsletter bimonthly and An Official Guide to Writing Programs. A national nonprofit organization to promote and foster creative-writing programs, encourage development of college and university curricula and staff, and conduct policy studies of the writer in higher education. Sponsors competitions for awards and publication. Cosponsors a literary festival with Old Dominion University. Offers institutional memberships for faculty and students.

Association of American University Presses
584 Broadway
New York, NY 10012
(212) 941-6610; Fax (212) 941-6618

A nonprofit organization that consists of more than 100 presses, ranging in size from those producing a handful of titles to those publishing hundreds each year. Organizes national and regional meetings, sponsors workshops and seminars, produces publishing-related books and catalogs, and operates cooperative exhibits programs.

Austin Writers' League
1501 West Fifth Street, Suite E2
Austin, TX 78703
(512) 499-8914

Membership approximately 1,600. Publishes Austin Writer monthly. Conducts statewide readings, workshops, seminars, study groups, and meetings. Provides library resource center, audiotapes, and technical assistance. Sponsors a writers-in-the-schools programs, Violet Crown Book Awards, Young Texas Writers Awards, and Word Is Art Awards.

Authors Guild
330 West 42nd Street
New York, NY 10036
(212) 563-5904; Fax (212) 564-5363; E-mail: Authors@pipeline.com

Membership approximately 6,500. A national membership organization dealing with the business and professional interests of authors (i.e., copyrights, contracts, subsidiary rights, taxes, etc.). Publishes *The Bulletin* quarterly. To be eligible for membership, a writer must have a book published by an established publisher within the last seven years or three works, fiction or nonfiction, published by a magazine within the last eighteen months.

Authors League of America, Inc.
330 West 42nd Street
New York, NY 10036
(212) 564-8350; Fax (212) 564-5363; E-mail: Authors@pipeline.com

Membership approximately 14,500. Restricted to authors and dramatists who are members of The Authors Guild and The Dramatists Guild. A corporation of national membership to promote professional interests of authors and dramatists, procure satisfactory copyright legislation, guard freedom of expression, and support fair tax treatment for writers.

Authors Resource Center, Inc. (TARC)
P.O. Box 64785
Tucson, AZ 85728-1785
(606) 325-4733

Membership approximately 300. Founded for aspiring and published authors who want to enhance their professional income. Publishes a bimonthly newsletter. Offers classes, workshops, and seminars yearly on a variety of subjects. Manuscript critiques and consultations available.

Aviation/Space Writers Association
17 South High Street, #1200
Columbus, OH 43215
(614) 221-1900

Membership approximately 800. Publishes an annual directory, an association newsletter, and other publications. Dedicated to establishing and maintaining high standards for reporting aeronautical information. Provides advice on covering aviation and space events through individual contacts, referrals, seminars, meetings, and affiliations with local chapters or regions.

Before Columbus Foundation
The Ginn House
660 13th Street, Suite 203
Oakland, CA 94612
(510) 268-9772

A nonprofit service organization that provides information, research, consultation, and promotional services for contemporary American multicultural writers and publishers. Publishes *Before Columbus Review* quarterly. Sponsors the Annual American Book Awards as well as a variety of classes, workshops, readings, and public events.

Beyond Baroque
Literary/Arts Center
681 Venice Boulevard
P.O. Box 2727
Venice, CA 90291
(310) 822-3006

Membership 600. A nonprofit arts organization founded to encourage and promote new literature. Is expanding into an interarts center to provide a forum for readings and so on. Presents a year-round reading and performance series, writing workshops, advanced poetry workshops for selected participants, and free open readings.

Biola University Writers Institute
Biola Avenue
La Mirada, CA 90639
(310) 903-4805

Sponsors an annual article-writing contest, open to all, with prizes awarded for both published and unpublished writers, as well as a poetry contest. Hands-on classes, video correspondence, and year-round manuscript services available. Offers an annual conference to serve more than 400 attendees of beginner, intermediate, and advanced levels.

California Writers' Club
2241 Derby Street
Berkeley, CA 94705
(510) 841-1217

Membership approximately 900. Serves professional writers. Publishes *California Writers' Club Bulletin* monthly. Conducts an annual writers conference as well as yearlong workshops in fiction, nonfiction, and poetry. Branches conduct their own workshops and contests.

Callanwolde Poetry Committee
980 Briarcliff Road, N.E.
Atlanta, GA 30306
(404) 872-5338

Presents an annual weekend conference that offers workshops, panels, manuscript critique, a writers contest, and an evening reading open to fiction and poetry writers of all levels. The conference is held at the Callanwolde Fine Arts Center, a Tudor-style mansion, where a variety of programs ranging from one-day workshops to ten-day classes is offered to adults and children.

Christian Writer's Guild
260 Fern Lane
Hume, CA 93628
(209) 335-2333

Membership approximately 3,500. Publishes *Quill o' the Wisp* quarterly. Primarily for members of the Guild and students but open to everyone. Sponsors three-year home-study course and one-day workshops.

Council of Literary Magazines and Presses
154 Christopher Street, Suite 3C
New York, NY 10014
(212) 741-9110; Fax (212) 741-9112

Membership approximately 435. A national nonprofit organization providing services to noncommercial literary magazines and book publishers. Publishes *Directory of Literary Magazines* annually and *CCLM News* triquarterly or quarterly. Assists with cooperative advertising.

Sponsors award programs for literary magazines and presses.

Editorial Freelancers Association (EFA)
36 East 23rd Street, Room 9R
New York, NY 10159
(212) 677-3357; Fax (212) 777-8207

Membership of approximately 1,000. Publishes a newsletter bimonthly. Also publishes a directory, resume book, and rates survey. Offers links with other professional freelance editors, indexers, writers, translators, production specialists, proofreaders, and researchers. Provides educational services, insurance programs, and meetings to share information about current business practices and trends. This nonprofit volunteer organization is open to professional freelancers.

Education Writers Association (EWA)
1331 H Street, NW
Washington, DC 20036
(202) 637-9700; Fax (202) 872-9707

Membership approximately 600. Publishes a bimonthly newsletter, *Education Reporter*, and a guide and directory, *Covering the Education Beat*. Sponsors the National Awards for Education Reporting, open to all writers, and offers an annual, national seminar. Also sponsors an annual special research seminar on major educational issues, open to twenty to twenty-five members who are selected by an outside judge from all who apply. Members include education reporters from newspapers, magazines, television, and radio.

Florida Freelance Writers Association
Affiliate of Cassell Network of Writers
Maple Ridge Road
North Sandwich, NH 03259
(603) 284-6367; Fax (603) 284-6648

Membership approximately 1,200. Publishes *Freelance Writer's Report* monthly, *Directory of Florida Markets for Writers* annually, and *Guide to Florida Writers* annually. Affiliated with Chastely Network of Writers. Conducts regular seminars and updates computer database of Florida writers by location and areas of expertise.

Freelance Editorial Association
Box 835
Cambridge, MA 02238
(617) 729-8164

Membership approximately 500. A nonprofit, voluntary organization for freelance editors, writers, proofreaders, indexers, researchers, and translators who work for trade, technical, business, and educational publishers. Publishes *Freelance Editorial Association News* quarterly and *Freelance Editorial Association Yellow Pages* and *Code of Fair Practice* annually. Sponsors projects to provide advocacy and establish standards of fair business practice. Provides formal and informal meetings as well as a telephone network for members.

Garden Writers Association of America
10210 Leatherleaf Court
Manassas, VA 22111
(703) 257-1032; Fax (703) 257-0213

Membership approximately 1,100. Publishes *Quill and Trowel*, a monthly newsletter. Sponsors an annual writers contest and an annual award program for published articles and books.

Golden Triangle Writers Guild (GTWG)
4245 Calder
Beaumont, TX 77706
(409) 898-3078

Membership approximately 900. Publishes *Scene and Sequel* monthly. Open to all interested writers. Holds monthly meetings and provides a writers support group. Sponsors an annual conference with workshops, an editorial panel, writing contests, and synopsis critiques.

Hellgate Writers, Inc.
Center for the Literary Arts
2210 North Higgins
P.O. Box 7131
Missoula, MT 59807
(406) 721-3620

Membership 150. Publishes a quarterly newsletter. Sponsors reading tours, administers an outreach program to schools, and hosts conferences.

Horror Writers of America
P. O. Box 1077
Eden, NC 27288

Membership of 400 includes active members who are novelists, associate members who are editors, agents, and producers, and affiliate members.

Illinois Writers, Inc. (IWI)
Illinois State University
Normal, IL 61761-6901
(309) 438-7705

Membership approximately 500. Publishes *IWI Monthly* and the *Illinois*

Writers Review semiannually. Dispenses information to Illinois writers and publishers. Reviews Illinois small press publications as well as books of national interest. Provides commentary on issues in contemporary writing.

Independent Writers of Chicago
7855 Gross Point Road, Suite G-4
Skokie, IL 60077
(708) 673-3784

Membership approximately 350. Publishes *STET* monthly newsletter and annual membership directory. Conducts monthly meetings and four workshops per year that deal with the business aspects of independent writing. Provides a writers line job referral and a speaker's bureau.

Independent Writers of Southern California
130 Via Xanthe
Newport Beach, CA 92663

Membership approximately 450. Professional organization of writers that provides a forum for writers to share ideas and information on business issues. Publishes *Independent* monthly. Provides a networking service. Incorporates a grievances and ethics committee. Serves as a liaison between purchasers of writing and writers. Offers group health insurance. Conducts monthly professional seminars and workshops.

International Association of Business Communications (IABC)
One Hallidie Plaza, Suite 606
San Francisco, CA 94102
(415) 433-3400; Fax (415) 362-8762

Membership approximately 1,750. Founded to foster research and education in the communication of business, industry, government, and nonprofit organizations. Members include authors, editors, professors, training directors, professional business writers, consultants, and more than 800 institutional members. Publishes *Journal of Business Communication* and *ABC Bulletin* quarterly. Sponsors regional conferences and an international convention annually.

International Association of Crime Writers, Inc.
JAF Box 1500
New York, NY 10116
(212) 757-3915

Membership approximately 200. Formed to promote communication among crime writers worldwide and to enhance awareness and encourage translations of the genre in the United States and abroad. Publishes *Border Patrol* quarterly.

International Black Writers (IBW)
Box 1030
Chicago, IL 60690
(312) 924-3818

Membership approximately 1,000. Publishes *Black Writer Magazine* quarterly and *In Touch* monthly newsletter. Formed to provide legal protection to black writers of fiction, nonfiction, poetry, children's, media writing, inspirational, and scriptwriting.

International Food, Wine and Travel Writers Association (IFW&TWA)
P.O. Box 13110
Long Beach, CA 90803
(310) 433-5969; Fax (310) 438-6384

Membership approximately 350. Publishes a monthly newsletter and a membership roster. Hosts an annual conclave. Sponsors an annual one-day conference open to food, wine, and travel writers of all levels.

International John Steinbeck Society
Ball State University
Muncie, IN 47306
(317) 285-5688

Membership approximately 600. Formed to provide research advice on Steinbeck. Publishes *Steinbeck* quarterly. Conducts conferences and sponsors speakers and workshops.

International Society for Humor Studies (ISHS)
Arizona State University
Tempe, AZ 85287-2803
(602) 965-7788

Attracts approximately 1,000 participants from the United States and thirty-five foreign countries for an international four-day study conference where more than thirty authors give presentations.

International Society of Dramatists
Box 1310
Miami, FL 33143

Membership approximately 10,500. Publishes *Dramatist's Bible* annually, *Globe Newsletter* monthly, and *Plays and Playwrights* annually. Administers several play-writing awards annually, including the Adriatic Award for a full-length play produced or unproduced. Provides a writers registration service for novels, plays, and nonfiction works. Offers a script-evaluation service for plays and screenplays.

International Women's Writing Guild (IWWG)

Box 810
Gracie Station
New York, NY 10028
(212) 737-7536; Fax (212) 737-9469

Membership approximately 2,000. Formed to provide a women's network for empowerment through writing. Publishes *Network* bimonthly. Provides manuscript referral and exchange, annual writing conferences and events, group rates for health and life insurance, legal aid, regional clusters, and job referrals.

Investigative Reporters and Editors (IRE)

Box 838
Columbia, MO 65205
(314) 882-2042; Fax (314) 882-5431

Membership approximately 3,000. Publishes a monthly newsletter, the *IRE Journal*, a book of summaries by reporters and editors, and a membership directory. Promotes high professional standards in investigative journalism. Provides educational services and supports an on-line computer database from newspapers, magazines, and television and radio stations. Sponsors regional conferences periodically around the country, conferences on specialized topics, and programs for college instructors.

Just Buffalo Literary Center

493 Franklin Street
Suite 209
Buffalo, NY 14202
(716) 881-3211

Publishes a monthly events calendar, *Response* newsletter, and *Words Over Easy*. Sponsors the annual Labor-in-Literature and Western New York Writer-in-Residence writing competitions. Founded to provide literary services and activities to the Western New York community. This includes workshops and classes, short- and long-term writers residencies, readings, lectures, panel discussions, and performances. Also assists writers and organizations with applications for grants, awards, and competitions.

Lane Literary Guild

164 West Broadway
Eugene, OR 97401
(503) 485-2278

Membership 150. Manages the Poets-in-the-Schools Programs and publishes a bimonthly newsletter, *Writer's Access*, and *Pacifica*. Conducts readings by local and regional writers, weekly workshops, special events, and information sessions.

Loft

Pratt Community Center
66 Malcolm Avenue, SE
Minneapolis, MN 55414
(612) 379-8999

Membership approximately 2,000. Founded to foster a writing community, promote the artistic development of individual writers, and develop an audience for literature in the Upper Midwest. Publishes *A View from the Loft* monthly. Conducts classes, workshops, and a mentor series. Sponsors the Loft-McKnight Award Program and Awards of Distinction. Sponsors readings, contests, and other events. Distributes grants and awards. Provides a meeting place for regularly scheduled writers groups. Makes available information and referral services.

**Maine Writers and Publishers
Alliance (MWPA)**
12 Pleasant Street
Brunswick, ME 04011-2201
(207) 729-6333

Membership 1,500. Publishes *Maine in
Print,* a monthly newsletter. Offers
statewide reading series, workshops,
conferences, special events, the MWPA
Book Distribution Service and performance space, a literary archive, and a book
gallery.

Media Alliance
Fort Mason
Building D, Second Floor
San Francisco, CA 94123
(415) 441-2557; Fax (415) 441-4067

Membership approximately 2,500.
Publishes *Media File* bimonthly;
Propaganda Review quarterly; *Media How-
to Notebook* and *People behind the News.*
Conducts educational programs, literary
fairs, and conferences. Assists with
medical plans, computer training,
referrals, and job files.

Melville Society
1016 Live Oak Lane
Arlington, TX 76012

Membership approximately 650.
Publishes *Melville Society Extracts*
quarterly. Cosponsors conferences with
the Modern Language Association and
conducts annual and special meetings.

Mystery Writers of America, Inc.
17 East 47th Street, Sixth Floor
New York, NY 10017
(212) 888-8171

Membership approximately 2,500. Open
to professional writers and students and

fans of mystery. Includes published
writers, novice writers, and people in
related detective story fields. Publishes
The Third Degree monthly and the *Mystery
Writers Annual Anthology.* Formed to
enhance the prestige of mystery story and
fact-crime writing. Holds a convention
and presents the Edgar Allan Poe and
Raven Awards. Also operates a reference
library and sponsors workshops.

**National Association of Black
Journalists (NABJ)**
P.O. Box 17212
Washington, DC 20041
(703) 648-1270; Fax (703) 476-6245

Membership of 1,700 includes those who
are employed in the production,
dissemination, and distribution of news
by newspapers, magazines, and radio and
television. Publishes *NABJ Journal* ten
times a year. Works with high schools to
identify potential journalists. Awards
scholarships to minorities. Acts as a
national clearinghouse for job information. Holds an annual conference.

**National Association of Science
Writers (NASW)**
Box 294
Greenlawn, NY 11740
(516) 757-5664

Membership includes approximately
1,700 writers and editors who prepare
scientific information. Publishes *Guide to
Careers in Science Writing* and a quarterly
newsletter. Sponsors three annual
Science-in-Society Awards for work
appearing in newspapers and magazines
and on television or radio. Includes
writers, editors, broadcasters, and
filmmakers who disseminate science news

and writers and communicators employed by scientific institutions, such as universities, hospitals, government agencies, corporations, and museums.

National Association of Young Writers (NAYW)
P.O. Box 228
2151 Hale Road
Sandusky, MI 48471
(810) 648-5102

Membership of 800 includes authors; editors; teachers of English, creative writing, and language arts; institutions; and interested individuals and groups. Promotes public awareness of children's creative writing. Provides speakers, consultations, and workshops. Publishes a quarterly newsletter and an annual directory of professional writers, *NAYW Directory: Poets and Writers in the Classroom*. Sponsors a young writers competition, awards, and an annual convention.

National Book Critics Circle (NBCC)
Los Angeles Times
Times Mirror Square
Los Angeles, CA 90012
(213) 237-5000

Membership approximately 653. A professional nonprofit organization formed to improve the quality of book reviewing throughout the country and to help extend book review coverage. Publishes *NBCC* quarterly. Sponsors annual awards honoring the best American works of fiction, general nonfiction, biography/autobiography, poetry, and criticism. Awards annual citation for excellence in reviewing.

National Conference of Editorial Writers
6223 Executive Boulevard
Rockville, MD 20853
(301) 984-3015

Membership approximately 575. Publishes *The Masthead* quarterly and *Editorial Excellence, Vol. II*. Cosponsors the Wells Award for exemplary leadership in offering minorities employment in journalism. Sponsors seminars, regional critique meetings, and an annual foreign tour for members. Offers an outreach critique service to nonmember papers.

National Endowment for the Arts (NEA)
Nancy Hanks Center
1100 Pennsylvania Avenue, NW
Washington, DC 20506
(202) 682-5451; Fax (202) 682-5610

Independent agency of the federal government. Allocates grants to eligible arts and cultural organizations. Awards fellowships to qualified individuals. Sponsors fellowships for arts administrators. Produces films and publishes newsletters, pamphlets, and directories.

National Federation of Press Women, Inc. (NFPW)
Box 99
1105 Main Street
Blue Springs, MO 64013-0099
(816) 229-1666

Membership of more than 5,000 full-time and freelance communicators. Publishes *Press Woman* monthly. Sponsors educational workshops and youth projects. Operates a speaker's bureau, grants journalism scholarships, holds an annual convention and an annual communications contest, and presents an annual award to a woman of accomplishment.

National League of American Pen Women
Pen Arts Building
1300 17th Street, NW
Washington, DC 20036
(202) 785-1997

Membership approximately 5,000. A professional, national organization that sponsors regional conferences, workshops, and literary competitions, and provides scholarships. Qualifications for membership must be met by professional writers, artists, or composers. Publishes *Pen Woman* monthly.

National Writers Club, Inc. (NWC)
1450 South Havana, Suite 620
Aurora, CO 80012
(303) 751-7844; Fax: (303) 751-8593

Membership of approximately 3,400 consists of professional as well as associate members. Publishes *Authorship* bimonthly, *Flash Market Update* monthly, *NWC Newsletter* bimonthly, *Freelancers Market* regularly, and *Professional Freelance Writers Directory* annually. Operates a library. Sponsors contests and a home-study magazine writing course. Periodically holds conventions to serve new and established freelance writers.

National Writers Union, UAW, AFL-CIO
873 Broadway, #203
New York, NY 10003
(212) 254-0279; Fax (212) 254-0673

Membership more than 3,000. An organization founded for better treatment of freelance writers by publishers. Assists with grievance procedures. Helps negotiate union contracts with publishers, works with health insurers, and holds conferences. Publishes *American Writer* quarterly and local chapter newsletters. Membership is open to all writers who have published a book, a play, three articles, five poems, one short story, or an equivalent amount of newspaper, publicity, technical, commercial, government, or institutional copy. Eligibility also includes those with an equal amount of unpublished material who are actively writing and attempting to publish work.

New England Poetry Club
Two Farrar Street
Cambridge, MA 02138

Membership approximately 500. Publishes *The Writ*, a quarterly bulletin, and *Best Published Poems of the Year*. Professional society for published poets. Meets monthly at the Harvard Faculty Club. Sponsors various poetry contests and workshops as well as an ongoing reading series. Founded by Amy Lowell, Robert Frost, and Conrad Aiken, the club sponsors poetry contests and programs. Membership is open to practicing poets who have achieved a level suitable for publication.

New Hampshire Writers and Publishers Project (NHWPP)
The Button Factory
855 Islington Street, #210
P.O. Box 150
Portsmouth, NH 03802-0150
(603) 436-6331

A nonprofit organization that provides programming in the literary arts and acts as a literary resource center for the state. Publishes a bimonthly newsletter, *Ex Libris*, and an annual catalog of books by New Hampshire writers or publishers or about New Hampshire. Sponsors such special events as readings, conferences, and workshops. Membership is open to all.

North Carolina Writers' Network (NCWN)
Box 954
Carrboro, NC 27510
(919) 967-9540

Membership approximately 1,650. Established to support the work of writers, writing organizations, and writing programs in North Carolina. Publishes a bimonthly newsletter, a literary resource guide, an annual chapbook, and a textbook, *Skills for Practical Writing*. Serves as a resource center, book gallery, and writers exchange. Sponsors a writers and readers series, a poetry chapbook competition, a nonfiction competition, and a black writers competition. Offers workshops, programs, and conferences statewide.

North Central Region of West Virginia Writers, Inc.
525 Grove Street
Morgantown, WV 26505
(304) 296-7564

A nonprofit writers organization supported by the West Virginia State Department of Culture and History, the West Virginia Humanities Council, and local businesses and universities. Conducts an annual conference for writers of all levels, including a book fair, exhibit, and computer demonstrations.

Novelists, Inc.
Box 1166
Mission, KS 66222

Membership approximately 350. Publishes a monthly newsletter and a confidential roster of members. Provides networking opportunities for members to further their professional status. Sponsors an annual conference. To qualify for membership, the applicant must have published at least two novels by recognized publishers within the last five years. Open to published authors of popular fiction, including the horror, mystery, romance, science fiction/fantasy, and western genres.

Oregon Association of Christian Writers
17768 SW Pointe
Forest Court
Aloha, OR 97006
(503) 642-9844

Membership approximately 300. Publishes a newsletter and sponsors conferences, workshops, and seminars for beginning and advanced writers. Provides guest speakers and critiques by professional writers.

Outdoor Writers Association of America, Inc.
2017 Cato Avenue, Suite 101
State College, PA 16801
(814) 234-1011

Membership approximately 1,900. Publishes *Outdoors Unlimited* monthly. An organization of professional authors, journalists, and so on, who cover hunting, fishing, camping, canoeing, and similar outdoor sports. Administers several writing contests for members only and an extensive scholarship program. Workshops held at the annual conference.

Panhandle Professional Writers (PPW)

Box 19303
Amarillo, TX 79114
(806) 352-3889

Membership approximately 200. Holds bimonthly meetings, featuring morning critique sessions and afternoon speakers. In conjunction with Amarillo College, sponsors an annual conference for all levels of writers that includes an awards luncheon honoring winners of writing contests, full faculty panel discussions, and study group sessions.

PEN American Center

568 Broadway
New York, NY 10012
(212) 334-1660; Fax (212) 334-2181

Membership approximately 2,500. Publishes *PENewsletter* quarterly, *Grants and Awards Available to American Writers*, and *Freedom to Write* publications and pamphlets. A division of International PEN consisting of writers, poets, playwrights, essayists, editors, novelists, and translators whose purpose is to bring about better understanding among writers of all nations. Has more than eighty centers in Europe, Asia, Africa, Australia, and the Americas. Membership is by invitation after nomination. PEN Prison Writing Program, a division of PEN, provides sources of information on writing to prisoners and sponsors an annual writing competition for writers in prison. Winning pieces are published in *Fortune News*.

PEN Center USA West

672 South Lafayette Park Place, Suite 41
Los Angeles, CA 90057
(213) 365-8500; Fax (213) 365-9616

Membership approximately 850. An international association consists of poets, playwrights, screenwriters, essayists, editors, novelists, historians, critics, journalists, and translators. Founded to foster a sense of community among writers in the western United States to advance freedom to write throughout the world. Publishes *PEN Center USA West Newsletter* quarterly.

Philadelphia Writers Organization (PWO)

Box 42497
Philadelphia, PA 19101
(215) 641-0342

Membership approximately 400. Publishes a membership directory and the monthly *PWO Bulletin*. Sponsors program meetings, fundraisers, panels, workshops, and the Writers Meeting Editors Marketplace annually.

Poetry Alive!

P.O. Box 9643
Asheville, NC 28815
(800) 476-8172; Fax (704) 298-5491; E-mail: AllanWolf@aol.com

A national touring group that presents poetry as theater to 600,000 students, teachers, and poetry lovers yearly. Also conducts teacher in-service programs, a residency at Warren Wilson College, and the annual Asheville Poetry Festival.

Poetry Center and American Poetry Archives
San Francisco State University
1600 Holloway Avenue
San Francisco, CA 94132
(415) 338-1056

Membership 250. Publishes *American Poetry Archives News* and *American Poetry Archives Catalog of Videotape Holdings.* Provides readings on campus and around the Bay Area. Administers a national book award and poetry contests. Maintains a video and audio collection of literary readings and performances.

Poetry Center of Chicago
37 South Wabash Avenue, Room 301
Chicago, IL 60603
(312) 368-0905

Serves 3,000 annually. Hosts the longest lived poetry reading series in Illinois. Provides readings, workshops, outreach programs, and a forum in a downtown location.

Poetry Project, Ltd.
Saint Mark's Church
Second Avenue and 10th Street
New York, NY 10003
(212) 674-0910

Publishes two literary magazines and a quarterly newsletter. Sponsors the annual Poets Theater Festival of plays written, directed, and performed by poets. Offers a reading series, a lecture series, and writing workshops, and provides a printing and distribution center.

Poetry Resource Center of Michigan
111 East Kirby
Detroit, MI 48202
(313) 972-5580

Membership approximately 300. A nonprofit organization founded to promote the reading, writing, and publishing of poetry in Michigan through readings, writing workshops, advisory sessions, benefits, and book parties. Publishes a monthly newsletter and the annual *Directory of Michigan Literary Publishers.*

Poetry Society of America
15 Gramercy Park
New York, NY 10003
(212) 254-9628

Membership 2,500. A national organization with regional branches. Publishes *PSA Newsletter.* Provides readings, lectures, symposia, workshops, annual prizes, and the Van Voorhis Library. Awards monthly and annual awards for poetry. The oldest group of its kind, membership includes more than 1,700 professional poets. Associate members include critics, lecturers, librarians, educators, and patrons.

Poets and Writers, Inc.
72 Spring Street
New York, NY 10012
(212) 226-3586; Fax (212) 226-3963

An information clearinghouse, service organization, and national nonprofit information center for those interested in contemporary American literature. Publishes *Poets and Writers* newsletter biannually as well as informative books such as writer's directories, guides, and handbooks. Maintains biographical archives on poets and fiction writers and provides a telephone information service. Lists writers who perform their work and are available for lectures and readings.

Sponsors literary events, readings, and workshop programs.

Poet's House
72 Spring Street
New York, NY 10012
(212) 431-7920

Membership 900. Publishes *Directory of American Poetry* books. Maintains the Reed Foundation Library and provides a meeting place for poets and the public. Sponsors readings, panel discussions, exhibits, and poets in the schools.

Private Eye Writers of America
330 Surrey Road
Cherry Hill, NJ 08002
(609) 482-1018

A national organization to promote private eye literature. Sponsors the annual Shamus Award for the best in private eye fiction. Eligibility requirements.

Romance Writers of America
13700 Veterans Memorial Drive, Suite 315
Houston, TX 77014
(713) 440-6885

Membership approximately 5,000 published and unpublished writers. Consists of individuals in ten foreign countries and has more than sixty local chapters. Organized to promote the recognition of the genre of romance writing as a serious book form. Publishes *Chapter Advisory Letter* monthly and *Romance Writers Report* bimonthly. Sponsors the annual Golden Heart Award, the Golden Medallion Award, and the RITA Awards. Conducts workshops and sponsors national and regional conferences and awards for members.

Science Fiction and Fantasy Writers of America, Inc. (SFWA)
Five Winding Brook Drive, #B
Guilderland, NY 12084
(518) 869-5361

Membership approximately 1,250 includes science fiction and fantasy writers of stories, novels, radio plays, teleplays, and screenplays. Publishes *SFWA Forum* bimonthly, *Bulletin* quarterly, and an annual membership directory. Sponsors conferences, discussions, lectures, seminars, and a competition for the Nebula Awards.

Science Fiction Research Association, Inc.
6354 Brooks Boulevard
Mentor, OH 44060
(216) 257-3646

Membership includes students, teachers, professors, librarians, futurologists, readers, authors, booksellers, editors, publishers, and scholars from twelve countries. Organized for the professional study of science fiction and fantasy. Publishes *Science Fiction and Fantasy Book Review*, the *SFRA Newsletter*, and an annual membership directory. Sponsors an annual scholar award as well as workshop awards and prizes. Maintains archives at the University of Kansas, Lawrence.

Small Press Genre Association
P.O. Box 6301
Concord, CA 94524
(510) 254-7442

An international service organization for

writers of any genre related to science fiction, fantasy, horror, western, mystery, and their subgenres. Publishes *Genre Press Digest*. Provides critique, grievance arbitration, and research assistance.

Small Press Writers and Artists Organization (SPWAO)
2131 South 227th Drive
Buckeye, AZ 85326-3872

Membership of 350 writers, artists, poets, and publishers dedicated to promoting science fiction, fantasy, and horror. Publishes *SPWAO Newsletter*. Provides critiques, grievance arbitration, and research assistance.

Society of American Travel Writers (SATW)
4101 Lake Boone Trail, Suite 201
Raleigh, NC 27607
(919) 787-5181

Membership approximately 900. A nonprofit organization dedicated to serving the interests of the traveling public and providing unbiased, objective reporting of information on travel topics. Publishes an annual membership directory, the *Travel Photo Source Book*, and an official periodical, *The Travel Writer*. Membership is by invitation only; applicants must be sponsored by two members.

Society of Children's Book Writers (SCBW)
22736 Vanowen Street, Suite 106
West Hills, CA 91307
(818) 888-8760

A national organization of more than 6,700 authors, editors, publishers, illustrators, filmmakers, librarians, and educators. Devoted to the interests of children's literature. Publishes *SCBW Bulletin* bimonthly. Sponsors meetings at the regional level. Awards four grants and the Golden Kite Award. Convenes annually. Eligibility requirements.

Society of Environmental Journalists
9425 Stenton Avenue, Suite 209
Philadelphia, PA 19118
(215) 247-9710; Fax (215) 247-9712; E-mail: SEJOffice@aol.com

Membership 900. Issues a quarterly journal. Provides national and regional conferences, a computer bulletin board service, a mentoring program, and an annual directory.

Society of Professional Journalists
16 South Jackson Street
Greencastle, IN 46135-0077
(317) 653-3333

Serves more than 16,000 members through 300 chapters. Publishes *The Quill*. Offers legal counsel, a jobs-for-journalists career-search program, professional development seminars, and awards. Promotes ethics and freedom of information.

Southwest Writers
Department CC-SG
P.O. Box 14632
Albuquerque, NM 87191
(505) 298-1653

Membership approximately 700. Publishes a monthly newsletter. Sponsors an annual writing contest judged by professional editors. Conducts an annual conference for writers of all levels, with featured speakers and book signings.

Space Coast Writers Guild
Box 804
Melbourne, FL 32902
(407) 727-0051

Membership approximately 375. A nonprofit national organization of professional and novice authors and writers of all media. Publishes a membership-activity book and periodic newsletters. Conducts a national conference, workshops, and writing contests and sponsors scholarships.

Texas Writers Association
219 Preston Royal Shopping Center, No. 3
Dallas, TX 75230

Membership approximately 800. Publishes *Writer's News* monthly. Supports and informs writers in every discipline of writing and promotes writers, writing, literature, and literacy. Sponsors conferences, workshops, study groups, and classes.

University of Arizona Poetry Center
1216 North Cherry Avenue
Tucson, AZ 85719
(602) 321-7760

No membership. Readings and library are open to the public; visitors are welcome. Publishes a biannual newsletter. Provides community workshops, outreach to prisoners, high school students, and senior citizens. Has a guest house for visiting writers and offers a summer residency program.

Walt Whitman Cultural Arts Center
Second and Cooper Streets
Camden, NJ 08102
(609) 964-8300

Membership 250. Sponsors the Notable Poets and Writers Series, Walt Whitman Poetry Series, Schools Program, Adult Theater Series, Children/Family Theater Series, Summer Children's Theater Series, Exhibitions Program, and residencies.

Washington Independent Writers (WIW)
220 Woodward Building
733 15th Street, NW
Washington, DC 20005
(202) 347-4973

Membership approximately 2,300. Established to promote the mutual interests of freelance writers. Publishes *WIW Newsletter* monthly, *Questions Writers Ask about Agents*, and a directory of members. Provides a variety of services to members.

Western Writers of America
416 Bedford Road
El Paso, TX 79922-1204
(915) 584-1001

Membership 600 freelance writers who specialize in western fiction and nonfiction. Dedicated to the spirit and reality of the West, past and present. Publishes *The Roundup* quarterly. Sponsors the Golden Saddleman Awards, the Spur Awards, the Owen Wister Award, and the Medicine Pipe Bearer's Award. Eligibility requirements.

Willamette Writers
9045 SW Barbur Boulevard, #5A
Portland, OR 97219
(503) 452-1592

A nonprofit organization. Publishes a monthly newsletter. Holds monthly meetings with speakers, provides opportunities to meet other writers, and sponsors seminars and workshops.

Wisconsin Regional Writers' Association (WRWA)
Route One
Pebble Beach Road
Cedar Grove, WI 53013
(414) 668-6267

Membership approximately 1,075 amateur and professional writers. Formed to encourage literary expression as well as cultural aspects of regional Wisconsin life. Publishes a quarterly newsletter. Provides networking opportunities and sponsors scholarships and writing contests. Sponsors spring and fall conferences for writers of all levels.

Women in Communications, Inc.
2101 Wilson Boulevard, Suite 417
Arlington, VA 22201
(703) 528-4200; Fax (703) 528-4205

Membership approximately 11,500. Serves members who work in advertising, education, film, magazines, newspapers, photo-journalism, public relations, publishing, broadcasting, and technical writing. Incorporates 100 campus chapters and 82 professional chapters. Publishes *Professional Communicator*, a national magazine. Sponsors national conference for communication professionals.

Women's National Book Association, Inc. (WNBA)
160 Fifth Avenue
New York, NY 10010
(212) 675-7804; Fax (212) 989-7542

Publishes *The Bookwoman* three times a year. Founded to advance women in the world of books. Open to women and men in all occupations allied to the publishing industry. Serves as a network for professionals. Individual chapters sponsor workshops and discussion groups. An award is presented biennially to a distinguished bookwoman who has made an outstanding contribution to the world of books.

Woodstock Guild
34 Tinker Street
Woodstock, NY 12498
(914) 679-2079

A nonprofit guild founded to promote the study and development of the arts, crafts, literature, drama, and music. Sponsors annual conference consisting of workshops and talks by editors, publishers, agents, and writers.

World Congress of Poets
3146 Buckeye Court
Placerville, CA 95667
(916) 626-4166; Fax (916) 626-5922

Established under the auspices of the nonprofit World Academy of Arts and Culture, Inc. Functions to promote world unity and peace and to facilitate the interchange of diverse cultures through poetry and literature. Members meet biennially in different parts of the world. The official languages are Arabic, Chinese, English, French, and Spanish.

Writers and Books
740 University Avenue
Rochester, NY 14607
(716) 473-2590

Membership 1,000. Runs the Writers & Poets Bookstore, The Cell Writers' Center of the Finger Lakes retreat and conference facility, and The Cell Gallery.

Sponsors monthly readings, the Visiting Writers Series, workshops, outreach programs, and literary exhibitions.

Writers at Work
P.O. Box 1146
Centerville, UT 84014-5146
(801) 292-9285

A nonprofit organization founded to support creative writing in Utah. The primary activity is an annual, week-long, summer conference of workshops, panels, seminars, and readings. Private consultations available to those submitting manuscripts in advance. Fellowships are offered in fiction and poetry. Scholarships are granted on the basis of need and manuscript submission.

Writer's Center
4508 Walsh Street
Bethesda, MD 20815-2004
(301) 654-8664

Membership approximately 2,200. A nonprofit, membership-service organization that sponsors readings and workshops in writing, word processing, design, and phototypesetting. Publishes *Carousel*, a bimonthly newsletter, and *Poet Lore*, a quarterly literary magazine. Has an independent press and sponsors special literary events, such as conferences, lectures, and meetings.

Writers Center of Indianapolis
Marian College P.O. Box 88386
Indianapolis, IN 46208
(317) 929-0625

Membership 500. Publishes *Literally* and *Flying Island*. Houses a resource library and presents readings, workshops, lectures, and the annual Jazz/Poetry Session.

Writers Conferences and Festivals
P.O. Box 102396
Denver, CO 80250
(303) 759-0519; Fax (303) 759-0519

A nonprofit professional service organization of conference and retreat directors. Publishes a biannual newsletter and membership directory. Provides a teacher/faculty recommendation service, a writer's referral service, and group advertising discount rates. Awards an annual conference scholarship to a writer in financial need. Membership is open to the director of any writer's conference or retreat.

Writers Connection
275 Saratoga Avenue, Suite 103
Santa Clara, CA 95050-6664
(408) 554-2090; Fax (408) 554-2088

Membership approximately 2,500. Publishers *Writers Connection* monthly newsletter and books on marketing, publishing, and writing. Produces videotapes, maintains a resource library, and operates a job shop for writers. Sponsors conferences and seminars.

Writers Guild of America (WGA) East, Inc.
555 West 57th Street
New York, NY 10019
(212) 767-7800

Membership approximately 3,000 writers living east of the Mississippi. A labor union representing professional writers in motion pictures, television, and radio. Publishes *WGA East* monthly. Professional memberships available only.

Writers Guild of America (WGA) West, Inc.
8955 Beverly Boulevard
West Hollywood, CA 90048
(310) 550-1000

Membership approximately 7,500 writers living west of the Mississippi. A labor union representing professional writers in motion pictures, television, and radio. Publishes *WGA Journal* monthly. Professional memberships available only.

Writer's Information Network (WIN)
P.O. Box 11337
Bainbridge Island, WA 09910
(206) 842-9103

Founded to provide Christian writers with opportunities to further their professional development, meet other Christian writers, and connect with members of the religious publishing industry. Publishes a bimonthly newsletter. Provides seminars, lectures, consultations, manuscript critique, author referral services, and free consultation on any Christian writing problem.

Writers League
219 Tuxedo
San Antonio, TX 78209

A national organization of working professional mystery authors. Publishes *ACWL BULLETin*, which features articles by experts and information and advice for professional writers. Eligibility requirements.

Writers Place
Midwest Center for the Literary Arts, Inc.
3607 Pennsylvania
Kansas City, MO 64111
(816) 753-1090

Membership 350. Publishes *The Keep*. Provides a professional seminar series and Young Writers in the Schools, as well as readings of poetry and fiction. Sponsors workshops, a library, and art gallery.

Writers Room, Inc.
153 Waverly Place, Fifth Floor
New York, NY 10014
(212) 807-9519

The Room has served more than 600 writers and is currently enrolled at capacity with a waiting list. Provides a quiet place to work for up to 140 writers per quarter. The Room welcomes writers from around the country who are visiting New York. Other services include a newsletter, an in-house job bank, a communal ink-jet printer for residents' use, an internship program for New York college students, monthly readings, and occasional workshops.

Writer's Voice
West Side YMCA
Five West 63rd Street
New York, NY 10023
(212) 875-4124

No membership; open to the public. Flagship center of the national Writer's

Voice Project. Includes several series of readings, workshops, and master-level workshops offered through the Writers Community. Presents the Capricorn Poetry and Fiction Awards, the Open Voice, and the New Voice Prizes for poetry and fiction and sponsors residency programs, a reading series, and peer studios (workshops without instructors).

Writing Center
416 Third Avenue
San Diego, CA 92101-6803
(619) 230-0670

Very young organization; over 520 members. Provides a gathering place for writers and those who want to find and explore their voice. Holds classes, groups, workshops, readings, and more.

10

Teaching Institutions

Listed in this chapter are colleges and universities known for either their creative-writing programs or their sponsorship of creative-writing seminars or conferences. Also included are schools that offer graduate writing programs through which you can obtain a traditional master's (M.A.) degree or a master of fine arts (M.F.A.) degree. Both can prepare you for entrance into a doctorate (Ph.D.) program. Traditional master's degree students concentrate more on literature, and M.F.A. students read more contemporary fiction and enroll in workshops where their own works are studied. Both can help you become a better writer.

Make a special note of colleges that produce academic publications. Some encourage students to become involved and even to serve on the staffs of these literary journals. Many offer opportunities to work on their magazines to earn credit.

Use these listings to inquire further about workshops and their prerequisites and about any outreach community programs that may be offered. I also suggest that you contact the creative writing, English, or humanities department at the community college, city college, or state university in your region for information regarding not only the specific writing courses or workshops offered on campus, but also literary events in the area that you might be interested in attending. These sources can often supply you with information on local writing groups and readings, too. Some colleges house poetry centers and provide access to audio- or videotapes of writers reading from their works. Many serve as a resource of sorts and maintain bulletin boards where advertisements for a variety of writing services and needs are posted.

With the increase in demands made on our educational systems and the fluctuating funding, colleges are adding component schools and losing certain curricula and special programs. For this reason, I suggest that you review *Lovejoy's College Guide*, which you will find in the reference section of your library, or contact the school for class schedules and catalogs. You may also want to check the *Catalogue of Programs*, which covers U.S. and Canadian academic institutions offering nondegree programs, extension courses, and brief summer seminars.

Alderson-Broaddus College
Director: Creative Writing Studies
Phillippi, WV 26416
(304) 457-9880
Private college affiliated with the
American Baptist Church. Publishes
Grab-a-Nickel.

Alma College
Director: Creative Writing Studies
Alma, MI 48801-1511
(517) 463-7111
Private college affiliated with the
Presbyterian Church USA.

Alverno College
Director: Great Lakes Writers Workshop
3401 South 39th Street
Milwaukee, WI 53204
(414) 382-6008
Private college affiliated with the
Roman Catholic Church.

Amarillo College
Director: Panhandle Professional
Writers Conference
Box 447
Amarillo, TX 79178
(806) 371-5353

American University, The
English/Creative Writing Graduate
Program
4400 Massachusetts Avenue, NW
Washington, DC 20016
(202) 885-1000
Publishes *Folio.*

Anderson College
Director: Academic Affairs/Writers'
Conferences
316 Boulevard
Anderson, SC 29621
(803) 231-2145

Antioch University
English/Creative Writing Graduate
Program
405 Corry Street
Yellow Springs, OH 45387
(513) 767-7047

Arizona State University
ISHS Director: International Humor
Conference
English/Creative Writing Graduate
Program
Tempe, AZ 85287-2803
(602) 965-2604
Publishes *Hayden's Ferry Review.*

Arkansas Tech University
Creative Writing Studies
818 Lexington Avenue
Fort Smith, AR 72901-4942
(501) 783-7436

Ashland University
Creative Writing Studies
401 College Avenue
Ashland, OH 44805
(419) 289-5133
Private university affiliated with the
Brethren Church.

Auburn University
English/Creative Writing Graduate
    Program
Auburn, AL 35849-5203
(334) 844-4000
Publishes *Southern Humanities Review*.

Augusta College
Director: Sandhills Writers' Confer-
    ence
Office of Continuing Education
2500 Walton Way
Augusta, GA 30910
(404) 731-7962

Augustana College
Director: Mississippi Valley Writers
    Conference
College Center
Rock Island, IL 61201-2296
(309) 794-7000

Austin Peay State University
English/Creative Writing Graduate
    Program
Clarkesville, TN 37044
(615) 648-7011
Publishes *Zone 3*.

Ball State University
Director: Midwest Writers Workshop
Department of Journalism
Muncie, IN 47306
(317) 285-8200

Bank Street College of Education
Director: Irma Simonton Black Award
1341 G Street, NW
Washington, DC 20005-3105
(202) 347-5813

Bard College
Creative Writing Studies
Annandale-on-Hudson, NY 12504
(914) 758-7472
Private college affiliated with the
    Association of Episcopal Colleges.

Barnard College
Director: Writers on Writing
3009 Broadway
New York, NY 10027-6598
(212) 854-7489
Private college.

Baylor University
English/Creative Writing Graduate
    Program
Waco, TX 76701
(817) 755-1011
Private university controlled by the
    Baptist General Convention of
    Texas.

Beloit College
Creative Writing Studies
Beloit, WI 53511
(608) 365-3391
Private college affiliated with the
    United Church of Christ.

Bennington College
Director: Summer Writing Workshops
Bennington, VT 05201
(802) 442-5401
Private college.

Biola University
Writers Institute/Writers Conference
13800 Biola Avenue
La Mirada, CA 90639-0001
(310) 903-6000
Private university affiliated with the
    Evangelical Church.

Boston University
English/Creative Writing Graduate
    Program
236 Bay State Road
Boston, MA 02215
(617) 353-2318
Publishes *Agni* and the *Partisan Review.*

Bowling Green State University
English/Creative Writing Graduate
    Program
Bowling Green, OH 43403
(419) 372-2086
Publishes *Mid-American Review* and
    Clues: A Journal of Detection.

Brevard College
Creative Writing Studies
Brevard, NC 28712
(704) 883-8292
Private college affiliated with the
    Methodist Church.

Brigham Young University
English/Creative Writing Graduate
    Program
Provo, UT 84602
(801) 378-2507
Private university affiliated with the
    Church of Latter Day Saints.
    Publishes *Inscape* and *BYU Studies.*

**Brooklyn College/City University of
    New York**
English/Creative Writing Graduate
    Program
Brooklyn, NY 11210
(718) 780-5485
Publishes *Brooklyn Review.*

Brown University
Creative Writing Studies
45 Prospect Street
Box 1876
Providence, RI 02912
(401) 863-2378
Private university.

Bucknell University
Director: Stadler Center for Poetry
Director: Seminar for Younger Poets
English/Creative Writing Graduate
    Program
Lewisburg, PA 17837
(717) 524-1853
Private university. Publishes *Red
    Wheelbarrow, Giving Voice, Tapestry,*
    and *West Branch.*

Burlington College
Director: Writing and Literature
95 North Avenue
Burlington, VT 05401
(800) 862-9616

Butler County Community College
Creative Writing Conference
    Coordinator
901 South Haverhill Road
El Dorado, KS 67042
(316) 321-2222

Campbellsville College
Creative Writing Studies
200 West College Street
Campbellsville, KY 42718
(502) 465-8158
Private college affiliated with the
    Southern Baptist Church.

Canyonlands Field Institute
Director: Desert Writers Workshop
P.O. Box 68
Moab, UT 84532
(801) 259-7750
Private school.

Carnegie-Mellon University
Creative Writing Studies
5000 Forbes Avenue
Pittsburgh, PA 15213
(412) 268-2082
Private university.

Case Western Reserve
English/Creative Writing Graduate
  Program
Cleveland, OH 43403
(216) 368-4450
Private university.

Central Community College
Chair: Nebraska Writing and
  Storytelling Festival
Box 4903
Grand Island, NE 68602-4903
(308) 389-6406

Central State University
English/Creative Writing Graduate
  Program
100 North University Drive
Edmond, OK 73060-0163
(405) 341-2980

Chapman College
English/Creative Writing Graduate
  Program
333 North Glassell Street
Orange, CA 92666
(714) 997-6711
Private college affiliated with the
  Disciples of Christ Christian
  Church. Publishes *Calliope, Califor-
  nia Quarterly*, and *Calliope II.*

Christopher Newport College
Continuing Education/Director:
  Writers' Conference
50 Shoe Lane
Newport News, VA 23606-2988
(804) 594-7015

City University of New York
Creative Writing Studies
101 West 31st Street, Sixth Floor
New York, NY 10001-3503
(212) 947-4800

Cleveland State University
Director: Writers Conference and
  Workshop
Cleveland, OH 44115
(216) 687-3986, Fax (216) 687-9366
Publishes *The Gamut* and *Whiskey
  Island Magazine.*

College of the Redwoods
Director: Mendocino Coast Writers
  Conference
1211 Del Mar Drive
Fort Bragg, CA 95437
(916) 625-4846

College of Wooster
Creative Writing Studies
Wooster, OH 44691
(216) 263-2270
Private college affiliated with the
Presbyterian Church. Publishes
Artful Dodge.

Colorado Mountain College
Director: Colorado Mountain Writer's
Workshop
Spring Valley Center
3000 County Road, 114
Glenwood Springs, CO 81601
(303) 945-7481

Colorado State University
English/Creative Writing Graduate
Program
Fort Collins, CO 80523
(303) 491-6909
Publishes *Colorado Review* and *Greyrock
Review.*

Columbia College
Creative Writing Studies
Columbia, SC 29203
(803) 786-3871
Private college affiliated with the
United Methodist Church.

Columbia College—Chicago
English/Creative Writing Graduate
Program
500 South Michigan
Chicago, IL 60613
(312) 663-1600
Private college. Publishes *Hair Trigger.*

**Columbia University—School of the
Arts**
Director: Summer Writers Festival
Writing Division
404 Dodge Hall
New York, NY 10027
(212) 854-4391
Private university. Publishes *Columbia:
A Magazine of Poetry and Prose.*

Connecticut College
Creative Writing Studies
270 Mohegan Avenue
New London, CT 06320
(860) 439-2200
Private college.

Cornell University
Director: Adult University/Summer
Writing Workshops
English/Creative Writing Graduate
Program
Smith Hall
Ithaca, NY 14850-2490
(607) 255-5241
Private university. Publishes *Epoch.*

Cuyahoga Community College
Director: Writers Conference
4250 Richmond Road
Highland Hills Village, OH 44122
(216) 987-2024

Davis and Elkins College
Creative Writing Studies
Elkins, WV 26241
(304) 636-5850
Private college affiliated with the
Presbyterian Church.

Denison University
Creative Writing Studies
P.O. Box H
Granville, OH 43023
(614) 587-5276
Private university.

Dickinson College
Cumberland Valley Fiction Writers
    Workshop
Department of English
Carlisle, PA 17013
(717) 243-5121
Private college.

Dominican College of San Rafael
Creative Writing Studies
1520 Grand Avenue
San Rafael, CA 94901
(415) 457-4440
Private college affiliated with the
    Catholic Church.

Duke University
Director: Writers Workshops
Duke Young Writers' Camp
The Bishop's House
Durham, NC 27708
(919) 684-6259
Private university affiliated with the
    United Methodist Church.

East Carolina University
English/Creative Writing Graduate
    Program
Greenville, NC 27858-4353
(919) 757-6640
Publishes *The Rebel* and *Tar River Poetry*
    and North Carolina Literary Review.

Eastern College
Creative Writing Studies
Fairview Drive
Saint Davids, PA 19087
(215) 341-5967
Private college affiliated with the
    American Baptist Church.

Eastern Illinois University
Creative Writing Studies
Charleston, IL 61920
(217) 581-2223

Eastern Kentucky University
Director: Writing Conference
Department of English
Richmond, KY 40475
(606) 622-5861

Eastern Oregon State College
Oregon Literature Series
English Department
La Grande, OR 97850
(503) 963-1393

Eastern Washington University
Young Writers Conference
English/Creative Writing Graduate
    Program
Cheney, WA 99004
(509) 359-2397
Publishes *Willow Springs.*

Eckerd College
Creative Writing Division
4200 54th Avenue South
Saint Petersburg, FL 33711
(813) 864-8331
Private college affiliated with the
    Presbyterian Church, USA.

Edison Community College
Director: Southwest Florida Writers'
    Conference
P.O. Box 06210
Fort Meyers, FL 33906-6210

Emerson College
English/Creative Writing Graduate
    Program
Ploughshares International Fiction
    Writing Seminar
100 Beacon Street
Boston, MA 02116
(617) 578-8600
Private college. Publishes *Ploughshares*.

Emory and Henry College
Creative Writing Studies
Emory, VA 24327
(705) 944-3121
Private college affiliated with the
    United Methodist Church.

Emory University
Summer Writing Institute
300 White Hall
Atlanta, GA 30322
(404) 727-6036
Private university affiliated with the
    Methodist Church.

Faulkner University
Metropolitan Writers Guild and
    Faulkner State University Writers
    Conference
5345 Atlanta Highway
Montgomery, AL 36117
(334) 272-5820

**Florida Community College at
    Jacksonville**
Registrar: Florida First Coast Writers'
    Festival
501 West State Street
Jacksonville, FL 32202-4030
(904) 633-8300
Publishes *Kalliope*.

Florida Institute of Technology
English/Creative Writing Graduate
    Program
Southgate Building A
Melbourne, FL 32901-6988
(305) 768-8000

Florida International University
South Beach Writers Conference
    Manager
Division of Continuing Education
North Miami, FL 33181
(305) 940-5669, Fax (305) 956-5484
Publishes *Gulf Stream Magazine*.

Florida State University
English/Creative Writing Graduate
    Program
Williams Building
Tallahassee, FL 32306
(904) 599-3796
Publishes *Sundog, Southeast Review,* and
    Kudzu Review.

Foothill College
Director: Foothills Writers Conference
12345 El Monte Road
Los Altos Hills, CA 94022-4599
(415) 949-7316

Four Corners School of Outdoor Education
Department SG/Writing Programs
East Route
Monticello, UT 84535
Private school.

Francis Marion College
English Department/Writers Conference Director
(803) 661-1232
Florence, SC 29501-0547

Fresno State University
English/Creative Writing Graduate Program
Fresno, CA 93740-0098
(209) 294-2191
Publishes *The Joaquin*.

Frostburg State University
Business Office/Western Maryland Writers' Workshop
Frostburg, MD 21532-1099
(301) 689-4152

Geneva College
Creative Writing Studies
Beaver Falls, PA 15010
(412) 847-6500
Private college affiliated with the Reformed Presbyterian Church of North America.

George Mason University
English/Creative Writing Graduate Program
4400 University Drive
Fairfax, VA 22030
(703) 323-2109
Publishes *Phoebe*.

Georgia State University
English/Creative Writing Graduate Program
Atlanta, GA 30303
(404) 651-2365
Publishes *GSU Review*.

Goddard College
Director: Writing Program
Box 98
Plainfield, VT 05667
(800) 468-4888

Grand Canyon University
Creative Writing Studies
3300 West Camelback Road
P.O. Box 11097
Phoenix, AZ 85017
(602) 249-3300
Private university affiliated with Arizona Southern Baptist Convention.

Grand Rapids Baptist College and Seminary
The Write Place
1001 East Beltline Avenue
Grand Rapids, MI 49505
(616) 949-5300
Private college.

Hamilton College
Creative Writing Studies
Clinton, NY 13323
(315) 859-4421
Private college.

Hampshire College
Creative Writing Studies
Amherst, MA 01002
(413) 549-4600
Private college. Publishes *Object Lesson*.

Hartwick College
Director: Catskill Poetry Workshop
Special Programs Office
Oneonta, NY 13820
(607) 431-4415

Harvard and Radcliffe Colleges
Summer Writing Programs
51 Brattle Street
Cambridge, MA 02138
(617) 495-4024
Private colleges.

High Point College
Creative Writing Studies
933 Montlieu Avenue
High Point, NC 27262
(919) 841-9216
Private college affiliated with the
United Methodist Church.

Hindman Settlement School
Director: Appalachian Writers Work-
shop
Hindman, KY 41822
Private school.

Hofstra University
Director: Summer Writers Conference
University College for Continuing
Education
205 Davison Hall
110 Hofstra University
Hempstead, NY 11550-1090
(516) 463-5016, Fax (516) 463-4833
Private university.

Houghton College
Creative Writing Studies
Houghton, NY 14744
(716) 567-2211
Private college affiliated with the
Wesleyan Church of America.

**Idyllwild School of Music and the
Arts**
Creative Writing Workshops
Box 38
Idyllwild, CA 92349
(213) 622-0355
Private school.

Illinois State University
Director: Illinois Writers, Inc.
English/Creative Writing Graduate
Program
Stevenson Hall
Normal-Bloomington, IL 61761
(309) 438-7705
Publishes *Spoon River Quarterly* and
Pikestaff Review.

Illinois Wesleyan University
Director: Hemingway Days and IWU
Writers Conferences
P.O. Box 2900
Bloomington, IL 61702
(309) 556-3031
Private university affiliated with the
Methodist Church. Publishes
Clockwatch Review.

Indiana State University
Department of English
Terre Haute, IN 47809
(812) 237-2968
Publishes *African American Review.*

Indiana University
Director: Writers Conference
English/Creative Writing Graduate
Program
Ballantine Hall 464
Bloomington, IN 47405
(812) 855-1877
Publishes *Indiana Review.*

Iowa State University
English/Creative Writing Graduate
   Program
203 Ross Hall
Ames, IA 50011
(515) 294-5836
Publishes *The Poet and Critic* and
   *Journal of Business and Technical
   Communication.*

Johns Hopkins University
Director: Writing Seminars
English/Creative Writing Graduate
   Program
34th and Charles Streets
Baltimore, MD 21219
(301) 338-8171
Private university. Publishes *Lemniscate*
   and *Zeniada.*

Johnson County Community College
Director: Center for Literary Culture/
   Writers Conference
12345 College at Quivira
Overland Park, KS 66210
(913) 829-8742

Johnson State College
Creative Writing Studies
Stowe Road
Johnson, VT 05656
(802) 635-2356

Kansas State University
English/Creative Writing Graduate
   Program
Denison Hall
Manhattan, KS 66506
(913) 532-6250
Publishes *Kansas Quarterly, Literary
   Magazine Review,* and *Touchstone.*

Kent State University
Creative Writing Division
Kent, OH 44242
(216) 672-2444

**Kent State University—Stark
   Campus**
Director: Midwest Writers Conference
6000 Frank Avenue, NW
Canton, OH 44720
(216) 499-9600

Knox College
Creative Writing Studies
Galesburg, IL 61401
(309) 353-0110
Private college.

Lakeland College
Creative Writing Division
P.O. Box 359
Sheboygan, WI 53082-0359
(414) 565-1217
Private college affiliated with the
   United Church of Christ. Publishes
   Seems.

Lehman College
English/Creative Writing Graduate
   Program
City University of New York
Bronx, NY 10468
(718) 960-8000
Publishes *Footnotes.*

Lewis and Clark College
Director: Northwest Writing Institute
Box 100
Portland, OR 97219
(503) 768-7745
Private college affiliated with the
   Presbyterian Church.

Linfield College
Creative Writing Studies
McMinnville, OR 97128
(503) 472-4121
Private college affiliated with the
American Baptist Church.

Long Beach State University
English/Creative Writing Graduate
Program
1250 Bellflower Boulevard
Long Beach, CA 90840
(213) 498-4111
Publishes *Rip Rap.*

**Long Island University at
Southhampton**
Southhampton Writers Conference
Southhampton, NY 11968
(516) 283-4000

**Long Island University—University
Center**
Creative Writing Studies
Brookville, NY 11548
(516) 299-2413
Private university.

Loras College
Creative Writing Studies
1450 Alta Vista
Dubuque, IA 52001
(319) 588-7236
Private college affiliated with the
Roman Catholic Church.

Lord Fairfax Community College
Director: Shenandoah Valley Writers'
Guild Conference
Box 47
Middletown, VA 22645
(540) 869-1120

Los Angeles State University
Writing Institute/Writers Conference
English Department
5151 State University Drive
Los Angeles, CA 90032
(213) 224-0111

Macalester College
Creative Writing Studies
1600 Grand Avenue
Saint Paul, MN 55105
(612) 696-6357
Private college affiliated with the
Presbyterian Church.

Maharishi International University
English/Creative Writing Program
Faculty Box 1058
Fairfield, IA 52557
(515) 472-1166
Private university. Publishes *Fairfield
Source* and *MIU Review.*

Manhattanville College
Summer Writers Workshops/Special
Programs
Office of Adult and Special Programs
Director: Writers' Week
Purchase, NY 10577
(914) 694-2200
Private college.

Mankato State University
English/Creative Writing Graduate
Program
Mankato, MN 56001
(507) 389-1822
Publishes *Mankato Poetry Review.*

Maple Woods Community College
Community Education
Director: Writers Conference
2601 NE Barry Road
Kansas City, MO 64156

Marymount Manhattan College
Director: Writers Conferences
Reba and Dave Williams Writing
   Center
221 East 71st Street
New York, NY 10021
(212) 517-0564, Fax (212) 628-4208
Private college affiliated with the
   Catholic Church.

**Massachusetts Institute of
   Technology**
Director: MIT Writing Programs
Office of the Summer Session Pro-
   grams
50 Ames Street, Room E19-356
Cambridge, MA 02139
(617) 253-2101, Fax (617) 253-8042
Private school. Publishes *Drama Review*.

McMurry College
Creative Writing Studies
Box 278
Abilene, TX 79697
(915) 691-6226
Private college affiliated with the
   United Methodist Church.

McNeese State University
English/Creative Writing Graduate
   Program
Lake Charles, LA 70609
(318) 475-5151

Memphis State University
English/Creative Writing Graduate
   Program
Patterson Hall
Memphis, TN 38152
(901) 454-2169
Publishes *River City Review*.

Mesa Community College
Writers Readings
English Department
1183 West Southern
Mesa, AZ 85202
(602) 969-5587

Metropolitan State College
Creative Writing Studies
1006 11th Street
Denver, CO 80204
(303) 556-3058

Miami University
English/Creative Writing Graduate
   Program
East High Street
Oxford, OH 45056
(513) 529-2531
Publishes *Oxford Magazine*.

Michigan State University
Director: Clarion Writers Workshops
Lyman Briggs School
English/Creative Writing Graduate
   Program
E-35 Holmes Hall
East Lansing, MI 48824-1107
(517) 353-6486
Publishes *Red Cedar Review*.

Middlebury College
Director: Bread Loaf Writers'
   Conference
Middlebury, VT 05753
(802) 388-3711
Private college. Publishes *New England
   Review*.

Mills College
Director: Summer Writers Institute/
NetWork Programs
Summer Programs: Bay Area Writers
Workshops
English/Creative Writing Graduate
Program
5000 MacArthur Boulevard
Oakland, CA 94613
(510) 430-2019
Private college. Publishes *The Walrus*.

Mississippi State University
English/Creative Writing Graduate
Program
Starkville, MS 39762
(601) 325-2224
Publishes *The Jabberwock*.

Moody Bible Institute
Director: Moody Write-to-Publish
Conference
820 North LaSalle Boulevard
Chicago, IL 60610
(509) 448-2555
Private school.

Morehead State University
English/Creative Writing Graduate
Program
Morehead, KY 40351
(606) 783-2008
Publishes *Inscape*.

Mount Holyoke College
Director: Writers Conference
Box 3213-D
South Hadley, MA 01075
(413) 538-2308

**Nantucket Island School of Design
and the Arts**
Institute for Published Writers
Box 958
Nantucket, MA 02554
Private school.

Napa Valley College
Director: Writers Conference
1088 College Avenue
Saint Helena, CA 94574
(707) 967-2900

Naropa Institute
Jack Kerouac School of Disembodied
Poetics/Summer Writing Program
English/Creative Writing Graduate
Program
2130 Arapahoe Avenue
Boulder, CO 80302
(303) 333-0202
Private school in the Buddhist contem-
plative tradition. Publishes *Bombay
Gin* and *Exit*.

New College of California
English/Creative Writing Graduate
Program
777 Valencia Street
San Francisco, CA 94110
(415) 626-1694
Publishes *Prosodia*.

New Mexico State University
English/Creative Writing Graduate Pro-
gram
Box 3E
Las Cruces, NM 88005
(505) 277-2446
Publishes *Puerto del Sol*.

New School/Eugene Lang College
Creative Writing Studies
65 West 11th Street
New York, NY 10011
(212) 741-5665
Private school.

New York State University at Albany
Writers Institute
English/Creative Writing Graduate Program
1400 Washington Avenue
Albany, NY 12222
(518) 442-5435
Publishes *13th Moon* and *The Little Magazine*.

New York State University at Brockport
Director: The Writers Forum
Kenyon Street
Brockport, NY 14420
(716) 395-2752

New York University
Director: Writers Conferences
School of Education, Office of Special Programs
32 Washington Place, Room 62
New York, NY 10003-6644
(212) 998-5090
Publishes *Pequod*.

North Carolina State University
Creative Writing Studies
Box 7103
Raleigh, NC 27695
(919) 737-2437
Publishes *Obsidian*.

North Cascades Institute
Director: Nature Writing Programs
2105 Highway 20
Sedro Woolley, WA 98284
(360) 856-5700
Private school.

Northeastern Junior College
Creative Writing Studies
Sterling, CO 80751
(303) 522-6600

Northeast Missouri State University
English/Creative Writing Graduate Program
Kirksville, MO 63501
(816) 785-4114
Publishes *Chariton Review, Paintbrush,* and *Cat's Eye.*

Northeast Texas Community College
Director: NETWO Writers Conference
P.O. Box 1307
Mount Pleasant, TX 75455
(903) 572-9868

Northern Arizona University
Communications School: High School Journalism Workshop for Minority Students
English/Creative Writing Graduate Program
Box 6001
Flagstaff, AZ 86011
(602) 523-5511
Publishes *Northern Arizona Review.*

Northern Michigan University
English/Creative Writing Graduate Program
Marquette, MI 49855
(906) 227-2650

Oakland University
Director: Detroit Women Writers Conference
Continuing Education
Rochester, MI 48309-4401
(313) 370-3120
Publishes *Witness*.

Oberlin College
Creative Writing Studies
Oberlin, OH 44074
(216) 775-8411
Private college. Publishes *Field*.

Ohio State University
Director: Writing Series
English/Creative Writing Graduate
    Program
363 Denney Hall
164 West 17th Avenue
Columbus, OH 43210-1370
(614) 292-3980
Publishes *The Journal* and *Literary*
    Magazine of OSU.

Ohio University
Creative Writing Studies
Athens, OH 45701
(614) 593-4100
Publishes *Ohio Review.*

Oklahoma Arts Institute
Program Director: Writing Workshops
P.O. Box 18154
Oklahoma City, OK 73154
(405) 842-0890
Private school.

Oklahoma Christian College
Creative Writing Studies
Box 11000
Oklahoma City, OK 73136-1100
(405) 425-5050
Private college affiliated with the
    Church of Christ.

Oklahoma City Community College
Writing Series, Continuing Education
7777 South May Avenue
Oklahoma City, OK 73159
(405) 682-7583

Oklahoma State University
English/Creative Writing Graduate
    Program
Stillwater, OK 74078-0135
(405) 774-6861
Publishes *Midland Review* and *Cimarron*
    Review.

Old Dominion University
Associated Writing Programs
Norfolk, VA 23529
(804) 683-3637

Olympic Park Institute
Director: Olympic Field Seminar
    Writing Series
HC 62 Box 9T
Port Angeles, WA 98362
(360) 928-3720
Private school.

Omega Institute for Holistic Studies
Director: Writing Workshops
Rural Delivery 2, Box 377
Rhinebeck, NY 12572
Private school.

Pasadena City College
Office of Community Education/
    Writers Forum
1570 East Colorado Boulevard
Pasadena, CA 91106-2003
(818) 449-5229

Penn State University
English/Creative Writing Graduate
    Program
Burrowes Building
University Park, PA 16802
(814) 865-5471

Pima College
Minority Writers Reading Series
Director: Pima Writers Workshop
2202 West Anklam Road
Tucson, AZ 85709
(602) 884-6974

Pittsburgh Theological Seminary
Continuing Education/Writing
   Workshops
616 North Highland Avenue
Pittsburgh, PA 15206
(412) 362-5610
Private school.

Portland State University
Director: Haystack Program in the Arts
   and Sciences
English/Creative Writing Graduate
   Program
P.O. Box 751
Portland, OR 97207
(800) 547-8887
Publishes *Portland Review.*

Prairie State College
Director: Writers Conference
202 South Halsted Street
Chicago Heights, IL 60411
(708) 709-3546, Fax (708) 755-2587

Purdue University
English/Creative Writing Graduate
   Program
West Lafayette, IN 47906
(317) 494-1776
Publishes *Sycamore Review.*

Radford University
Director: Appalachian Writers Associa-
   tion
Director: Highland Summer Confer-
   ences
P.O. Box 6935
Radford, VA 24142-6935
(703) 831-5366

Rappahannock Community College
Director: Chesapeake Writers'
   Conference
Glenns, VA 23149
(804) 333-6700

Rice University
Director of Programs
Publishing Conference
P.O. Box 1892
Houston, TX 77006
(713) 527-4036
Private university.

Roanoke College
Director: Blue Ridge Writers
   Conference
Community Education and Special
   Events
Salem, VA 24153
(703) 375-2270
Private college affiliated with the
   Lutheran Church.

Roger Williams College
Director: Writers' Conference
Creative Writing Programs
Old Ferry Road
Bristol, RI 02809
(401) 254-3046
Private college. Publishes *Aldebaran
   Literary Magazine* and *Calliope.*

**Rutgers University—Camden
   College of Arts and Sciences**
English/Creative Writing Graduate
   Program
Camden, NJ 08102
(201) 932-3770
Publishes *Mickle Street Review.*

Saint Cloud University
Director: Mississippi River Creative
   Writers Workshop
Saint Cloud, MN 56303
(612) 255-3061

Saint Leo College
Creative Writing Studies
P.O. Box 2008
Saint Leo, FL 33574
(904) 588-8283
Private college affiliated with the
Roman Catholic Church.

Saint Mary's College
Creative Writing Studies
Notre Dame, IN 46556
(219) 284-4587
Private college affiliated with the
Roman Catholic Church.

Saint Mary's College of Maryland
Director: The Literary Festivals
Lexington Park, MD 20653
(301) 862-0239

Saint Xavier University
Director: Taste of Chicago Writing
Conference
Continuing Education
3700 West 103rd Street
Chicago, IL 60655-3105
(312) 779-8661

Salem State College
Director: Eastern Writers' Conference
English Department
Salem, MA 01970
(508) 741-6270
Publishes *Sounding East.*

Salve Regina College
Creative Writing Studies
Ochre Point Avenue
Newport, RI 02840
(401) 847-6650
Private college affiliated with the Sisters
of Mercy.

San Diego State University
Extension Programs/Writers
Conference
English/Creative Writing Graduate
Program
San Diego, CA 92182-0723
(619) 594-5384
Publishes *Pacific Review* and *Fiction
International.*

San Francisco State University
Director: American Poetry Archives
The Poetry Center
1600 Holloway Avenue
San Francisco, CA 94132
(415) 338-2227
Publishes *Transfer* and *Ink.*

Santa Monica College
Writers Conference
Department of English
1900 Pico Boulevard
Santa Monica, CA 90405
(310) 450-5150

Sarah Lawrence College
Summer Seminars for Writers
English/Creative Writing Graduate
Program
One Meadway
Bronxville, NY 10708
(914) 395-2510
Private college. Publishes *One Meadway,
Sarah Lawrence Review,* and *Dark
Phrases.*

Seattle Pacific University
Christian Writers Conference
Coordinator
Humanities Department
Seattle, WA 98119
(206) 281-2036
Private university affiliated with the
Free Methodist Church.

Seton Hall University
Director: Metropolitan Writers Group
    of Seton Hall
Continuing Education
Bayley Hall
400 South Orange Avenue
South Orange, NJ 07079
(201) 761-9430
Private university.

Shimer College
Creative Writing Studies
438 North Sheridan Road
Waukegan, IL 60085
(708) 662-9631
Private college.

Simmons College
Director: New England Writers
    Workshop
The Fenway
Boston, MA 02115
(617) 521-2090
Private college.

Sinclair Community College
Director: Writers' Workshop
444 West Third Street
Dayton, OH 45402
(513) 226-2500

Skidmore College
Director: New York State Summer
    Writers Institute
Special Programs
Saratoga Springs, NY 12866
(518) 584-5000
Private college. Publishes *Salmagundi.*

Snake River Institute
Writers Workshops
P.O. Box 7724
Jackson Hole, WY 83001
(307) 733-2214
Private school.

**Southeastern Massachusetts
    University**
Creative Writing Studies
North Dartmouth, MA 02747
(508) 999-8605

Southern Methodist University
Creative Writing Studies
P.O. Box 296
Dallas, TX 75275
(214) 768-3648
Private university affiliated with the
    Methodist Church.

Southern Nazarene University
Creative Writing Studies
6729 NW 39th Expressway
Bethany, OK 73008
(405) 789-6400
Private university affiliated with the
    Church of the Nazarene.

Southwest Missouri State University
English/Creative Writing Graduate
    Program
901 South National
Springfield, MO 65804
(417) 836-5517
Publishes *Type.*

Southwest Texas State University
English/Creative Writing Graduate
    Studies
San Marcos, TX 78666-4616
(512) 245-2364

Stanford University
Director: Creative Writing Program
Director: Professional Publishing
    Course
Stanford, CA 94305-2087
(415) 723-2537, Fax (415) 725-0755

State University of New York at Brockport
Director: Brockport Writers' Forum
Summer Workshops
Brockport, NY 14420
(716) 395-5713

Sterling College
Director: Wildbranch Writing Workshops
Craftsbury Common, VT 05827
(802) 586-7711

Sweet Briar College
Creative Writing Studies
Sweet Briar, VA 24595
(804) 381-6142
Private college.

Syracuse University
English/Creative Writing Graduate Program
Hall of Languages
Syracuse, NY 13244-1170
(315) 443-3611
Publishes *Ridin' the Signifier, Shared Works, Poems and Stories,* and *Salt Hill Journal.*

Taos Institute of Arts
Director: Writing Workshop Series
P.O. Box 1389
Taos, NM 87571
(505) 758-2793

Temple University
English/Creative Writing Graduate Program
Anderson Hall
Philadelphia, PA 19122
(215) 787-7000
Public/private university. Publishes *Border Lines: Works in Translation.*

Texas A&M University
English/Creative Writing Graduate Program
College Station, TX 77843-4227
(409) 845-1031
Publishes *Litmus* and *Inksled Press.*

Texas Christian University
Director: Chisholm Trail Writers' Workshop
P.O. Box 32927
Fort Worth, TX 76129
(817) 921-7130

Trenton State College
Director: Annual Writers Conference
Department of English
Hillwood Lakes, NJ 08650-4700
(609) 771-3254

University of Alabama
English/Creative Writing Graduate Program
Box 870244
Tuscaloosa, AL 35487-0244
(205) 348-5666
Publishes *Black Warrior Review* and *Marr's Field Journal.*

University of Alaska at Fairbanks
Director: Midnight Sun Writers Conference
Fairbanks, AK 99775
(907) 474-7521

University of Anchorage
English/Creative Writing Graduate Program
3211 Providence Drive
Anchorage, AK 99508
(907) 786-1525
Publishes *Alaska Quarterly Review* and *Inklings.*

University of Arizona
English/Creative Writing Graduate
    Program
Tucson, AZ 85721-0007
(602) 621-3237
Publishes *Sonora Review.*

University of Arkansas
Director: Arkansas Poetry Award
201 Ozark Avenue
Fayetteville, AR 72701
(501) 575-3246, Fax (501) 575-6044
Publishes the *Ogalala Review.*

University of Bridgeport
Creative Writing Studies
Bridgeport, CT 06602
(203) 576-4552
Private university.

University of California at Berkeley
National Writing Project Network
Bay Area Writing Project
5627 Tolman Hall
Berkeley, CA 94720
(415) 642-2949
Publishes *Representations.*

**University of California at Berkeley
    Extension**
Director: The Writing Program
2223 Fulton Street
Berkeley, CA 94720
(510) 642-1063; Fax (510) 643-7062

University of California at Davis
Creative Writing Workshops
English Department
Davis, CA 95615
(916) 752-2971

University of California at Irvine
English/Creative Writing Graduate
    Program
Irvine, CA 92717
(714) 856-6703

**University of California at Irvine
    Extension**
Director: Summer Writers Conference
Arts and Humanities
Box 6050
Irvine, CA 92716-6050
(714) 824-6335

**University of California at Los
    Angeles**
UCLA Extension Writers Program
10995 LeConte Avenue, #313
Los Angeles, CA 90024
(213) 825-3101

**University of California at Los
    Angeles Extension**
Director: Writers Program
10995 LeConte Avenue, Suite 440
Los Angeles, CA 90024
(310) 825-9415

University of California at Riverside
University Extension/Creative Writing
    Programs
Riverside, CA 92521-0112
(714) 787-4531

**University of California at San
    Diego**
Creative Writing Studies
Z-021-R
La Jolla, CA 92093
(619) 534-3160

University of Chicago
Creative Writing Studies
1116 East 59th Street
Chicago, IL 60615
(312) 702-8650

University of Cincinnati
English/Creative Writing Graduate
    Program
ML0069
Cincinnati, OH 45221
(513) 558-3784
Publishes *Cincinnati Poetry Review,*
    American Drama, Mystics Quarterly,
    and *Clifton Magazine.*

University of Colorado at Denver
Creative Writing Studies
1200 Larimer Street
Denver, CO 80204-5300
(303) 556-2275

University of Connecticut
English/Creative Writing Graduate
    Program
Storrs, CT 06269
(203) 486-3137
Publishes *Lit.*

University of Delaware
English/Creative Writing Graduate
    Program
Newark, DE 19716
(302) 451-8123
Publishes *D.H. Lawrence Review* and
    Journal of Irish Literature.

University of Denver
Director: Publishing Institute
2075 South University Boulevard, D-
    114
Denver, CO 80210
(303) 871-2036, Fax (303) 871-2501
Publishes *Denver Quarterly.*

University of Findlay
Creative Writing Studies
1000 North Main Street
Findlay, OH 45840
(419) 424-4540
Private university affiliated with the
    Churches of God—General Confer-
    ence.

University of Florida
English/Creative Writing Graduate
    Program
4008 Turington Hall
Gainesville, FL 32601
(904) 392-1365
Publishes *Mangrove Review.*

University of Hawaii
Director: Manoa Writing Program
Bilger Hall, Room 104
Honolulu, HI 96822
(808) 956-6660, Fax (808) 956-9170
Publishes *Hawaii Review* and *Manoa.*

University of Houston
English/Creative Writing Graduate
    Program
Houston, TX 77204-3012
(713) 749-2321
Publishes *Gulf Coast.*

University of Illinois at Chicago
English/Creative Writing Graduate
    Program
Box 4348
Chicago, IL 60680
(312) 996-0998
Publishes *Red Shoes Review* and *Other*
    Voices.

University of Iowa
Director: Iowa Summer Writing
  Festival
Division of Continuing Education
116 International Center
Iowa City, IA 52242
(319) 335-2534
Publishes *Iowa Review* and *Iowa Journal
  of Literary Studies*.

University of Kansas
Director: Center for the Study of
  Science Fiction Writers Workshop
Department of English
3116 Wescoe Hall
Lawrence, KS 66045-2115
(913) 864-3380, Fax (913) 874-4298
Publishes *Cottonwood*.

University of Kentucky
Director: Women Writers Conference
Donovan Scholars Program
Director: Council on Aging/Writing
  Workshops
106 Frazee Hall
Lexington, KY 40506-0031
(606) 257-3295

University of Maine at Orono
Downeast Poetry Workshop
Conference and Institute Division
304 Neville Hall
Orono, ME 04469
(207) 581-1561
Publishes *Paideuma*.

**University of Maryland at College
  Park**
English/Creative Writing Graduate
  Program
College Park, MD 20742
(301) 454-5550
Publishes *Ethos*.

University of Massachusetts
Indian Summer Writers Workshop
Continuing Education
English/Creative Writing Graduate
  Program
Amherst, MA 01003
(413) 545-0222
Publishes *Massachusetts Review* and
  Spectrum.

**University of Massachusetts at
  Dartmouth**
English/Creative Writing Graduate
  Program
Old Westport Road
North Dartmouth, MA 02747
(508) 999-8605
Publishes *Temper*.

**University of Massachusetts at
  Lowell**
Director: Writers Conference
Continuing Education
One University Avenue
Lowell, MA 01854
(508) 934-2405, Fax (508) 934-3008

University of Miami
Creative Writing Studies
Box 240825
Coral Gables, FL 33124
(305) 284-4323

University of Michigan
Engineering Writing Conference
English/Creative Writing Graduate
   Program
Haven Hall
Ann Arbor, MI 48109
(313) 764-9265
Publishes *Michigan Quarterly Review.*

University of Minnesota
Director: Split Rock Arts Program
English/Creative Writing Graduate
   Program
306 Wesbrook Hall
77 Pleasant Street, SE
Minneapolis, MN 55455
(612) 624-6800
Publishes *Agassiz Review.*

University of Mississippi
Director: Faulkner and Yoknapatawpha
   Conference
Center for the Study of Southern
   Culture
English/Creative Writing Graduate
   Program
University, MS 38677
(601) 232-5993
Publishes *Studies in English.*

University of Missouri at Kansas City
College of Arts and Sciences
Director: Ozark Writers Conference
Director: Mark Twain Creative Writing
   Workshop
English/Creative Writing Graduate
   Program
5100 Rockhill Road
Kansas City, MO 64110-2499
(816) 235-2558; Fax (816) 235-2611
Publishes *Number One* and *New Letters.*

University of Montana
Center for Continuing Education
Director: Environmental Writing
   Institute
Director: Yellow Bay Writers Workshop
English/Creative Writing Graduate
   Program
Missoula, MT 59812
(406) 243-6486; Fax (406) 243-2047
Publishes *Cutbank.*

University of Nebraska at Lincoln
English/Creative Writing Graduate
   Program
Lincoln, NE 68688-0333
(402) 472-3620
Publishes *Prairie Schooner.*

University of Nebraska at Omaha
ASH 215
Omaha, NE 68181-0324
(402) 554-2771
Publishes *Nebraska Review.*

University of Nevada
Reading and Writing the West
  Conference
English Department
Reno, NV 89557-0031
(702) 784-6865

University of Nevada at Las Vegas
English/Creative Writing Graduate
  Program
Las Vegas, NV 89154
(702) 739-3443
Publishes *Interim.*

University of Nevada at Reno
Sierra Nevada Writing Institute
Reno, NV 89557
(702) 784-6856

University of New Hampshire
English/Creative Writing Graduate
  Program
Camden, NH 03824
(603) 862-1360
Publishes *Aegis.*

University of New Mexico
English/Creative Writing Graduate
  Program
Albuquerque, NM 87131
(505) 843-2111
Publishes *Blue Mesa Review.*

University of New Orleans
International Study Programs
English/Creative Writing Graduate
  Program
New Orleans, LA 70148
(504) 286-6595
Publishes *Ellipsis.*

University of North Carolina
English Department
Charlotte, NC 28223
(704) 547-4336
Publishes *Southern Poetry Review.*

**University of North Carolina at
  Greensboro**
English/Creative Writing Graduate
  Program
134 Melver
Greensboro, NC 27412
(919) 334-5243
Publishes *Greensboro Review.*

University of North Dakota
Director: Writers Conference
English/Creative Writing Graduate
  Program
Box 8237
Grand Forks ND 58202
(701) 777-4195
Publishes *North Dakota Quarterly.*

University of North Texas
Director: Association for Business
 Communication International
 Convention
College of Business Administration
Denton, TX 76203
(817) 565-2681

University of Oklahoma
English/Creative Writing Graduate
 Program
760 Van Vleet Oval
Norman, OK 73019-0240
(405) 325-6963

University of Oregon
English/Creative Writing Graduate
 Program
Eugene, OR 97403
(503) 686-3201
Publishes *Northwest Review.*

University of Pennsylvania
College of General Studies/Young
 Writers at Penn
3440 Market Street, #100
Philadelphia, PA 19104-3335
(215) 243-9880

University of Pittsburgh
English/Creative Writing Graduate
 Program
Bruce Hall
Pittsburgh, PA 15260
(412) 624-7488
Publishes *Pennsylvania Review.*

University of Pittsburgh at Bradford
Creative Writing Studies
300 Campus Drive
Bradford, PA 16701-0990
(814) 266-9661

**University of Pittsburgh at
 Johnstown**
Creative Writing Studies
Johnstown, PA 15904
(814) 362-3801

University of South Carolina
English/Creative Writing Graduate
 Program
Columbia, SC 29208
(803) 777-4057
Publishes *Portfolio.*

University of South Dakota
English/Creative Writing Graduate
 Program
414 East Clark Street
Vermillion, SD 57069
(605) 677-5434
Publishes *South Dakota Review, The
 Absolute Ceiling,* and *Vermillion
 Literary Arts Magazine.*

University of Southern California
Director: Professional Writing Program
WPH 404
Los Angeles, CA 90089-4034
(213) 740-3252, ext. 45
Publishes *Southern California Anthology.*

University of Southern Indiana
Director: Rope Walk Writers Retreat
Continuing Education
8600 University Boulevard
Evansville, IN 47712
(800) 467-8600

University of Southern Maine
Director: Stonecoast Writers
    Conference
Summer School Office
96 Falmouth Street
Portland, ME 04103
(207) 780-4291

University of South Florida
Creative Writing Studies
4202 East Fowler Avenue
Tampa, FL 33620
(813) 974-3350

**University of South Florida—Saint
    Petersburg Campus**
Director: Florida Suncoast Writers'
    Conference
140 Seventh Avenue
Saint Petersburg, FL 33701

**University of Southwestern
    Louisiana**
Director: Deep South Writers
    Conference
Drawer 44691
Lafayette, LA 70504
(318) 482-6918

University of Tampa
Creative Writing Studies
401 West Kennedy Boulevard
Tampa, FL 33606
(813) 253-6228
Publishes *Tampa Review*.

**University of Tennessee at
    Chattanooga**
English/Creative Writing Graduate
    Program
McCallie Avenue
Chattanooga, TN 37403
(423) 755-4662
Publishes *Poetry Miscellany* and *Tennes-
see Philological Bulletin*.

University of Tennessee at Knoxville
English/Creative Writing Graduate
    Program
Knoxville, TN 37996-0430
(423) 974-2184
Publishes *The Phoenix*.

University of Texas at Dallas
Director: American Literary Translators
    Association
Director: Writers Conference
Center for Continuing Education
P.O. Box 830688
Dallas, TX 75083-0688
(214) 690-2204

University of Texas at El Paso
Creative Writing Studies
University Avenue at Hawthorne
El Paso, TX 79968
(214) 690-2341

University of the South
Director: Sewanee Writers' Conference
310G Saint Luke's Hall
735 University Avenue
Sewanee, TN 37375-1000
(615) 598-1141
Private university affiliated with the
    Episcopal Church. Publishes *Sewanee
Review*.

University of Toledo
Division of Continuing Education/
    Writing Seminars
Toledo, OH 43606-3390
(419) 537-2696

University of Utah
English/Creative Writing Graduate
    Program
Salt Lake City, UT 84112
(801) 581-7281
Publishes *Western Humanities Review*
    and Quarterly West.

University of Vermont
Director: Summer Writing Program
322 South Prospect Street
Burlington, VT 05401-3505
(800) 639-3210

University of Virginia
English/Creative Writing Graduate
    Program
Wilson Hall
Charlottesville, VA 22903
(804) 924-7751
Publishes *Callaloo.*

University of Washington
English/Creative Writing Graduate
    Program
Padleford Hall
Seattle, WA 98195
(206) 764-2245
Publishes *Seattle Review* and
    Metamorfosis.

University of West Florida
Director: English Department
Pensacola, FL 32514-5751
(904) 474-2923
Publishes *Panhandler Magazine.*

University of Wisconsin
Director: Brittingham Prize in Poetry
Madison, WI 53706
(608) 262-1234

**University of Wisconsin at Eau
    Claire**
Director: Northern Waters Writers
    Conference
English/Creative Writing Graduate
    Program
Eau Claire, WI 54702-4004
(715) 836-2031

University of Wisconsin at Madison
Director: School of the Arts at
    Rhinelander
Continuing Education
Lowell Hall, Suite 727
610 Langdon Street
Madison, WI 53703
(608) 263-3494

**University of Wisconsin at
    Milwaukee**
English/Creative Writing Graduate
    Program
P.O. Box 749
Milwaukee, WI 53201
(414) 229-4801
Publishes *Cream City Review.*

University of Wyoming
English/Creative Writing Graduate
    Program
Box 3353
University Station
Laramie, WY 82070
(307) 766-5160
Publishes *Owen Wister Review.*

Utah State University
Director: Logan Canyon Writers
    Workshop
Conference and Institute Division
Logan, UT 84322-5005
(800) 538-2663

Vassar College
Director: Institute of Publishing and
    Writing
Box 300
Poughkeepsie, NY 12601
(914) 437-5903

**Vermont College of Norwich
    University**
English/Creative Writing Graduate
    Program
Montpelier, VT 05602
(802) 828-8750

Villanova University
Director: Writers Workshops
Villanova, PA 19085
(215) 654-4620

Virginia Commonwealth University
English/Creative Writing Graduate
    Program
1015 Grove Avenue
Richmond, VA 23284-9022
(804) 828-2772
Publishes *Richmond Arts Magazine* and
    The Writer's Corner.

Virginia Intermont College
Creative Writing Studies
600 Harmeling Street
Bristol, VA 24201-1477
(540) 669-9515
Private college affiliated with the
    Baptist Association of Virginia.

Warren Wilson College
Director: Writing Program
P.O. Box 9000
Asheville, NC 28815-9000
(704) 298-3325, ext. 380

Washington University
English/Creative Writing Graduate
    Program
Box 1122
One Brookings Drive
St. Louis, MO 63130
(314) 935-5010

Webster University
Creative Writing Studies
470 East Lockwood
Webster Groves, MO 63119
(314) 968-7000
Private university. Publishes *Webster
    Review.*

Wesleyan University
Director: Wesleyan Writers Conference
Middletown, CT 06459
(203) 347-9411, ext. 2448
Private university.

Westark Community College
Writers Workshops
P.O. Box 3649
Fort Smith, AR 72913
(501) 788-7000

Western Kentucky University
English/Creative Writing Graduate
    Program
Bowling Green, KY 42101
(502) 745-2551
Publishes *Zephyrus.*

Western Michigan University
Director: Western Michigan Writers
  Conference
English/Creative Writing Graduate
  Program
221 South Quarterline Road
Muskegon, MI 49442-1432
(616) 777-3444

Western Montana College
Director: Writers Conference
Summer School Office
Dillon, MT 59725
(800) 962-6668

Western Washington University
Creative Writing Studies
Bellingham, WA 98225
(206) 676-3440
Publishes *Jeopardy.*

West Virginia University
English/Creative Writing Graduate
  Program
Morgantown, WV 26505
(304) 293-2121
Publishes *Calliope.*

Wichita State University
English/Creative Writing Graduate
  Program
1845 Fairmount
Box 14
Wichita, KS 67208
(316) 689-3085
Publishes *Microcosmos.*

Wright State University
English/Creative Writing Graduate
  Program
1001 Xenia Avenue
Yellow Springs, OH 45387-1600
(513) 864-2505
Publishes *Nexus.*

Yellowstone Institute
Coordinator: Writing Workshops
P.O. Box 117
Yellowstone National Park, WY 82190
(307) 344-7749

11

Major Resource Listing

Do not mistake the finger pointing at the moon for the moon, as the wise teacher once said. This directory serves as a guide; a resource for you to browse and investigate. It does not say, "Here, this one is for you." Instead it urges you to venture and discover. You are given an opportunity to experience serendipity. As you search far and wide for the group that you think you want, you may, to your delight and surprise, find another, even better group in your own backyard.

This comprehensive roster ranges from small, regional group listings to large, national conventions and includes a substantial selection of workshops, clubs, and conferences that function in between at varying capacities and dimensions. These include circles, courses, workshops, groups, clubs, gatherings, associations, societies, leagues, unions, guilds, fellowships, alliances, confederations, colonies, retreats, salons, festivals, forums, conclaves, book fairs, exhibits, forums, panels, scholarships, residencies, sessions, centers, foundations, fellowships, programs, and more.

None of these groups have paid to be listed. Requests have arrived scribbled on postcards, been transmitted through e-mail, and been left on the answering machine. I have obtained most of these listings by scouring some very fine written catalogs, whose authors and editors I thank. I suggest that you check them out, too.

The Guide to Writers Conferences (Shaw Associates, Coral Gables, FL 33134) provides dates, locations, and other details based on information obtained from questionnaires and personal interviews with conference sponsors. *Poets and Writers Magazine* (72 Spring Street, New York, NY 10012) runs announcements about writers' programs and conferences and publishes an annual guide.

Many conferences and seminars are advertised in *Writer's Digest Magazine* (1507 Dana Avenue, Cincinnati, OH 45207) and are featured in its annual

Writer's Market publication. Some are advertised in *The Writer* (120 Boylston Street, Boston, MA 02116-4615) and are featured in its annual *Writer's Handbook*.

The Literary Market Place (R. R. Bowker, 121 Chanlon Road, New Providence, NJ 07974), a directory of the U.S. book publishing industry with industry yellow pages, lists a number of workshops. You can also contact the National Writers Club (1450 South Havana, Suite 620, Aurora, CO 80012) for their *Directory of Local Writers' Organizations*. More information is offered by the Associated Writing Programs (Tallwood House, Mail Stop 1E3, George Mason University, Fairfax, VA 22030) in its official guide. Additional associations are listed in *Gale's Encyclopedia of Associations* and the *Encyclopedia of Associations*, which should be available in your public library.

Writers Conferences and Festivals (P.O. Box 102396, Denver, CO 80250) is a nonprofit service organization open to anyone interested in writers conferences, workshops, and festivals and how they are run. As such, it is not a writers organization, per se, but it focuses on the administration of these programs.

I mention all of these publications because in the rapidly changing world of writers, it is difficult to keep tabs on what is currently available. My aim is to do everything possible to make the experience easier and more productive for you.

There is a time lag between the research for this book and the actual publication. Consequently, if you are interested in calling any of the resources listed here, you might want to call the operator for the current telephone number. Because telephone numbers change more frequently than mailing addresses, it's usually best to write. In fact, many of the associations have requested that I not list telephone or fax numbers here in case a new number is issued after this book goes to press.

It is almost impossible to keep a list such as this as current as I would like. Not only do phone numbers and mailing addresses change, but locations change and groups disband. Also, many groups are operating on grants and little else, consequently they are understaffed and underfunded, staffing offices part-time and depending greatly on volunteers. Instead of forcing staffers to spend valuable time fielding questions that could easily be answered by reading their literature, they would prefer that you inquire by mail, including a self-addressed, stamped envelope. This enables them to respond efficiently and effectively with brochures, pamphlets, guidelines, and, if appropriate, applications. In some cases, you may receive a personal response, perhaps a suggestion or referral, or even a follow-up phone call.

I invite your updates, additions, and deletions. Please send them to:

Eileen Malone
c/o Wiley Books for Writers Series
John Wiley & Sons, Inc.
Professional, Reference and Trade Group
605 Third Avenue
New York, NY 10158

I look forward to hearing from you!

A

About Books, Inc., Phone (719) 395-2459, Box 1500, 425 Cedar Street, Buena Vista, CO 81211

Academy of American Poets, Phone (212) 274-0343, Fax (212) 427-4489, 584 Broadway, Suite 1208, New York, NY 10012-3250

Act 1 Creativity Center, Phone (816) 753-0383, Box 10153, Kansas City, MO 64111

Advanced Writing and Interviewing Workshop, Phone (800) 444-2942, Effective Communications, 309 Windsor Terrace, Ridgewood, NJ 07450

Affiliated Writers of America, Inc., Phone (307) 327-5328, Fax (307) 327-5705, P.O. Box 343, Encampment, WY 82325

Akron Manuscript Club, Phone (216) 923-2094, P.O. Box 1011, Cuyahoga Falls, OH 44223

Akumal, Mexico, Writers Conference, Phone (800) 662-8351, Box 21922, Santa Barbara, CA 93121

Alabama State Council on the Arts, Phone (334) 242-4076, Fax (334) 240-3269, One Dexter Avenue, Montgomery, AL 36130

Alabama Writers' Conclave, Phone (205) 871-6855, 117 Hanover Road, Homewood, AL 35209

Alaska Adventure in Travel Writing, Phone (907) 586-3067, P.O. Box 21494, Juneau, AK 99802

Alaska State Council on the Arts, Phone (907) 279-1558, Fax (907) 279-4330, 411 West 4th Avenue, Suite 1E, Anchorage, AK 36130

Alden B. Dow Creativity Center, Phone (517) 837-4478, Northwood Institute, 3225 Cook Road, Midland, MI 48640-2398

AlianzaSi Writers Workshops, 600 South Bryant Street, Denver, CO 80219 (inquire with SASE)

Alliance of New York Writers and Publishers, Inc., 194 Soundview Drive, Rocky Point, NY 11778 (inquire with SASE)

American Academy and Institute of Arts and Letters, Phone (212) 368-5900, 633 West 155th Street, New York, NY 10032

American Academy of Arts and Sciences, Phone (617) 491-2600, Fax (617) 576-5088, Nortons Woods, 136 Irving Street, Cambridge, MA 02138

American Association of Community and Junior Colleges, Phone (202) 728-0200, Fax (202) 223-9390, One Dupont Circle, Washington, DC 20036

American Association of Sunday and Feature Editors, Phone (703) 648-1286, Fax (703) 620-4557, Box 17407, Dulles Airport, Washington, DC 20041

American Auto Racing Writers and Broadcasters, Phone (818) 842-7005, Fax (818) 842-2070, 922 North Pass Avenue, Burbank, CA 91505

American Baptist Assembly, Phone (800) 558-8898, Green Lake Conference Center, Green Lake, WI 54941-9599

American Black Book Writers Association, P.O. Box 10458, Venice, CA 90295 (inquire with SASE)

American Book Producers Association, Phone (212) 645-2368, Fax (212) 989-7542, 160 Fifth Avenue, New York, NY 10011-7000

American Booksellers Association, Phone (800) 637-0037, 137 West 25th Street, New York, NY 10001

American Christian Writers, Phone (800) 21-WRITE, P.O. Box 5168, Phoenix, AZ 85010

American Council on Education, Phone (202) 939-9380, Fax (202) 833-4760, One Dupont Circle, Washington, DC 20036

American Dialect Society, Phone (217) 474-7056, MacMurray College, English Department, Jacksonville, IL 62650

American Federation of Television and Radio Artists, 260 Madison Avenue, New York, NY 10016 (inquire with SASE)

American Film Institute, Phone (800) 999-4234, TOP, 2021 North Western Avenue, Los Angeles, CA 90027

American Heritage Library, Phone (212) 206-5107, Fax (212) 620-2332, 60 Fifth Avenue, New York, NY 10011

American Historical Association, Phone (202) 544-2422, Fax (202) 544-8307, 400 A Street, SE, Washington, DC 20003

American Jewish Historical Society, Phone (617) 891-8110, Two Thornton Road, Waltham, MA 02154-7711 (inquire with SASE)

American Library Association, Phone (312) 944-6780, Fax (312) 440-9374, 50 East Huron Street, Chicago, IL 60611

American Literacy Council, Phone (212) 662-0650, 106 Morningside Drive, Suite 79, New York, NY 10027

American Literary Translators (ALTA), Phone (214) 690-2093, Fax (214) 690-2989, Internet: ert@UTDallas.edu, University of Texas, Dallas, Box 830688, Richardson, TX 75083-0688

American Medical Writer's Association, Phone (800) 444-2942, 9650 Rockville Pike, Bethesda, MD 20814-3928

American Newspaper Syndicate, Phone (714) 559-8047, 9 Woodrush Drive, Irvine, CA 92714

American Poetry Archives, Phone (415) 338-1056, San Francisco State University, 1600 Holloway Avenue, San Francisco, CA 94132

American Poetry Association, Box 1803, 250A Potrero Street, Santa Cruz, CA 95061-1803 (inquire with SASE)

American-Scandinavian Foundation, Phone (212) 879-9779, 725 Park Avenue, New York, NY 10021

American Society of Business Press Editors, 4445 Gilmer Lane, Cleveland, OH 44143 (inquire with SASE)

American Society of Composers, Authors, and Publishers, Phone (212) 595-3050, Fax (212) 721-0955, One Lincoln Plaza, New York, NY 10023

American Society of Indexers, Phone (512) 749-4052, Fax (512) 749-6334, 1700 18th Street, NW, Washington, DC 20009

American Society of Journalists and Authors, Inc., Phone (212) 997-0947, Fax (212) 768-7414, 1501 Broadway, Suite 1907, New York, NY 10036

American Society of Magazine Editors, Phone (212) 752-0055, Fax (212) 888-4217, 575 Lexington Avenue, New York, NY 10022

American Translators Association, Phone (703) 941-1500, 3818 North Ridgeview Road, Arlington, VA 22207

American Writers Theatre Foundation, Box 810, Times Square Station, New York, NY 10108 (inquire with SASE)

Amy Foundation, Phone (517) 323-6233, P.O. Box 16091, Lansing, MI 48901

Anniston Spring Conference, 1616 Kestwick Drive, Birmingham, AL 35226 (inquire with SASE)

Antioch Writers Workshop of Yellow Springs, Phone (513) 866-9060, P.O. Box 494, Yellow Springs, OH 45387

Appalachian Mountain Club, Phone (617) 523-0636, Fax (304) 535-2667, 5 Joy Street, Boston, MA 02108

Appalachian Mountain Club, Phone (603) 466-2727, P.O. Box 844, Gorham, NH 03581

Appalachian Trail Conference, Phone (304) 535-6331, Fax (304) 535-2667, Box 807, Harpers Ferry, WV 25425

Appalachian Writers, Phone (606) 785-5475, Box 844, Hindman, KY 41822

Appalachian Writers Association Conference, Phone (703) 831-5269, Radford University, P.O. Box 6935, Radford, VA 24142-6936

Appalachian Writers Workshop, Phone (704) 262-2120, Appalachian State University, University Hall, Boone, NC 28608

Arizona Authors' Association, Phone (602) 942-4240, 3509 East Shea Boulevard, Suite 117, Phoenix, AZ 85028-3339

Arizona Christian Writers, Phone (602) 838-4919, P.O. Box 5168, Phoenix, AZ 85010

Arizona Commission on the Arts, Phone (602) 255-5882, 417 West Roosevelt, Phoenix, AZ 85003

Arizona Poetry Center, Phone (602) 321-7760, University of Arizona, 1216 North Cherry Avenue, Tucson, AZ 85719

Arkansas Arts Council, Phone (501) 324-9766, 1500 Tower Building, 323 Center Street, Little Rock, AR 72201

Arkansas Writers' Conference, Phone (501) 225-0166, 1115 Gillette Drive, Little Rock, AR 72207

Art of the Wild, Phone (916) 752-1658, University of California at Davis, Department of English, Davis, CA 95616

Art without Walls Prison Program, 72 Fifth Avenue, New York, NY 10010 (inquire with SASE)

Artist Trust Fellowship, Phone (206) 467-8734, Fax (206) 467-9633, 1402 Third Avenue, Suite 415, Seattle, WA 98101

Artists Foundation, Inc., 110 Broad Street, Boston, MA 02110 (inquire with SASE)

Arts at Menucha, Phone (503) 771-4270, Creative Community Arts, P.O. Box 4958, Portland, OR 97208

Arts Indiana, Inc., Phone (317) 632-7894, 47 South Pennsylvania, Suite 701, Indianapolis, IN 46204

Asheville Poetry Festival, Phone (800) 476-8172, Fax (704) 298-5491, Internet: AllanWolf@aol.com, P.O. Box 9643, Asheville, NC 28815

Asian American Journalists Association, Phone (415) 346-2051, 1765 Sutter Street, Room 1000, San Francisco, CA 94115 (inquire with SASE)

ASJA Writers Conference, Phone (212) 997-0947, Fax (212) 768-7414, 1501 Broadway, #302, Room 1907, New York, NY 10036

Aspen Writers' Conference, Phone (303) 923-4144, Fax (303) 923-4485, Box 5840, Snowmass Village, CO 81615

Aspen Writers' Foundation, Phone (800) 925-2526, Drawer 7726, Aspen, CO 81612

Assisi Screenplay Workshop (Italy), Phone (212) 691-1159, 463 West Street, 1028H, New York, NY 10014

Associated Authors, Inc., Phone (813) 449-2777, 692 Bayway Boulevard, Clearwater Beach, FL 34630

Associated Business Writers of America, Inc., Phone (303) 751-7844, Fax (303) 751-8593, 1450 South Havana Street, Suite 620, Aurora, CO 88012

Associated Press, Phone (212) 621-1500, 50 Rockefeller Plaza, New York, NY 10020

Associated Writing Programs, Phone (804) 683-3839, Old Dominion University, Norfolk, VA 23529-0079

Association for Business Communication International Convention, Phone (817) 565-2681, University of North Texas, College of Business Administration, Denton, TX 76203

Association for Education in Journalism and Mass Communications, Phone (803) 777-7700, University of South Carolina, College of Journalism, Columbia, SC 29208

Association of American Colleges and Universities, Phone (202) 387-3760, Fax (202) 265-9532, 1818 R Street, NW, Washington, DC 20009

Association of American Publishers, Phone (212) 689-8920, Fax (212) 696-0131, 220 East 23rd Street, New York, NY 10010

Association of American University Presses, Phone (212) 941-6610, Fax (212) 941-6618, 584 Broadway, New York, NY 10012

Association of Authors Representatives, Phone (212) 353-3709, 10 Astor Place, Third Floor, New York, NY 10003

Association of Editorial Businesses, Phone (202) 232-8484, 116 Fourth Street, SE, Washington, DC 20003

Association of Jewish Libraries, Phone (212) 535-6700, Fax (212) 879-9763, YIVO Institute for Jewish Research, 1048 Fifth Avenue, New York, NY 10028

Association of Petroleum Writers, *Oil and Gas Journal,* Box 1260, Tulsa, OK 74101 (inquire with SASE)

Association of Professional Translators, Phone (412) 234-5751, Fax (412) 234-0214, Three Mellon Bank Center, Suite 2523, Pittsburgh, PA 15259

Athenaeum of Philadelphia, Phone (215) 925-2688, 219 South Sixth Street, Philadelphia, PA 19106

Atlantic Center for the Arts, Phone (904) 427-6975, 1414 Art Center Avenue, New Smyrna Beach, FL 32168

Austin Writers' League, Phone (512) 499-8914, 1501 West Fifth Street, Suite E-2, Austin, TX 78703

Author and Agent, Phone/Fax (415) 381-6431, 609 Northern Avenue, Mill Valley, CA 94941

Authors and Artists Group, Inc., Phone (212) 944-9898, Fax (212) 944-6484, 19 West 44th Street, Suite 1602, New York, NY 10036

Authors and Artists Resource Center, Phone (602) 325-4733, P.O. Box 64785, Tucson, AZ 85740-1785

Authors Guild, Phone (212) 563-5904, 330 West 42nd Street, New York, NY 10036

Authors in the Park, Phone (407) 658-4520, P.O. Box 85, Winter Park, FL 32790-0085

Authors League of America, Inc., Phone (212) 564-8350, Fax (212) 564-8363, 330 West 42nd Street, New York, NY 10036

Authors of the Flathead, P.O. Box 189, Kila, MT 59920 (inquire with SASE)

Authors Unlimited, Inc., Phone (212) 481-8484, Fax (212) 481-9582, 31 East 32nd Street, Suite 300, New York, NY 10016

Autumn Authors' Affair, Phone (708) 862-9797, 1507 Burnham Avenue, Calumet City, IL 60409

Aviation/Space Writers Association, Phone (614) 221-1900, Fax (614) 221-1989, 17 High Street, #1200, Columbus, OH 43215

Avila Writers Conference, Phone (816) 942-8400, Avila College, 11901 Wornall Road, Kansas City, MO 64143

B

BABRA (Bay Area Book Reviewers Association), Phone (415) 883-2353, Fax (415) 883-4280, 11A Commercial Boulevard, Novato, CA 94949

Baker Street Irregulars, 34 Pierson Avenue, Norwood, NJ 07648 (inquire with SASE)

Baptist Writers Workshop, Phone (615) 251-2939, Baptist Sunday School Board, 127 Ninth Avenue, Nashville, TN 37234

Bard Society, Phone (904) 398-5352, 1358 Tiber Avenue, Jacksonville, FL 32207

Bay Area Book Reviewers Association, Phone (415) 883-2353, Fax (415) 883-4280, 11A Commercial Boulevard, Novato, CA 94949

Bay Area Lawyers for the Arts, Fort Mason Center, Building C, San Francisco, CA 94123 (inquire with SASE)

Bay Area Writers League, P.O. Box 1426, Friendswood, TX 77546 (inquire with SASE)

Bay Area Writers Workshop, Phone (510) 430-3127, Box 620327, Woodside, CA 94062

Bay Area Writing Project, Phone (415) 642-2949, University of California, 5627 Tolman Hall, Berkeley, CA 94720

Before Columbus Foundation, Phone (510) 268-9772, The Ginn House, 660 13th Street, Suite 203, Oakland, CA 94612

Bellagio Residencies at Villa Serbelloni, Phone (212) 852-8431, The Rockefeller Foundation, 1133 Avenue of the Americas, New York, NY 10036

Belles, Beaux and Bayous, Phone (318) 487-9917, 43 Westwood Boulevard, Alexandria, LA 71301

Bennington Summer Writing Workshops, Phone (802) 442-5401, ext. 160, Fax (802) 442-6164, Bennington College, Bennington, VT 05201

Bernard Shaw Society, Phone (212) 989-7833, Box 1159, Madison Square Station, New York, NY 10163

Beyond Baroque Literary Arts Center, Phone (213) 822-3006, 681 Venice Boulevard, Box 806, Venice, CA 90291

Bigfork Gathering, Phone (406) 837-4885, P.O. Box 1230, Bigfork, MT 59911

Biola University Writers Institute, Phone (800) 759-6737, 13800 Biola Avenue, La Mirada, CA 90639

Bisbee Poetry Festival, P.O. Box 500, Bisbee, AZ 85603 (inquire with SASE)

Black Hills Writers Workshop, Box 1539, Rapid City, SD 57709 (inquire with SASE)

Black Writers and Artists, Inc., International, Phone (415) 532-6179, 5312 Normandie, Oakland, CA 94619

Blooming Grove Writers, Phone (309) 828-5092, Fax (309) 829-8369, Box 515, Bloomington, IL 61702

Blue Mountain Center, Phone (518) 352-7391, Blue Mountain Lake, New York, NY 12812

Blue Ridge Christian Writers' Conference, Phone (704) 669-8421, Box 188, Black Mountain, NC 28711

Blue Ridge Mountains Writers Retreat, Phone (800) 551-9453, 1200 Midland Building, Des Moines, IA 50309

Blue Ridge Writers Conference, Phone (703) 345-8557, 2515 Laburnum Avenue, SW, Roanoke, VA 24015

Bluegrass Writers Workshop, Phone (609) 275-2947, Box 3098, Princeton, NJ 08543-3098

Bold Productions, Phone (817) 468-9924, P.O. Box 152281, Arlington, TX 76015

Book Builders, Inc., Phone (212) 737-8210, Fax (212) 879-0860, 18 East 80 Street, Suite B, New York, NY 10021

Book Industry Study Group, Inc., Phone (212) 929-1393, Fax (212) 989-7542, 160 Fifth Avenue, New York, NY 10010

Book Passage Writers' Conference, Phone (800) 999-7909, 51 Tamal Vista Boulevard, Corte Madera, CA 94925

Book Publishing Workshops, Phone (805) 968-7277, Box 423261, Santa Barbara, CA 93140-4232

Bookbuilders of Boston, Phone (617) 933-6878, Fax (617) 935-0132, 112 Cummings Park, Woburn, MA 01801

Border Playwrights Project, Phone (602) 882-8607, Borderlands Theater, P.O. Box 2791, Tucson, AZ 87702

Bozeman Authors, 6413 Cattle Drive, Bozeman, MT 59715 (inquire with SASE)

Branham Ranch, Phone (505) 776-2622, P.O. Box 220, San Cristobal, NM 87564

Bread Loaf Writers' Conference, Phone (802) 388-3711, Middlebury College, Middlebury, VT 05753

Brockport Writers Forum, Phone (716) 395-5713, English Department, State University of New York, Brockport, NY 14420

Brooklyn Poetry Circle, 2550 Independence Avenue, Bronx, NY 10463 (inquire with SASE)

Brooklyn Writers Club, Phone (718) 837-3484, Box 184, Bath Beach Station, Brooklyn, NY 11214

Brooklyn Writers Network Workshops, Phone (718) 377-4945, 2509 Avenue K, Brooklyn, NY 11210

Bumbershoot Bookfair, Phone (206) 622-5123, P.O. Box 9750, Seattle, WA 98109-0750

Bush Artist Fellowships, Phone (612) 227-5222, The Bush Foundation, First National Bank Building, 332 Minnesota Street, Saint Paul, MN 55101

Business Writing Workshop, Phone (319) 588-6316, Clarke College, 1550 Clarke Drive, Dubuque, IA 52001

Byliners of Corpus Christi, P.O. Box 6015, Corpus Christi, TX 78466-6015 (inquire with SASE)

Byrdcliffe Arts Colony, Phone (914) 679-2079, 34 Tinker Street, Woodstock, NY 12498

C

California Arts Council, Phone (916) 227-2550, Public Information Office, 2411 Alhambra Boulevard, Sacramento, CA 95817

California Community Foundation, Phone (213) 413-4042, 606 South Olive Street, Suite 2400, Los Angeles, CA 90014-1526

California Literacy, Inc., Phone (818) 282-2196, Fax (818) 282-0134, 339 South Mission Drive, San Gabriel, CA 91776-1105

California Poets in the Schools, Phone (415) 399-1565, Fax (415) 399-1566, 870 Market Street, Suite 657, San Francisco, CA 94102

California Writers' Club, Phone (510) 841-1217, 2214 Derby Street, Berkeley, CA 94705

Callanwolde Poets' and Writers' Weekend Workshop, Phone (404) 872-5338, 980 Briarcliff Road, NE, Atlanta, GA 30306

Canton Midwest Writers Conference, 6000 Frank Avenue, NW, Canton, OH 44720 (inquire with SASE)

Canyonlands Field Institute, Phone (801) 259-7750, P.O. Box 68, Moab, UT 84532

Cape Cod Writers' Center, Phone (508) 375-0516, 1135 Route 132, West Barnstable, MA 02668

Cape May Institute, Phone (609) 884-7117, Writing by the Sea, 1511 New York Avenue, Cape May, NJ 08204

Caribbean Writers Summer Institute, Phone (305) 284-2182, Fax (305) 284-5635, University of Miami, P.O. Box 248145, Coral Gables, FL 33124-4632

Carolina Publishing Institute, Phone (800) 845-8640, Fax (919) 962-2061, Internet: rmd.ce@mhs.unc.edu, P.O. Box 3392, Chapel Hill, NC 27515-3392

Carter Caves State Resort Writers Workshops, Phone (502) 245-0643, Carter Caves State Resort Park, Olive Hill, KY 41164

Cassell Network of Florida Freelance Writers, Phone (603) 284-6367, Fax (603) 284-6648, Maple Ridge Road, North Sandwich, NH 03259

Cassell Network of Writers, Phone (800) 351-9278, Fax (603) 284-6648, Maple Ridge Road, North Sandwich, NH 03259

Catholic Press Association, Phone (516) 471-4730, Fax (516) 471-4804, 355 Veterans Memorial Highway, Ronkonkoma, NY 11779

Catskill Poetry Workshops, Phone (607) 431-4415, Hartwick College, Oneonta, NY 13820

Celebration of Childrens Literature, Phone (207) 780-5215, University of Southern Maine, 305 Bailey Hall, Gorham, ME 04038

Center for Book Arts, Phone (212) 460-9768, Fax (212) 475-0242, 626 Broadway, New York, NY 10012

Center for Literary Culture, Phone (913) 469-3836, JCCC, 12345 College at Quivira, Overland Park, KS 66210

Center for the Study of Science Fiction, Phone (913) 864-3380, University of Kansas, 3116 Wescoe Hall, Lawrence, KS 66045-2115

Center for the Study of Science Fiction Writers Workshop, Phone (913) 864-3911, University of Kansas, Department of English, 3116 Wescoe Hall, Lawrence, KS 66045-2115

Center for the Study of Southern Culture, Phone (601) 232-5993, University of Mississippi, University, MS 38677

Central Indiana Writers Association, Phone (317) 784-6118, 5968 South Keystone Avenue, Indianapolis, IN 46227

Centrum Foundation, Phone (360) 385-3102, Fax (360) 385-2470, Port Townsend Writers Conference, P.O. Box 1158, Port Townsend, WA 98368

Charleston Writers Conference, Phone (803) 953-5822, Fax (803) 953-1454, College of Charleston, SC 29424

Chattanooga Conference on Southern Literature, Phone (615) 267-1218, Box 4203, Chattanooga, TN 37405

Chautauqua Writer's Center, Phone (716) 357-6255, Box 408, Chautauqua, NY 14722

Cheesecake: A Working Retreat, Phone (707) 895-2876, Box 654, Mendocino, CA 95460

Chesapeake Writers Conference, Phone (804) 758-5324, Rappahonnock Community College, Glenns, VA 23149

Chicago Art Institute, Phone (312) 443-3540, Fax (312) 443-0849, Michigan Avenue at Adams Street, Chicago, IL 60603

Chicago Writing Conference, Phone (312) 779-3300, Saint Xavier College, 3700 West 103rd Street, Chicago, IL 60655

Children's Book Council, Inc., Phone (212) 966-1990, Fax (212) 966-2073, 568 Broadway, Suite 404, New York, NY 10012

Children's Book Guild, Phone (301) 320-6356, 5700 Ridgefield Road, Bethesda, MD 20816

Children's Book Publishing and Illustration Workshops, Phone (713) 527-4036, Rice University, P.O. Box 1892, Houston, TX 77251-1892

Children's Book Writers, 1242 Amsterdam Drive, Colorado Springs, CO 80908 (inquire with SASE)

Children's Book Writers and Illustrators Pocono Mountains Retreat, Society of Children's Book Writers, 303 Main Avenue, Clarks Summit, PA 18411 (inquire with SASE)

Children's Book Writers Conference, North Central Texas Chapter, 19804 Tameria, Irving, TX 75060 (inquire with SASE)

Children's Literature Conference, Phone (312) 955-5597, 1321 East 56th Street, Chicago, IL 60637-1762

Children's Picture Book Seminar, East Arkansas Community College, Newcastle Road, Forrest City, AR 72335 (inquire with SASE)

Children's Picture Book Writing Seminar, 6507 East Holly Street, Scottsdale, AZ 85257 (inquire with SASE)

Chisholm Trail Writers Workshop, Phone (817) 921-7130, Fax (817) 921-7333, Texas Christian University, P.O. Box 32927, Fort Worth, TX 76129

Christian Artisan's Guild, 3172 43rd Street, Long Island City, NY 11103-2702 (inquire with SASE)

Christian Communicator Conferences, Phone (800) 959-6737, 3133 Puente Street, Fullerton, CA 92635

Christian Communicators Conference, LaSierra University, Box 5005, Westlake Village, CA 91359 (inquire with SASE)

Christian Writers, Phone (602) 634-4421, P.O. Box 529, Cornville, AZ 86325

Christian Writer's and Communicator's Workshop, Phone (616) 471-3303, Andrews University, Berrien Springs, MI 49104

Christian Writer's Club, 14801 East 111th Street, Broken Arrow, OK 74011-3904 (inquire with SASE)

Christian Writer's Conference, Phone (602) 838-4919, P.O. Box 5168, Phoenix, AZ 85010

Christian Writer's Conference, Phone (408) 335-4466, Fax (408) 335-9218, Mount Hermon Association, P.O Box 413, Mount Hermon, CA 95041

Christian Writer's Conference and Workshop, Phone (708) 653-4200, Christian Writer's Institute, 388 East Gunderson Drive, Wheaton, IL 60188

Christian Writer's Fellowship, Phone (509) 662-8392, 1818 Skyline Drive, #31, Wenatchee, WA 98801

Christian Writer's Fellowship of Orange County, 2420 North Briston Street, Santa Ana, CA 92706 (inquire with SASE)

Christian Writer's Guild, Phone (209) 335-2333, 260 Fern Lane, Hume, CA 93628

Christian Writer's Guild Seminar, Phone (619) 748-0565, 14140 Mazatlan Court, Poway, CA 92064

Christian Writer's Institute, 177 East Crystal Lake Avenue, Lake Mary, FL 32746 (inquire with SASE)

Christian Writer's Workshop, Phone (513) 244-8181, Cincinnati Bible College and Seminary, 2700 Glenway Avenue, Cincinnati, OH 45204

Christian Writer's Workshop, Phone (216) 352-6363, 34200 Ridge Road, #110, Willoughby, OH 44094

Christina Baldwin Seminars, Phone (612) 823-4424, Keane and Communicators, 3252 Lyndale Avenue South, Minneapolis, MN 55408

Christopher Newport College Writer's Conference, Phone (804) 594-7158, 50 Shoe Lane, Newport News, VA 23606-2998

Cincinnati Bible College and Seminary, Phone (513) 244-8181, 2700 Glenway Avenue, Cincinnati, OH 45204

Citizen Exchange Council's Writers' Seminars in the Former USSR, 12 West 31st Street, New York, NY 10001 (inquire with SASE)

Clarion West SciFi and Fantasy Writers' Workshop, Phone (206) 322-9083, Clarion West, 340 15th Avenue East, Suite 350, Seattle, WA 98112

Clarion Workshop in Science Fiction and Fantasy Writing, Phone (517) 353-6486, Fax (517) 336-2758, Michigan State University, Lyman Briggs School, Holmes Hall, East Lansing, MI 48814-1107

Clark Poetry Seminars, P.O. Box 24824, San Jose, CA 95154 (inquire with SASE)

Clearing, Phone (414) 854-4088, P.O. Box 65, Ellison Bay, WI 54210

Cleveland Heights/University Heights Mini Writers Workshops, Phone (216) 352-6363, 34200 Ridge Road, #110, Willoughby, OH 44094

Coalition for the Advancement of Jewish Education, Phone (212) 268-4210, Fax (212) 268-4214, 261 West 35th Street, Floor 12A, New York, NY 10001

Coconino Center for the Arts, P.O. Box 296, Flagstaff, AZ 86002 (inquire with SASE)

Colorado Authors League, Phone (303) 480-5363, P.O. Box 24905, Welshire Postal Station, Denver, CO 80224

Colorado Center for the Book, Phone (303) 866-6876, Colorado State Library, 201 East Colfax, Suite 309, Denver, CO 80203

Colorado Christian Communicators Retreat, 1294 Amsterdam Drive, Colorado Springs, CO 80907-4004 (inquire with SASE)

Colorado Christian Writers, Phone (303) 823-5718, 67 Seminole Court, Lyons, CO 80540

Colorado Council on the Arts, Phone (303) 894-2619, Fax (303) 894-2615, 750 Pennsylvania Street, Denver, CO 80203

Colorado Mountain Writer's Workshop, Phone (303) 945-7481, 114 Spring Valley Center, 3000 County Road, Glenwood Springs, CO 81601

Colorado River Writers Conference, 4416 West Court Street, Pasco, WA 99301 (inquire with SASE)

Colorado Visions Project, Phone (303) 894-2619, 750 Pennsylvania Street, Denver, CO 80203-3699

Columbia Gorge Writers Conference, 2479 Lichens Drive, Hood River, OR 97031 (inquire with SASE)

Columbus Christian Writers Workshop Christian Alliance, 3732 Shoreline Drive, Columbus, OH 43232 (inquire with SASE)

Comedy/Humor Writers Association, P.O. Box 211, San Francisco, CA 94101 (inquire with SASE)

Committee of Small Magazine Editors and Publishers, P.O. Box 703, San Francisco, CA 94101 (inquire with SASE)

Commonwealth Club of California, Phone (415) 597-6700, Fax (415) 597-6722, 595 Market Street, San Francisco, CA 94105

Commonwealth of Pennsylvania Council on the Arts, Phone (717) 787-6883, 216 Finance Building, Harrisburg, PA 17120

Communicators Workshops, Phone (800) 661-1500, Southern College, Box 370, Collegedale, SC 37315

Compas: Writers and Artists in the Schools, Phone (612) 292-3254, 305 Landmark Center, 75 West Fifth Street, Saint Paul, MN 55102

Computer Press Association, 1260 25th Avenue, San Francisco, CA 94122 (inquire with SASE)

Comstock Writers Group, Phone (315) 475-0339, 907 Comstock Avenue, Syracuse, NY 13210

Connecticut Commission on the Arts, Phone (203) 566-4770, Fax (203) 566-6462, 227 Lawrence Street, Hartford, CT 06106

Connecticut Storytelling Center, Phone (203) 439-2764, Box 5295, 270 Mohegan, New London, CT 06320

Connecticut Writers League, Box 10536, West Hartford, CT 06110 (inquire with SASE)

Construction Writers Association, P.O. Box 259, Poolesville, MD 20837

Coos Bay Writers, Phone (503) 756-7906, Box 4022, Coos Bay, OR 97420

Copywriters Council of America—Freelance, Phone (516) 924-8555, Fax (516) 924-8555, CCA Building 102, Seven Putter Lane, Middle Island, NY 11953-0102

Cornell Summer Sessions, Phone (607) 255-4987, B20 Day Hall, Ithaca, NY 14853

COSMEP Conference, Phone (415) 922-9490, Cosmep, Inc., P.O. Box 420703, San Francisco, CA 94142-0703

COSMEP Prison Project, R.D. 1, Box 80, Greenfield Center, NY 12833 (inquire with SASE)

Council for the Advancement of Science Writing, Inc., P.O. Box 404, Greenlawn, NY 11740 (inquire with SASE)

Council of Biology Editors, 9650 Rockville Pike, Bethesda, MD 20814 (inquire with SASE)

Council of Literary Magazines and Presses, Phone (212) 741-9110, Fax (212) 741-9112, 154 Christopher Street, Suite 3C, New York, NY 10014

Council of Writers Organizations, One Auto Club Drive, Deerborn, MI 48126 (inquire with SASE)

Councils of Authors and Journalists, Phone (800) 476-4925, Box 830008, Stone Mountain, GA 30083-0001

Cowboy Poetry Gathering, Phone (702) 738-7508, P.O. Box 888, Elko, NV 89801

Craft of Writing, Phone (214) 690-2207, University of Texas, P.O. Box 830688, Richardson, TX 75083

Creating Your Own Story, P.O. Box 227, Maysville, GA 30558 (inquire with SASE)

Creative and Freelance Writing Workshops, Markel Enterprises, P.O. Box 209, Ambridge, PA 15003 (inquire with SASE)

Creative Arts International, Inc., Phone (212) 777-8323, 296 Elizabeth Street, Suite 2R, New York, NY 10012

Creative Christian Ministries Writing Seminars, Phone (703) 342-7511, P.O. Box 12624, Roanoke, VA 24027

Creative Communications, Phone (619) 459-8997, P.O. Box 2201, La Jolla, CA 92038

Creative Community Arts, Phone (503) 771-4270, Arts at Menucha, P.O. Box 4958, Portland, OR 97208

Creative Writing Workshop/Workshop, Phone (316) 321-2222, Community College, 901 South Haverhill Road, El Dorado, KS 67042

Cross-Cultural Communications, Phone (516) 868-5635, Fax (516) 379-1901, International Writers and Translators, 239 Wynsum Avenue, Merrick, NY 11566-4725

CSU Summer Arts, Phone (707) 826-4402, Humboldt State University, Arcata, CA 95521-8299

Cumberland Valley Fiction Writers' Workshop, Phone (717) 245-1231, Dickinson College, Department of English, Carlisle, PA 17013-2896

Cummington Community of the Arts, Phone (413) 634-2172, Rural Route 1, Box 145, Cummington, MA 01026

Curry Hill Writer's Retreat, Phone (912) 246-3369, P.O. Box 514, Bainbridge, GA 31717

Cuyahoga Community College Writer's Conference, Phone (216) 987-2046, 4250 Richmond Road, Highland Hills Village, OH 44122

D

D. H. Lawrence Summer Fellowship, Phone (505) 277-6340, Department of English, Humanities Building 217, University of New Mexico, NM 87131

Dallas National Magazine Editors Conference, Texas Writers Association, 219 Preston Royal Shopping Center, Suite 23, Dallas, TX 75230-3832

Davis and Elkins College, Phone (304) 636-5850, Creative Writing Studies, Elkins, WV 26241

Davis and Sacramento Writing Workshops, Phone (916) 752-2971, University of California at Davis, University Extension, Davis, CA 95616

Deaf Playwrights Conference, Phone (860) 526-4971, Fax (860) 526-9732, National Theater of the Deaf, Five West Main Street, Chester, CT 06412

Deep South Writers, Phone (318) 231-6908, Box 44691, Lafayette, LA 70504-4691

Delaware State Arts Council, Phone (302) 577-3540, Fax (302) 577-6561, 820 North French Street, Wilmington, DE 19801

Denver Metro Writers Club, Phone (303) 699-9569, 16075 Columbia Place, Aurora, CO 80013

Denver Publishing Institute, Phone (303) 871-2570, Fax (303) 871-2501, 2075 South University Boulevard, D-114, Denver, CO 80210

Des Moines Annual National Poetry Festival, Phone (515) 277-5091, P.O. Box 12196, Des Moines, IA 50312

Desert Dreams Romance Writers, 1018 East Caroline Lane, Tempe, AZ 85284 (inquire with SASE)

Desert Writers Workshop, Phone (801) 259-7750, Canyonlands Field Institute, P.O. Box 68, Moab, UT 84532

Desmond Communications Training, Box 30153, Santa Barbara, CA 93130 (inquire with SASE)

Detroit Women Writers Annual Writers Conference, Phone (313) 370-3120, Oakland University, Continuing Education, Rochester, MI 48309-4401

Dickens Project, Phone (408) 429-2705, University of California, Santa Cruz, CA 95069

Dillman's Sand Lake Lodge Writing Workshops, Phone (715) 588-3143, Lac du Flambeau, WI 54538

Dillon Authors Association, Box 414, Dillon, MT 59725 (inquire with SASE)

Diverse Visions Program, Phone (612) 627-4444, Intermedia Arts, 425 Ontario Street, SE, Minneapolis, MN 55414

Djerassi Foundation Resident Artists Program, Phone (415) 851-8395, Fax (415) 747-0105, 2325 Bear Gulch Road, Woodside, CA 94062

Dobie-Paisano Writing Fellowships, Phone (512) 471-7213, Fax (512) 471-7620, University of Texas, Austin, TX 78712

Dog Writers Association of America, Inc., Phone (717) 566-9843, P.O. Box E, Hummelstown, PA 17036

Donovan Scholars Program, Phone (606) 257-2000, University of Kentucky, Ligon House, Lexington, KY 40506-0442

Door Company, Phone (414) 854-4088, Box 65, Ellison Bay, WI 54210

Dorland Mountain Arts Colony, Phone (909) 676-5039, P.O. Box 6, Temecula, CA 92593

Dorothy Canfield Fisher's Writers Conference, Phone (802) 496-3271, League of Vermont Writers, Box 1058, Waitsfield, VT 05673

Dorset Colony House for Writers, P.O. Box 519, Dorset, VT 05251 (inquire with SASE)

Downeast Poetry Workshop, Conferences and Institutes Division, Phone (207) 947-1121, University of Maine, Orono, ME 04469

DownEast Maine Writers Workshops, Phone (800) 567-4339, Box 446, Stockton Springs, ME 04981

Dramatists Guild, 234 West 44th Street, New York, NY 10036 (inquire with SASE)

Drury College Writing for Children Workshop, Phone (417) 865-8731, 900 North Benton Avenue, Springfield, MO 65902

E

Easter Shore Writers Association, Internet: IOSONI@aol.com, P.O. Box 1773, Easton, MD 21801

Eastern Writers Conference, Phone (508) 741-6300, Salem State College, Continuing Education, Salem, MA 01970

Editcetera, Phone (510) 849-1100, 2490 Channing Way #507, Berkeley, CA 94704

Editorial Freelancers Association, Phone (212) 677-3357, Fax (212) 777-8207, 36 East 23rd Street, Room 9R, New York, NY 10159-2050

Edmonds Arts Commission, Phone (206) 775-2525, 700 Main Street, Edmonds, WA 98020

Education Writers Association, Phone (202) 429-9680, Fax (202) 872-4016, 1001 Connecticut Avenue, NW, Suite 310, Washington, DC 20036

Educational Press Association of America, Phone (609) 863-5346, Glassboro State College, Glassboro, NJ 08028

Edward F. Albee Foundation, Phone (212) 226-2020, 14 Harrison Street, New York, NY 10013

Effective Communications Group, Phone (201) 444-2942, 309 Windsor Terrace, Ridgewood, NJ 07450

El Dorado Poetry and Writing Workshops, Phone (310) 924-1972, 7550 East Spring, Long Beach, CA 92674

Ellen LaForge Memorial Poetry Foundation, Inc., Phone (617) 547-4648, Fax (617) 547-4230, 6 Plympton Street, Cambridge, MA 02138

Engineering Writing Conference, Phone (303) 764-7433, University of Michigan, Chrysler Center, North Campus, Ann Arbor, MI 48109

Englewood Cliffs Writing Center, Phone (201) 567-4017, 601 Palisade Avenue, Englewood Cliffs, NJ 07632

Environmental Writing Institute, Phone (406) 243-6486, Fax (406) 243-2047, University of Montana, Missoula, MT 59812

F

Falkirk Community Cultural Center, Phone (415) 485-3328, 1408 Mission Avenue, P.O. Box 60, San Rafael, CA 94915

Feminist Women's Writing Workshops, Inc., Phone (607) 734-5588, P.O. Box 6583, Ithaca, NY 14851

Feminist Writers Guild, P.O. Box 9396, Berkeley, CA 94709 (inquire with SASE)

Feminist Writers Guild, 1742 West Melrose, Chicago, IL 60657 (inquire with SASE)

Feminist Writers Guild, P.O. Box 25477, Chicago, IL 60625 (inquire with SASE)

Festival of Poetry, Phone (603) 823-5510, The Frost Place, Franconia, NH 03580

Festival of Poets and Poetry, Fiction Writing, Phone (301) 862-0200, Saint Mary's College of Maryland, Saint Mary's City, MD 20686

Fiction from the Heartlands Writers Conference, Phone (912) 262-3357, Mid-America Romance Authors, P.O. Box 32186, Kansas City, MO 64111

Fiction Group, 1638 Redcliff, Los Angeles, CA 90026 (inquire with SASE)

Film Writers Factory, Phone (703) 528-6273, 3113 North Pershing Drive, Arlington, VA 22201

Fine Arts Work Center in Provincetown, 24 Pearl Street, Provincetown, MA 02657 (inquire with SASE)

Fir Acres Workshop in Writing and Thinking, Phone (503) 293-2679, Lewis and Clark College, Campus Box 100, Portland, OR 97219

Fishtrap, P.O. Box 38, Enterprise, OR 97828 (inquire with SASE)

Florida Arts Council, Phone (904) 487-2980, Department of State, Division of Cultural Affairs, The Capitol, Tallahassee, FL 32399-0250

Florida Center for Writers, Phone (813) 974-1711, University of South Florida, CPR 358, Tampa, FL 33620

Florida Christian Writers, 2600 Park Avenue, Titusville, FL 32780 (inquire with SASE)

Florida Cultural Affairs, Phone (904) 487-2980, Fax (904) 922-5259, The Capitol, Tallahassee, FL 32399-0250

Florida First Coast Writers' Festival, Phone (904) 381-3620, 3939 Roosevelt Boulevard, Jacksonville, FL 32205

Florida Freelance Writers Association, Phone (800) 351-9278, Fax (603) 284-6648, Cassell Network, Maple Ridge Road, North Sandwich, NH 03259

Florida International University, Phone (305) 554-3421, Director: South Beach Writers Conference, North Miami, FL 33181

Florida Romance Writers, Inc., Phone (305) 389-5750, 417 Lakeview Drive, #102, Fort Lauderdale, FL 33326

Florida State Poets Association, Phone (305) 653-2875, Box 680-536, Miami, FL 33168

Florida State Writers Conference, P.O. Box 9844, Fort Lauderdale, FL 33310 (inquire with SASE)

Florida Studio Theatre, Phone (813) 366-9017, 1241 North Palm Avenue, Sarasota, FL 34236

Florida Suncoast Writers' Conference, Phone (813) 974-1711, University of South Florida, 140 Seventh Avenue South, Saint Petersburg, FL 33701

Food Writers Workshop, Phone (707) 963-0777, P.O. Box 663, Saint Helena, CA 94574

Football Writers Association of America, Phone (405) 341-4731, Box 1022, Edmond, OK 73083

Foothills Writers Conference, Phone (415) 949-7450, Foothills College, Los Altos Hills, CA 94022

Foundation Center, Phone (212) 620-4230, Fax (212) 807-3677, 79 Fifth Avenue, New York, NY 10003

Foundation for the Community of Artists, 280 Broadway, Suite 412, New York, NY 10007 (inquire with SASE)

Four Corners School of Outdoor Education, Phone (800) 525-4456, Writing Program, East Route, Monticello, UT 84535

Frances Anderson Center, 700 Main Street, Edmonds, WA 98020 (inquire with SASE)

Francis Marion Writers Retreat, Phone (803) 661-1500, Francis Marion College, Florence, SC 29501

Franconia Festival of Poetry, Phone (603) 823-5510, P.O. Box 74, Franconia, NH 03580

Freedom to Read Foundation, Phone (312) 944-6780, 50 East Huron Street, Chicago, IL 60611

Freelance Editorial Association, Phone (617) 729-8164, Box 835, Cambridge, MA 02238

Freelance Writers Network, P.O. Box 1290, Fairfield Bay, AR 72088 (inquire with SASE)

Free-Lance Writers, Inc., Phone (215) 368-6777, 300 Franklin Court, North Wales, PA 19454-1016

Friends of American Writers, Phone (708) 827-8339, Fax (708) 825-0001, 506 Rose, Des Plaines, IL 60016

Friends of Libraries, USA, Phone (215) 790-1674, Fax (215) 545-3821, 1326 Spruce Street, Suite 1105, Philadelphia, PA 19107

From Pen to Paycheck, Phone (406) 837-4885, Box 1490, Red Lodge, MT 59068

G

GAP Fellowship, Phone (206) 467-8734, Fax (206) 467-9633, Artist Trust, 1402 Third Avenue, Suite 415, Seattle, WA 98101-2118

Garden Writers Association of America, Phone (703) 257-1032, Fax (703) 257-0213, 10210 Leatherleaf Court, Manassas, VA 22111

Gary Provost's Writers Retreat Workshop, Phone (508) 368-0287, P.O. Box 139, South Lancaster, MA 01561

Gathering at Bigfork, Phone (406) 837-4885, P.O. Box 1230, Bigfork, MT 59911

Generoso Pope Writers Conference, Phone (914) 694-2200, Manhattanville College, Purchase, NY 10577

George Bennet Fellowship, Phillips Exeter Academy, Exeter, NH 03833 (inquire with SASE)

Georgia Council for the Arts, Phone (404) 651-7920, 530 Means Street, NW, Suite 115, Atlanta, GA 30318

Georgia Romance Writers, Phone (404) 587-5861, 440 Dogleg Court, Roswell, GA 30076

Georgia State Poetry Society, Inc., Phone (404) 633-1647, 1590 Riderwood Court, Decatur, GA 30033-1531

Geraldine R. Dodge Foundation Poetry Festival, Phone (201) 540-8443, Fax (201) 540-1211, 163 Madison Avenue, P.O. Box 1239, Morristown, NJ 07962-1239

Ghost Ranch Writers Retreat, Phone (505) 466-3505, 11 Bonito Court, Santa Fe, NM 87505

Gila Writers Conference, Phone (602) 986-1399, 11012 East Crescent Avenue, Apache Junction, NM 85220

Glacier Institute, Phone (406) 756-3911, P.O. Box 1457A, Kalispell, MT 59903

Golden Lake Writers Workshops, 12708 Second Avenue, NW, Seattle, WA 98177 (inquire with SASE)

Golden Triangle Writers Guild, Phone (409) 898-3078, 4245 Calder, Beaumont, TX 77706

Goldenrod Writers Conference, Phone (304) 296-7564, 525 Grove Street, Morgantown, WV 26505

Golf Writers Association of America, Box 37324, Cincinnati, OH 45222 (inquire with SASE)

Gordon Burgett Communications Unlimited, Phone (805) 937-8711, P.O. Box 6405, Santa Maria, CA 93456

Gordon Burgett Seminars, Phone (805) 937-8711, Communications Unlimited, P.O. Box 6405, Santa Maria, CA 93456

Grand Rapids Baptist College and Seminary, Phone (616) 949-5300, The Write Place, 1001 East Beltline Avenue, Grand Rapids, MI 49505

Great Falls Writers Conference, Box 6608, Great Falls, MT 59406-6608 (inquire with SASE)

Great Lake Christian Writers Conference, Phone (800) 558-8898, American Baptist Assembly, Green Lake, WI 54941-9599

Great Lake Symposium, Ohio State University Extension, 3200 West 65th Street, Cleveland, OH 44102 (inquire with SASE)

Great Lakes Writers Workshop, Phone (414) 382-6177, Alverno College, 3401 South 39th Street, Milwaukee, WI 53215

Great Pikes Peak Cowboy Poetry Gathering, Phone (719) 531-6333, Pikes Peak Library District, 5550 North Union Boulevard, Colorado Springs, CO 80918

Greater Gulf Coast Writers Workshop, Houston Council of Writers, Box 441381, Houston, TX 77244-1381 (inquire with SASE)

Green River Writers Retreat, Phone (502) 245-4902, 11906 Locust Road, Middletown, KY 40243

Greeting Card Association, 1350 New York Avenue, NW, Suite 615, Washington, DC 20005

Guadalupe Cultural Arts Center, Phone (210) 271-3151, Fax (210) 271-3480, 1300 Guadalupe Street, San Antonio, TX 78207

Guggenheim Memorial Foundation, Phone (212) 687-4470, 90 Park Avenue, New York, NY 10016

Guideposts Writers Workshops, 747 Third Avenue, New York, NY 10017 (inquire with SASE)

Guild Poetry Video Fest, 3404 North Troy, Chicago, IL 60618 (inquire with SASE)

H

H. H. Herbert School of Journalism and Mass Communications, Annual Short Course on Professional Writing, Copeland Hall, Norman, OK 73019-0270 (inquire with SASE)

Haiku North America Conference, Las Positas College, 3033 Collier Canyon Road, Livermore, CA 94550 (inquire with SASE)

Hambidge Center, Phone (404) 746-5718, P.O. Box 33, Rabun Gap, GA 30568

Hands-On Writers Workshops, Phone (903) 882-5591, Fax (903) 882-5710, P.O. Box 1380, Lindale, TX 75771-1380

Harriette Austin Writers Conference, Phone (800) 884-1381, Fax (706) 542-6596, Internet: Register@gacsrv.gactr.uga.edu, Georgia Center for Continuing Education, Athens, GA 30602-3603

Hattiesburg Writers Retreat, Phone (601) 264-7034, 404 Crestmont Avenue, Hattiesburg, MS 39401

Hawaii State Foundation on Culture and the Arts, Phone (808) 586-0302, Fax (808) 586-0308, 335 Merchant Street, Room 202, Honolulu, HI 96813

Haystack Writing Program, Phone (800) 547-8887, Portland State University, Summer Session, P.O. Box 751, Portland, OR 97207

Headland Center for the Arts, Phone (425) 331-2787, 944 Fort Barry, Sausalito, CA 94965

Heart of America Writers Conference, Phone (816) 942-8400, Fax (913) 469-4415, Johnson Community College, 12345 College Boulevard, Overland Park, KS 66210

Heart of Oregon Conference for Writers, 1210 Woodside Drive, Eugene, OR 97401-6414 (inquire with SASE)

Heartland Writers Guild, Phone (314) 888-3032, P.O. Box 652, Kennett, MO 63857

Heekin Group Foundation, Phone (503) 548-4147, P.O. Box 1534, Sisters, OR 97759

Heights Writers Conference, Phone (216) 481-1974, Box 24684, Cleveland, OH 44124-0684

Helena Writers Group, 1450 Prospect, #264, Helena, MT 59601 (inquire with SASE)

Hellgate Writers, Inc., Phone (406) 721-3620, Center for Literary Arts, 2210 North Higgins, P.O. Box 7131, Missoula, MT 59807

Hemingway Days Writers Workshop and Conference, P.O. Box 4045, Key West, FL 33041 (inquire with SASE)

Hendricks Creative Writing Conference, Phone (801) 586-1994, J. P. Hendricks, 351 West Center, Cedar City, UT 84720

High Country Writers, Phone (303) 879-8079, P.O. Box 775063, Steamboat Springs, CO 80477

Highland Summer Conference, Phone (703) 831-5366, Radford University, Box 6935, Radford, VA 24142

Highlights Foundation Writers Workshop, Phone (717) 253-1080, 711 Court Street, Honesdale, PA 18431

Hindman Settlement School, Phone (606) 785-5475, Appalachian Writers Workshop, Box 844, Hindman, KY 41822

Hispanic Arts Association, 200 East 87th Street, New York, NY 10028 (inquire with SASE)

Historical Writing Conference, Rural Route 3, Box 202, Bloomsburg, PA 17815 (inquire with SASE)

Hofstra Summer Writers' Conference, Phone (516) 463-5016, Hofstra University, Davison Hall, Room 208, Hempstead, NY 11550

Hollywood Film School for Writers, Hollywood Film Institute, Box 481252, Los Angeles, CA 90048 (inquire with SASE)

Hoosier Horizon Writers, Phone (219) 663-7077, Write-On, Hoosiers, Inc., P.O. Box 51, Crown Point, IN 46307

Horror Writers of America, P.O. Box 1077, Eden, NC 27288 (inquire with SASE)

Horror Writers of America, 112 Hadley Road, South Burlington, VT 05403 (inquire with SASE)

Housewife-Writers Forum, Phone (307) 786-4513, P.O. Box 780, Lyman, WY 82937-0780

Houston Council of Writers, Council, Greater Gulf Coast Writers Workshop, P.O. Box 441381, Houston, TX 77244-1381

Houston Write-On Writers Conference, 8826 Rowan, Houston, TX 78703 (inquire with SASE)

Humor Writers Convention, Phone (818) 796-4823, P.O. Box 1415, South Pasadena, CA 91031

I

Ibsen Society of America, Phone (718) 636-3794, Fax (718) 622-6174, DeKalb Hall Three, Pratt Institute, Brooklyn, NY 11205-3899

Idaho Commission on the Arts, Phone (208) 334-2119, Fax (206) 334-2488, 304 West State, Boise, ID 83720

Idaho Writers League Conference, Phone (208) 263-7202, Box 1043, Sand Point, ID 83864

Idyllwild Creative Writing Workshops, Phone (714) 659-2171, Fax (714) 659-5463, Idyllwild School of Music and the Arts, Box 38, Idyllwild, CA 92349

Illinois Arts Council, Phone (312) 814-6750, Fax (312) 814-1471, 100 West Randolph, Suite 10-500, Chicago, IL 60601

Illinois Writers, Inc., Phone (309) 438-7705, Illinois State University, Normal, IL 61761-6901

Independent Literary Agents Association, Inc., 432 Park Avenue South, Suite 1205, New York, NY 10016 (inquire with SASE)

Independent Writers of Chicago, Phone (708) 676-3784, 7855 Gross Point Road, Guide G4, Skokie, IL 60077

Indexing Workshops, Bayside Indexing Service, 265 Arlington Avenue, Kensington, CA 94707 (inquire with SASE)

Indian Summer Writers Workshop, Phone (413) 545-0474, University of Massachusetts, 610 Goodell, Amherst, MA 01004

Indiana Arts Commission, Phone (317) 232-1268, 402 West Washington Street, Room 072, Indianapolis, IN 46204-2741

Ingersoll Foundation, Phone (815) 964-5811, 934 North Main Street, Rockford, IL 61103

Institute for Readers Theatre, P.O. Box 17193, San Diego, CA 92177 (inquire with SASE)

International Art Workshop, 463 West Street, 1028H, New York, NY 10014 (inquire with SASE)

International Association of Business Communicators, Phone (415) 433-3400, Fax (415) 362-8762, One Hallidie Plaza, Suite 600, San Francisco, CA 94102

International Association of Crime Writers, Inc., North American Branch, Phone (212) 757-3915, JAF Box 1500, New York, NY 10116

International Black Writers, Phone (312) 924-3818, Box 1030, Chicago, IL 60690

International Food, Wine and Travel Writers Association, Phone (310) 433-5969, Fax (310) 438-6384, P.O. Box 13110, Long Beach, CA 90803

International John Steinbeck Society, Phone (317) 285-5688, Ball State University, Muncie, IN 47306

International Music Camp Creative Writing Workshop, Workshops, 1725 11th Street, SW, Minot, ND 58701

International Reading Association, Phone (302) 731-1600, P.O. Box 8139, Newark, DE 19714-8139

International Society for Humor Studies, Phone (602) 965-5490, Fax (602) 965-1608, Arizona State University, Tempe, AZ 85287-2803

International Society of Dramatists, Box 1310, Miami, FL 33153 (inquire with SASE)

International Society of Weekly Newspaper Editors, Phone (815) 753-0446, Department of Journalism, Northern Illinois University, DeKalb, IL 60115

International Study Programs, Phone (504) 286-6595, University of New Orleans, P.O. Box 1315, New Orleans, LA 70148

International Television Association, Phone (214) 869-1112, 6311 North O'Connor Road, Irving, TX 75039

International Women's Writing Guild, Phone (212) 737-7536, Fax (212) 737-9469, P.O. Box 810, Gracie Station, New York, NY 10028

International Writers and Translators Conference, Phone (516) 868-5635, Fax (516) 379-1901, Cross-Cultural Communications, 239 Wynsum Avenue, Merrick, NY 11566-4725

Intersection for the Arts, Phone (416) 626-ARTS, 446 Valencia Street, San Francisco, CA 94103

Interstate Religious Writers Association, Phone (319) 396-2732, 300 Cherry Hill Road, NW, Cedar Rapids, IA 52405

Investigative Reporters and Editors, Phone (314) 882-2042, Fax (314) 882-5431, Box 838, Columbia, MO 65205

Iowa Arts Council, Phone (515) 281-4451, Capitol Complex, Des Moines, IA 50319-0290

Iowa Summer Writing Festival, Phone (319) 335-2534, University of Iowa, 116 International Center, Iowa City, IA 52242

Irish Writers' Centre Workshop in Dublin, Phone (509) 359-7064, Summer Writing Workshop-MS 25, Eastern Washington University, 526 Fifth Street, Cheney, WA 99004-2431

Island Institute, Phone (907) 747-3794, Sitka Symposium, P.O. Box 2420, Sitka, AK 99835

Ithica House, Greenfield Review Literary Center, Two Middle Grove Road, Greenfield Center, NY 12833

J

Jack Kerouac School of Disembodied Poetics, Phone (303) 444-0202, Naropa Institute, 2130 Arapahoe Avenue, Boulder, CO 80302

Jack London Writers Conference, Phone (415) 342-9123, 135 Clark Drive, San Mateo, CA 94002

Jackson Hole Writing Workshops, Phone (800) 448-7801, Box 3972, University Station, WY 83001

James Joyce Society, Phone (212) 719-4448, Gotham Book Mart Gallery, 41 West 47th Street, New York, NY 10036

Jewish Book Council, Phone (212) 532-4949, 15 East 26th Street, New York, NY 10010

Journal Writing, Phone (800) 862-8890, Omega Institute for Holistic Studies, Lake Drive, Rural Delivery 2, Box 377, Rhinebeck, NY 12572

Journalism Education Association, Phone (913) 532-6250, Kedzie Hall 104, Kansas State University, Manhattan, KS 66506

Journalism Workshop for Minority Students, Phone (602) 523-3559, Fax (602) 523-9313, North Arizona University, Box 6001, Flagstaff, AZ 86011

Just Buffalo Literary Center, Phone (716) 881-3211, 493 Franklin Street, Suite 209, Buffalo, NY 14202

K

Kalamazoo Writers Conference, Phone (616) 383-8408, Department of English, Kalamazoo, MI 49008-5092

Kalani Honua, Box 4500, Pahoa-Kamaili, HI 96778 (inquire with SASE)

Kansas Arts Commission, Phone (913) 296-3335, Jayhawk Tower, 700 SW Jackson, Suite 1004, Topeka, KS 66603-3758

Keane and Communicators, Phone (612) 823-4424, Christina Baldwin Seminars, 3252 Lyndale Avenue, South, Minneapolis, MN 55408

Kentucky Arts Council, Phone (502) 564-3757, Fax (502) 564-2839, 31 Fountain Place, Frankfort, KY 40601

Kentucky Women Writers Conference, Phone (606) 257-1388, University of Kentucky, 208 Patterson Office Tower, Lexington, KY 40506-0027

Keswick Write-to-Publish Conference, 820 North LaSalle Boulevard, Chicago, IL 60610 (inquire with SASE)

Key West Literary Seminars, Phone (305) 293-9291, 419 Petronia Street, Key West, FL 33040

Key West Writers Workshops, Phone (305) 296-3573, Heritage House Museum, 410 Caroline Street, Key West, FL 33040

Konglomerati Foundation, Box 5001, Gulfport, FL 33737 (inquire with SASE)

L

Lacawac Sanctuary, Rural Delivery 1, Box 518, Lake Ariel, PA 18436 (inquire with SASE)

Laguna Poets, Phone (714) 497-8373, 384 Forest Avenue, #15, Laguna Beach, CA 92651

Lake Area Writers Guild, 202 South Union Street, Warsaw, IN 46580 (inquire with SASE)

Lakeland Community College Writers and Freelance Conference, 7700 Clocktower Drive, Mentor, OH 44060 (inquire with SASE)

Lamplight Reading Series, P.O. Box 76785702, Tucson, AZ 85702 (inquire with SASE)

Lancaster Writers Retreat Workshop, Phone (800) 642-2494, Fax (508) 368-0287, Box 139, South Lancaster, MA 01561

Lannan Foundation, Phone (310) 306-1004, Fax (310) 578-6445, 5401 McConnell Avenue, Los Angeles, CA 90066-7027

Lawyers for the Arts, 1285 Avenue of the Americas, Third Floor, New York, NY 10019 (inquire with SASE)

Lawyers for the Creative Arts, 213 West Institute, Suite 411, Chicago, IL 60610 (inquire with SASE)

LDS Writers Workshop, Phone (808) 293-3211, Brigham Young University, Laie, HI 96762

League of Vermont Writers, Phone (802) 496-3271, Dorothy Canfield Fisher's Writers Conference, Box 1058, Waitsfield, VT 05673

Lewis Carroll Society of North America, Phone (301) 593-7077, 617 Rockford Road, Silver Spring, MD 20902

Ligonier Valley Writers, Inc., Phone (412) 238-5749, Rural Route 4, Box 8, Ligonier, PA 15658

Lion Entertainment, 220 West 19th Street, #501, New York, NY 10011 (inquire with SASE)

Literary Nonfiction Workshops, Phone (303) 943-3232, Western State College, Bunnison, CO 81231

Literuption Writers Festival, Phone (503) 274-8830, 0215 SW Whiteaker, Portland, OR 97201

LitNet (The Literary Network), Phone (212) 741-9110, Fax (212) 741-9112, 154 Christopher Street, Suite 3C, New York, NY 10014-2839

Live Poets Society, Phone (516) 581-2214, P.O. Box 391, Islip, NY 11751-0391

Living Streams Christian Writers Retreat, P.O. Box 1321, Vicennes, IN 47591 (inquire with SASE)

Loft Literary Center, Phone (612) 379-8999, Fax (612) 627-2281, Pratt Community Center, 66 Malcolm Avenue, SE, Minneapolis, MN 55414

Logan Canyon Writers Workshop, Phone (800) 538-2663, Utah State University, Logan, UT 84322-5005

Long Beach Museum of Art Poetry Workshop, P.O. Box 20409, Long Beach, CA 90801 (inquire with SASE)

Long Island University at Southampton, Phone (516) 287-8349, Southampton Writers Conference, Southampton, NY 11968

Louisiana State Arts Council, Phone (504) 342-8200, Fax (504) 342-8173, Box 44247, Baton Rouge, LA 70804

Love Designers Writers Club, 1507 Burnham Avenue, Calumet City, IL 60409 (inquire with SASE)

Lowell Celebrates Kerouac, Lowell National Historical Park, 246 Market, Lowell, MA 01852 (inquire with SASE)

Lowell Historic Preservation Commission, Phone (508) 458-7653, 222 Merrimack Street, Suite 310, Lowell, MA 01852

M

M. E. Hughes Peripatetic Writing Workshop/Colony, P.O. Box 822, Village Station, New York, NY 10014 (inquire with SASE)

MacDowell Colony, Phone (603) 924-3886, 100 High Street, Peterborough, NH 03458

Magazine Publishers of America, Phone (212) 752-0055, Fax (212) 888-4217, 575 Lexington Avenue, New York, NY 10022

Magazine Publishing Congress Week, Six River Bend, P.O. Box 4949, Stamford, CT 06907-0949 (inquire with SASE)

Maine Arts Commission, Phone (207) 287-2724, Fax (207) 287-2335, 55 Capital Street, State House, Augusta, ME 04333

Maine Publishers and Writers Alliance, Phone (207) 729-6333, 12 Pleasant Street, Brunswick, ME 04011-2201

Maine Writers Conference, Phone (207) 934-5034, P.O. Box 296, Ocean Park, ME 04063

Maine Writers Workshops, Phone (207) 236-8581, Fax (207) 236-2558, The Workshop, Rockport, ME 04856

Manhattanville Writers Week, Phone (914) 694-3425, Manhattanville College, Purchase, NY 10577

Manoa Writing Program, Phone (808) 956-6660, Fax (808) 956-9170, University of Hawaii, Bilger Hall, Room 104, Honolulu, HI 96822

Maple Woods Community College Writers Conference, Phone (816) 734-4878, 2601 NE Barry Road, Kansas City, MO 64156

Marantha's Christian Writers Seminar, Phone (616) 798-2161, Bible and Missionary Conference Office, 4759 Lake Harbor Road, Muskegon, MI 49411

Marin Poetry Center, Phone (415) 485-3323, Falkirk Cultural Center, 1408 Mission, San Rafael, CA 94901-1971

Mark Twain Creative Writing Workshop, Phone (816) 235-2558, University of Missouri—Kansas City, 5100 Rockhill Road, Kansas City, MO 64110-2499

Mark Twain Writers Conference, Phone (314) 221-2462, 921 Center Street, Hannibal, MO 63401

Markle Enterprises, P.O. Box 209, Ambridge, PA 15003 (inquire with SASE)

Mars Art Space, Divergent Arts Poetry Series, 1201 South First Avenue, P.O. Box 20431, Phoenix, AZ 85003 (inquire with SASE)

Mary Anderson Center, Phone (812) 923-8602, 101 Saint Francis Drive, Mount Saint Francis, IN 47146

Maryland State Arts Council, Phone (410) 333-8232, Fax (410) 333-1062, 601 North Howard Street, Baltimore, MD 21201

Massachusetts Audubon Society, Phone (508) 349-2615, Wellfleet Bay Wildlife Sanctuary, P.O. Box 236, South Wellfleet, MA 02663

Massachusetts Cultural Council, Phone (617) 727-3668, 80 Boylston Street, 10th Floor, Boston, MA 02116-4802

Master Artists in Residence, Phone (904) 427-6975, Atlantic Center for the Arts, 1414 Art Center Avenue, New Smyrna Beach, FL 32168

Mature Poets, Phone (510) 644-6107, North Berkeley Senior Center, 1901 Hearst Street, Berkeley, CA 90025

Maui Writers Conference, Phone (808) 669-6109, Box 10307, Lahaina, HI 96761

McKendree Writers Association, Phone (618) 397-5388, Box 1522, Belleville, IL 62222

Media Alliance, Phone (415) 441-2557, Fax (415) 441-4067, Fort Mason, Building D, San Francisco, CA 94123

Meeman Center Writing for Children Conference, Special Studies, 2000 North Parkway, Memphis, TN 38112 (inquire with SASE)

Melville Society, 1016 Live Oak Lane, Arlington, TX 76012 (inquire with SASE)

Mendocino Coast Writers Conference, Phone (707) 961-1001, College of the Redwoods, 1211 Del Mar Drive, Fort Bragg, CA 95437

Mentorship Poetry Program, The Poetry Center, Box 553, Wayne, PA 19087 (inquire with SASE)

Metropolitan Writers Guild, Phone (205) 937-0429, P.O. Box 337, Stapleton, AL 36578

Metropolitan Writers Group of Seton Hall, Phone (201) 761-9430, Seton Hall University, South Orange, NJ 07079

Miami Earth Poets, Phone (305) 653-2875, Box 680-536, Miami, FL 33168

Michael Hauges Screenwriting, Phone (818) 995-8188, Hilltop Productions, P.O. Box 55728, Sherman Oaks, CA 91413

Michigan Arts Foundation, Phone (313) 964-2244, 2164 Penobscot Building, 645 Griswold Street, Detroit, MI 48226

Michigan Council for Arts and Cultural Affairs, Phone (313) 256-3731, Fax (313) 256-3781, 1200 Sixth Street, Suite 1180, Detroit, MI 48226-2461

Mid America Romance Authors, P.O. Box 32186, Kansas City, MO 64111 (inquire with SASE)

Mid-Atlantic Mystery Book Fair and Convention, Detecto Mysterioso Books, Society Hill Playhouse, 507 South Eighth Street, Philadelphia, PA 19147 (inquire with SASE)

Mid-Atlantic Society of Children's Book Writers Conference, P.O. Box 1707, Midlothian, VA 23112 (inquire with SASE)

Midland Authors Society, 840 East 87th Street, Chicago, IL 60619 (inquire with SASE)

Midland Writers Conference, Phone (517) 631-7151, Grace A. Dow Memorial Library, 1810 West Saint Andrews, Midland, MI 48640

Midnight Sun Writers' Conference, Phone (907) 474-6389, Fax (907) 474-7225, University of Alaska, English Department, Fairbanks, AK 99775

Midwest Society of Children's Book Writers, 2060 16th Terrace, NW, New Brighton, MN 55112 (inquire with SASE)

Midwest Travel Writers Association, Phone (800) 222-6012, Fax (402) 390-0539, P.O. Box 3535, 910 North 96th Street, Omaha, NE 68103

Midwest Writers Conference, Phone (216) 499-9600, Kent State University, Stark Campus, 6000 Frank Avenue, NW, Canton, OH 44720

Midwest Writers Conference, Phone (715) 425-3169, University of Wisconsin, River Falls, WI 54022

Midwest Writers' Workshop, Phone (317) 285-8200, Ball State University, Journalism Department, Muncie, IN 47306

Midwestern Playwrights Festival, Phone (419) 537-2202, University of Toledo, Department of Theatre, Toledo, OH 43606-3390

Mildred I. Reid Writers Colony, Phone (603) 746-3625, Penacook Road, Rural Route 5, Box 51, Contoocook, NH 03229

Millay Colony for the Arts, Phone (518) 392-3103, Steepletop, P.O. Box 3, Austerlitz, NY 12017-0003

Milwaukee Christian Writers, 10605 West Wabash Avenue, Milwaukee, WI 53224-2315 (inquire with SASE)

Mini Writers Conference, Phone (216) 352-6363, 34200 Ridge Road, #110, Willoughby, OH 44094

Minneapolis Writers Workshop, P.O. Box 24356, Minneapolis, MN 55424 (inquire with SASE)

Minnesota Men's Conference, Hidden Wine, 4521 Garfield Avenue South, Minneapolis, MN 55409 (inquire with SASE)

Minnesota State Arts Board, Phone (612) 297-2603, Fax (612) 297-4304, 432 Summit Avenue, Saint Paul, MN 55102

Minnesota Writers Guild, Phone (612) 475-1466, 15535 Holdridge Drive, Wayzata, MN 55391

Minority Writers Reading Series, Phone (602) 884-6974, Pima Community College, East Campus, 8202 East Poinciano Drive, Tucson, AZ 85730

Mississippi Arts Commission, Phone (601) 359-6030, 239 North Lamar Street, Suite 207, Jackson, MS 39201

Mississippi River Creative Writing Workshop, Phone (612) 225-3061, Saint Cloud State University, English Department, Saint Cloud, MN 56301

Mississippi Valley Writers, Phone (309) 762-8985, Augustana College, Union Center, Rock Island, IL 61201

Mississippi Writers Association, P.O. Box 1278, Jackson, MS 39215-1278 (inquire with SASE)

Missoula Book Fair, Phone (406) 721-2665, Missoula Public Library, 301 East Main Street, Missoula, MT 59802

Missouri Arts Council, Phone (314) 340-6845, Wainwright Office Complex, 111 North Seventh Street, Suite 105, Saint Louis, MO 63101-2188

Modern Language Association, Phone (212) 475-9500, Fax (212) 477-9863, 10 Astor Place, New York, NY 10003-6981

Mohonk Writers Retreat, Phone (914) 255-1000, Lake Mohonk, New Paltz, NY 12561

Molokai Writers, Box 61751, Honolulu, HI 96839 (inquire with SASE)

Montana Arts Council, Phone (406) 444-6430, 316 North Park Avenue, Suite 252, Helena, MT 59620

Montana Authors Coalition, P.O. Box 20818, Billings, MT 59104 (inquire with SASE)

Montana Institute of the Arts Writers Organization, P.O. Box 1872, Bozeman, MT 59771 (inquire with SASE)

Montgomery County Community College Writers' Club, Phone (610) 641-6369, P.O. Box 400, 340 DeKalb Pike, Blue Bell, PA 19422-0758

Montrose Bible Conference Writers Conference, P.O. Box 159, Montrose, PA 18801-0159 (inquire with SASE)

Moody Write to Publish Conference, Phone (800) 621-7105, Moody Bible Institute, 820 North LaSalle Boulevard, Chicago, IL 60610

Moon Fish Arts Program in Yachats, Phone (503) 547-4031, P.O. Box 605, Yachats, OR 97498

Moore-Norman Vocational Tech., Writers and Artists Workshops, 4701 12th Avenue, NW, Norman, OK 73069 (inquire with SASE)

Mount Hermon Association, Inc., Phone (408) 335-4466, Fax (408) 335-9218, Christian Writers Conference, P.O. Box 413, Mount Hermon, CA 95041

Mount Holyoke Writers Conference, Phone (413) 538-2308, Mount Holyoke College, South Hadley, MA 01075

Mountain West Center for Regional Studies, Phone (801) 750-3630, Fax (801) 750-3899, Utah State University, University Hill, Logan, UT 84322-0735

Mrs. Giles Whiting Foundation, 1133 Avenue of the Americas, New York, NY 10036 (inquire with SASE)

Multicultural Playwrights' Festival, Phone (206) 685-4969, Seattle Group Theatre, 3940 Brooklyn Avenue, NE, Seattle, WA 98105

Mystery Writers Midwest, Phone (708) 729-4538, Box 8, Techny, IL 60082

Mystery Writers of America Conference, Midwest Chapter, 200 South Garden Avenue, Roselle, IL 60172

Mystery Writers of America, Inc., Phone (212) 888-8171, 17 East 47th Street, Sixth Floor, New York, NY 10017

N

Nantucket Island School of Design and the Arts, Phone (508) 228-9248, Box 958, Nantucket, MA 02554

Napa Valley Writers Conference, Phone (707) 253-3070, Napa Valley College, 1088 College Avenue, Saint Helena, CA 94574

Naropa Institute, Phone (303) 444-0202, 2130 Arapahoe Avenue, Boulder, CO 80302

Nashville Writers Workshop, Box 24001, Nashville, TN 37203 (inquire with SASE)

Natchez Literary Celebration, Phone (800) 647-6724, Copiah-Lincoln Community College, Box 894, Natchez, MS 39121

Nathan Mayhew Seminars of Martha's Vineyard, Phone (508) 693-6603, P.O. Box 1125, Vineyard Haven, MA 02568

Nation Institute, Phone (212) 242-8400, 72 Fifth Avenue, New York, NY 10011

National Association for Young Writers, P.O. Box 228, 2151 Hale Road, Sandusky, MI 48471 (inquire with SASE)

National Association for Young Writers, 215 Valle del Sol Drive, Santa Fe, NM 87501 (inquire with SASE)

National Association of Agricultural Journalists, Phone (419) 433-5412, 312 Valley View Drive, Huron, OH 44839

National Association of Black Journalists, Phone (703) 648-1270, Fax (703) 476-6245, P.O. Box 17212, Washington, DC 20041

National Association of Real Estate Editors, Phone (602) 265-1699, Fax (602) 230-8504, 3101 North Central Avenue, Suite 560, Phoenix, AZ 85012

National Association of Science Writers, Phone (516) 757-5664, Box 294, Greenlawn, NY 11740

National Association of Third World Writers, 373 Fifth Avenue, Suite 1007, New York, NY 10016 (inquire with SASE)

National Book Critics Circle, Phone (212) 463-0889, Fax (212) 875-0148, 41 Union Square West, Room 804, New York, NY 10003

National Conference of Editorial Writers, Phone (301) 984-3015, 6223 Executive Boulevard, Rockville, MD 20852

National Contesters Association, 346 City View Drive, Fort Lauderdale, FL 33311 (inquire with SASE)

National Endowment for the Arts, Phone (202) 682-5786, Fax (202) 682-5610, Nancy Hanks Center, 1100 Pennsylvania Avenue, NW, Washington, DC 20506

National Federation of Press Women, Phone (816) 229-1666, Box 99, 1105 Main Street, Blue Springs, MO 64013-0099

National Federation of State Poetry Societies, Phone (513) 834-2666, 3520 State Route 56, Mechanicsburg, OH 43044

National Foundation for Advancement in the Arts, Phone (305) 573-0490, Fax (305) 573-4870, 3915 Biscayne Boulevard, Miami, FL 33137

National League of American Pen Women, Phone (202) 785-1997, Pen Arts Building, 1300 17th Street, NW, Washington, DC 20036

National Museum of Women in the Arts, Phone (202) 783-5000, Fax (202) 393-3235, 1250 New York Avenue, NW, Washington, DC 20005

National Panhellenic Editors Conference, 6750 Merwin Place, Worthington, OH 43085 (inquire with SASE)

National Poetry Association, Phone (415) 776-6602, Fort Mason Center, Laguna Street/Laguna Boulevard, Building D, Room 270, San Francisco, CA 94123

National Press Club, Phone (202) 662-7500, Fax (202) 879-6725, 529 14th Street, NW, Washington, DC 20045

National Society of Newspaper Columnists (NSNC), Phone (816) 234-4141, Box 22668, Louisville, KY 40252

National Turf Writers Association, 2362 Winston, Louisville, KY 40205 (inquire with SASE)

National University Continuing Education Association, Phone (202) 939-9380, Fax (202) 833-4760, One Dupont Circle, Washington, DC 20036

National Women's Music and Writers Festival, P.O. Box 1427, Indianapolis, IN 46206-1427 (inquire with SASE)

National Writers Club, Inc., Phone (303) 751-7844, Fax (303) 751-8593, 1450 South Havana, Suite 620, Aurora, CO 80012

National Writers Union, Phone (212) 254-0279, Fax (212) 254-0673, 873 Broadway, Suite 203, New York, NY 10003

National Writers Union Conference, P.O. Box 1073, Harvard Square Station, Cambridge, MA 02238 (inquire with SASE)

National Writers Union Local #3 Annual Conference, 236 West Portal Avenue, #232, San Francisco, CA 94127

National Writer's Voice Project, Phone (212) 875-4261, West Side YMCA Center for the Arts, Five West 63rd Street, New York, NY 10023

National Writing Project Network, Phone (415) 642-2949, University of California, 5627 Tolman Hall, Berkeley, CA 94720

Nebraska Arts Council, Phone (402) 595-2122, Fax (402) 595-2334, 3838 Davenport Street, Omaha, NE 68131-2329

Nebraska Sandhills Humor Writing Conference, Phone (800) 347-5237, Broken Bow, Box 96A, Route 1, Mern, NE 68856

Nebraska Writers Guild, Inc., Phone (402) 488-2530, 431 West Broadview Drive, Lincoln, NE 68505

Nebraska Writing and Storytelling Festival, Phone (402) 564-7132, Central Community College, Platte Campus, Box 1027, Columbus, NE 68602

Nevada State Council on the Arts, Phone (702) 687-6680, Fax (702) 687-6688, Capitol Complex, 100 Steward Street, Carson City, NV 89710

New Dramatists, 424 West 44th Street, New York, NY 10036 (inquire with SASE)

New England Poetry Club, Two Farrar Street, Cambridge, MA 02138 (inquire with SASE)

New England Small Press Association, 45 Hillcrest Place, Amherst, MA 01002 (inquire with SASE)

New England Society of Children's Book Writers, 12 Pine Street, Franklin, MA 02038 (inquire with SASE)

New England Writers Conference, P.O. Box 483, Windsor, VT 05089 (inquire with SASE)

New England Writers Workshop, Phone (617) 738-3131, Fax (617) 738-2099, Simmons College, 300 The Fenway, Boston, MA 02115

New Hampshire State Council on the Arts, Phone (603) 271-2789, Fax (603) 271-3584, 40 North Main Street, Concord, NH 03301-4974

New Hampshire Writers and Publishers Project, Phone (603) 436-6331, The Button Factory, 855 Islington Street, #210, P.O. Box 150, Portsmouth, NH 03802-0150

New Hope Foundation, Phone (212) 242-8400, 72 Fifth Avenue, New York, NY 10011

New Jersey Romance Writers, Phone (201) 747-0410, P.O. Box 646, Old Bridge, NJ 08857

New Jersey State Council on the Arts, Phone (609) 292-6130, Fax (609) 989-1440, Four North Broad Street, CN306, Trenton, NJ 08625

New Jersey Writers Conference, New Jersey Institute of Technology, Newark, NJ 07102 (inquire with SASE)

New Letters, Phone (816) 232-2736, University of Missouri–Kansas City, 215 SSB, 5100 Rockhill Road, Kansas City, MO 64110

New Mexico Arts Division, Phone (505) 827-6490, 228 East Palace Avenue, Santa Fe, NM 87501

New Orleans Writers, Phone (504) 566-5090, Fax (504) 566-5046, 1520 Sugar Bowl Drive, New Orleans, LA 70112

New Press Literary Society, Phone (718) 229-6782, 53-35 Hollis Court Boulevard, Flushing, NY 11365

New School, Phone (800) 319-4321, ext. 92, 66 West 12th Street, New York, NY 10011

New York Foundation for the Arts, Phone (212) 366-6900, Fax (212) 366-1778, 155 Avenue of the Americas, New York, NY 10013-1507

New York State Council on the Arts, Phone (212) 387-7028, 915 Broadway, New York, NY 10010

New York State Summer Writers Institute, Phone (518) 584-5000, Skidmore College, Saratoga Springs, NY 12866

New York State Writers Institute, Phone (518) 442-5620, Fax (518) 442-5621, Humanities 355, State University of New York at Albany, Albany, NY 12222

New York Writers Conference, Phone (212) 517-0530, 221 East 71st Street, New York, NY 10021

New York Writing Group, P.O. Box 192, 2440 Broadway, New York, NY 10024 (send 5–10 page sample)

Newspaper Guild, Phone (301) 585-2990, Fax (301) 585-0668, 8611 Second Avenue, Silver Spring, MD 20910

Niagara-Erie Writers, Western New York Literary Center, Seven West Northrup Place, Buffalo, NY 14214 (inquire with SASE)

Nitty-Gritty Writers Workshop, P.O. Box 412, Powhatan, VA 23139 (inquire with SASE)

Nonfiction Articles Writers Workshop, Phone (800) 944-4536, Glen Eyrie Conference Center, P.O. Box 6000, Colorado Springs, CO 80934

North Carolina Arts Council, Phone (919) 733-2111, Fax (919) 733-4834, Department of Cultural Resources, Raleigh, NC 27601-2807

North Carolina Literary and Historical Association, Phone (919) 733-7305, 109 East Jones Street, Raleigh, NC 27601-2807

North Carolina Writer's Network, Phone (919) 967-9540, Fax (919) 929-0535, P.O. Box 954, Carrboro, NC 27510

North Cascades Institute Workshops, Phone (206) 856-5700, 2105 Highway 20, Sedro Woolley, WA 98284

North Dakota Council on the Arts, Phone (701) 244-3954, 418 East Broadway, Suite 70, Bismark, ND 58501

North Dakota University Writers Conference, Phone (701) 777-3321, Box 8237, University Station, Grand Forks, ND 58202

North Dakota Writers Conference, Phone (701) 777-3321, University of North Dakota, P.O. Box 8237, Grand Forks, ND 58202

North Louisiana Romance Writers Conference, 1333 Pecan Square, Bossier City, LA 71112 (inquire with SASE)

Northeast Texas Writers Conference, Phone (903) 572-1911, Northeast Texas Community College, P.O. Box 1307, Mount Pleasant, TX 75455

Northern Virginia Christian Writers Fellowship, Phone (703) 698-7707, Box 629, Dunn Loring, VA 22027

Northern Waters Writers Conference, Phone (715) 836-2031, University of Wisconsin—Eau Claire, Eau Claire, WI 54702-4004

Northwest Writers, Inc., 0215 Southwest Whiteaker, Portland, OR 97201 (inquire with SASE)

Northwest Writers Workshop, 219 North 19th Street, Enid, OK 73701-4524 (inquire with SASE)

Northwest Writing Institute, Phone (503) 768-7745, Lewis and Clark College, Campus Box 100, Portland, OR 97219

Northwood Institute, Phone (517) 837-4478, Alden B. Dow Creativity Center, 3225 Cook Road, Midland, MI 48640-2398

Nourishing the Creative Woman Conference, Phone (415) 564-9453, National League of American Pen Women/Nob Hill Branch, 2730 39th Avenue, San Francisco, CA 94116

Novelists, Inc., P.O. Box 1166, Mission, KS 66222 (inquire with SASE)

Novels-in-Progress Workshop, Phone (502) 245-4902, 11906 Locust Road, Middletown, KY 40243

O

Oakland Writers Conference, Phone (810) 370-3120, Oakland University, Rochester, MI 48309-4401

Ocooch Mountain Writers Retreat, University of Wisconsin, 1200 Highway 14 West, Richland Center, WI 53581 (inquire with SASE)

Ohana Cultural Center, Phone (510) 832-2205, 4345 Telegraph Avenue, Oakland, CA 94612

Ohio Arts Council, Phone (614) 466-2613, 727 East Main Street, Columbus, OH 43205

Ohio-Kentucky-Indiana Writers Conference, 204 Walton Avenue, Lexington, KY 40502 (inquire with SASE)

Ohioana Library Association, Phone/Fax (614) 466-3831, 65 South Front Street, Room 1105, Columbus, OH 43215

Oklahoma Arts Institute Writing Workshop, Phone (405) 842-0890, P.O. Box 18154, Oklahoma City, OK 73154

Oklahoma Cowboy Poetry Gathering, Metropolitan Library System, 131 Dean A. McGee, Oklahoma City, OK 73102 (inquire with SASE)

Oklahoma State Arts Council, Phone (405) 521-2931, Jim Thorpe Building, Room 640, Oklahoma City, OK 97310

Oklahoma Writers' Federation, Federation Conference, P.O. Box 18472, Oklahoma City, OK 73154

Oklahoma Writers Federation Conference, P.O. Box 735, Laverne, OK 73848 (inquire with SASE)

Oklahoma Writers' Symposium and Workshop, Phone (918) 584-3333, Arts and Humanities Council of Tulsa, 2210 South Main, Tulsa, OK 74114-1190

Old Chatham Fiction Workshop, P.O. Box 211, Old Chatham, NY 12136 (inquire with SASE)

Old Pueblo Playwrights, P.O. Box 76785702, Tucson, AZ 85702 (inquire with SASE)

Older Travel Writers, Phone (802) 755-6774, Box 163, Albany, VT 05820

Olympic Field Seminars, Phone (206) 928-3720, Olympic Park Institute, HC 62, Box 9T, Port Angeles, WA 98362

Olympic Rainforest Writing Workshop for Photographers, Phone (904) 867-0463, Box 194, Lowell, FL 32663

Omega Institute for Holistic Studies, Phone (800) 862-8890, Lake Drive, Rural Delivery 2, Box 377, Rhinebeck, NY 12572

Orange County Christian Writers Fellowship, 2420 North Bristol Street, Santa Ana, CA 92706 (inquire with SASE)

Orange Ocean Poets, Phone (714) 366-1057, Box 1328, San Clemente, CA 92674

Oregon Arts Commission, Phone (503) 986-0082, 775 Summer Street, NE, Salem, OR 97310

Oregon Association of Christian Writers, Phone (503) 642-9844, 17768 SW Pointe, Forest Court, Aloha, OR 97006

Oregon Christian Writers Coaching Writers, Phone (503) 726-8320, 506 West Centennial, Springfield, OR 97477

Oregon Literature Series, Phone (503) 963-1393, Eastern Oregon State College, English Department, La Grande, OR 97850

Oregon Writers Colony, P.O. Box 15200, Portland, OR 97215 (inquire with SASE)

Outdoor Writers Association of America, Phone (814) 234-1011, Fax (814) 234-9692, 2017 Cato Avenue, Suite 101, State College, PA 16801-2768

Outreach Program, Phone (800) 999-4234, American Film Institute, 2021 North Western Avenue, Los Angeles, CA 90027

Ozark Creative Writers Conference, Phone (501) 751-7246, 511 Perry Road, Springdale, AR 72764

Ozark Creative Writers, Inc., Phone (505) 565-8889, 6817 Gingerbread Lane, Storybook Village, Little Rock, AR 72204

Ozark Writers and Artists Guild Conference, Phone (417) 451-3223 Crowder College, Neosho, MO 64850

Ozark Writers Conference, Phone (816) 235-2558, University of Missouri, 5100 Rockhill Road, Kansas City, MO 64110-2499

P

Pacific Northwest Booksellers Association, Phone (503) 324-8180, Route 1, Box 219B, Banks, OR 97106

Pacific Northwest Field Seminars, Phone (206) 553-2636, 83 South King Street, Suite 212, Seattle, WA 98104

Pacific Northwest Writers Conference, Phone (206) 443-3807, 2033 Sixth Avenue, Suite 804, Seattle, WA 98121

Pacifica Poetry Forum, Phone (415) 355-8811, Florey's Book Company, 2316 Palmetto, Pacifica, CA 94044

Padua Hills Playwrights Workshop, Phone (213) 913-2636, Box 461450, Los Angeles, CA 90046

Palenville Interarts Colony, Phone (212) 254-4614, Two Bond Street, New York, NY 10012

Palm Springs Writers' Conference, Phone (818) 564-9565, Fax (818) 564-0289, 948 Winston Avenue, San Marino, CA 91108

Panhandle Professional Writers, Phone (806) 352-3889, P.O. Box 19303, Amarillo, TX 79114

Panhandle-Plains Writers Workshops, Phone (806) 296-5521, Wayland Baptist University, 1900 West Seventh Street, Plainview, TX 79072

Paris-American Academy Writing Workshop, Phone (806) 889-3533, P.O. Box 102, HC 01, Plainview, TX 79072

Pasadena Writers Forum, Phone (818) 585-7603, Pasadena City College, Pasadena, CA 91106-2003

Paul Gillette's Writing Workshop, Phone (213) 461-9437, Fax (213) 876-4090, 3284 Barham Boulevard, Suite 201, Los Angeles, CA 90068

PEN American Center, Phone (212) 334-1660, Fax (212) 334-2181, 568 Broadway, New York, NY 10012

PEN Center West, Phone (213) 365-8500, Fax (213) 365-9616, 672 South Lafayette Park Place, Suite 41, Los Angeles, CA 90057

Pennsylvania Council on the Arts, Phone (717) 787-6883, Fax (717) 787-8614, Finance Building, Suite 216, Harrisburg, PA 17120

Pennwriters Conference, 122 Westward Ho Drive, Pittsburgh, PA 15235 (inquire with SASE)

Penpointers, Phone (303) 225-2347, 2902 Brumbaugh Drive, Fort Collins, CO 80526

Perceiving and Interpreting Wild Environments, Workshops, Wildlands Studies, Three Mosswood Circle, Cazadero, CA 95421

Perspectives in Children's Literature, Phone (413) 545-0474, University of Massachusetts, 226 Furcolo Hall, Amherst, MA 01003

Phi Beta Kappa Society, Phone (202) 265-3808, 1811 Q Street, NW, Washington, DC 10009-1696

Philadelphia Christian Writers, Phone (215) 626-6833, 316 Blanchard Road, Drexel Hill, PA 19026

Philadelphia Poetry Center, P.O. Box 355, Wayne, PA 19087 (inquire with SASE)

Philadelphia Writers Conference, 28 Home Road, Hatboro, PA 19040-2026 (inquire with SASE)

Philadelphia Writers Organization, Phone (215) 641-0342, P.O. Box 42497, Philadelphia, PA 19101

Phoenix Desert Rose Conference, Phone (602) 917-8041, Box 20193, Mesa, AZ 85277

Piedmont Literary Society, Phone (804) 384-2027, 1017 Spanish Moss Lane, Breaux Bridge, LA 70517

Pikes Peak Christian Writers Seminar, Phone (719) 685-9432, P.O. Box 8118, Colorado Springs, CO 80933

Pima Writers Workshop, Phone (602) 884-6974, Fax (602) 884-6975, Pima Community College West Campus, 2202 West Anklam Road, Tucson, AZ 85709

Pittsburgh Theological Seminary Writers Workshop, Phone (412) 362-5610, Writers Workshops, 616 North Highland Avenue, Pittsburgh, PA 15206

Ploughshares International Fiction Writing Seminar, Phone (617) 578-8600, Emerson College, 100 Beacon Street, Boston, MA 02116

PMR Screenwriting Workshop, Phone (312) 433-6573, 511 Green Bay Road, Highland Park, IL 60035

Poetry Alive!, Phone (800) 476-8172, Fax (704) 298-5491, Internet: AllanWolf@aol.com, P.O. Box 9643, Asheville, NC 28815

Poetry Center, Phone (212) 415-5760, 92nd Street YM-YWCA, 1395 Lexington Avenue, New York, NY 10128

Poetry Garden, Phone (310) 306-1004, Fax (310) 578-6445, Lannan Foundation, 5401 McConnell Avenue, Los Angeles, CA 90066-7027

Poetry Project at Saint Mark's, Phone (212) 674-0910, 10th Street and Second Avenue, New York, NY 10003

Poetry Resource Center of Michigan, Phone (313) 972-5580, 111 East Kirby, Detroit, MI 48202

Poetry Society of America, Phone (212) 254-9628, 15 Gramercy Park, New York, NY 10003

Poetry Society of Virginia, Box 773, Lynchburg, VA 24505 (inquire with SASE)

Poetry Video Festival, Guild Complex, 3404 North Troy, Chicago, IL 80901 (inquire with SASE)

Poetry West, Phone (719) 632-4874, P.O. Box 2413, Colorado Springs, CO 80901

Poets and Patrons, Eight Pembroke Avenue, Oak Brook, IL 60521 (inquire with SASE)

Poets and Writers, Inc., Phone (212) 226-3586, Fax (212) 226-3963, 72 Spring Street, New York, NY 10012

Poets Club of Chicago, Phone (708) 393-0417, 1725 West Patton Avenue, Arlington Heights, IL 60004

Poet's House, Phone (212) 431-7920, 72 Spring Street, New York, NY 10012

Poets Study Club of Terre Haute, Phone (812) 234-0819, 826 S Center, Terre Haute, IN 47804

Port Townsend Writers Conference, Phone (360) 385-3102, Fax (360) 385-2470, Centrum, P.O. Box 1158, Port Townsend, WA 98368

Portland Outdoor Writers Association of America, Phone (814) 234-1011, Fax (814) 234-9692, State College, 2017 Cato Avenue, Suite 101, Portland, PA 16801

Portland Poetry Festival, P.O. Box 8452, Portland, OR 97207 (inquire with SASE)

Portland Retreat for Writers, Phone (800) 547-8887, Box 1491, Portland, OR 97207-1491

Prague Summer Writers Workshop, Phone (310) 789-3330, University of Southern California, WPH 404, Los Angeles, CA 90089-4034

Presbyterian Writers Guild, Phone (314) 725-6290, 6900 Kingsbury Boulevard, Saint Louis, MO 63130

Professional Food Writers Workshop, Nestle USA, Inc., P.O. Box 663, Saint Helena, CA 94574 (inquire with SASE)

Professional Writers Conference, Phone (405) 325-2251, University of Oklahoma, 1704 Asp Avenue, Norman, OK 73037

Professional Writers League of Long Beach Writers, P.O. Box 20409, Long Beach, CA 90801 (inquire with SASE)

Professionalism in Writing School, Phone (918) 744-1876, Parkview Baptist Church, 5805 South Sheridan, Tulsa, OK 74105

Progoff Intensive Journal Writing Program, Phone (800) 221-5844, Dialogue House Associates, Inc., P.O. Box 1225, Old Chelsea Station, New York, NY 10113-1225

Progress in the Pressroom Seminar, R&E Council of the Graphic Arts Industry, Box 639, Chadds Ford, PA 19317 (inquire with SASE)

Proprioceptive Writing, Phone (800) 862-8890, Omega Institute for Holistic Studies, Lake Drive, Rural Delivery 2, Box 377, Rhinebeck, NY 12572

Provincetown Fine Arts Work Center, Phone (508) 487-9960, Box 565, Provincetown, MA 02657

Publication Services Guild, Phone (404) 525-0985, P.O. Box 19663, Atlanta, GA 30325

Publishers Marketing Association, 2401 Pacific Coast Highway, Suite 102, Hermosa Beach, CA 90254 (inquire with SASE)

Publishing Seminar, Glendale Community College, 544 West Colorado Street, Glendale, CA 91204-1102 (inquire with SASE)

Publishing Your Own Book, Phone (608) 263-3494, 225 Lowell Hall, 610 Langdon Street, Madison, WI 53703-1195

Puget Sound Freefall Workshops, Phone (206) 368-8054, 12708 Second Avenue, NW, Seattle, WA 98177

Pulitzer Prize Board, Phone (212) 854-3841, 702 Journalism, Columbia University, New York, NY 10027

Purchase Writers Workshop, Phone (914) 694-3425, Manhattanville College, 2900 Purchase Street, Purchase, NY 10577

Q

Quackenbush Children's Book Writing, Phone (212) 744-3822, 460 East 79th Street, New York, NY 10021

Quicksilvering Experiential Creative Writing Workshops, Phone/Fax (415) 756-5279, Webhallow Classroom, 1544 Sweetwood Drive, Colma, CA 94015-2029

Quill and Scroll Society, Phone (319) 335-2534, School of Journalism, University of Iowa, Iowa City, IA 52242

Quincy Writers Guild, Phone (217) 223-3117, P.O. Box 112, Quincy, IL 62306-0112

R

Ragdale Foundation, Phone (708) 234-1063, 1260 North Greenbay Road, Lake Forest, IL 60045

Rain Forest Writers Conference, Box 22889, Juneau, AK 99802

Randall House Publications Writers Conference, Box 17306, 114 Bush Road, Nashville, TN 37217 (inquire with SASE)

Rappahonnock Community College, Phone (804) 758-5324, Chesapeake Writers Conference, Glenns, VA 23149

Reader's Digest Writers Workshop, Phone (602) 523-2507, Northern Arizona University, Box 4092, Flagstaff, AZ 86011

Reading and Writing the West, Phone (702) 784-6865, University of Nevada, English Department, Reno, NV 89557-0031

Reading, Writing and Romance, Phone (513) 863-6053, 72 Cherokee Drive, Hamilton, OH 45013

Recursos de Santa Fe, Phone (505) 982-9301, Fax (505) 989-8608, Santa Fe Writers Conference, 826 Camino de Monte Rey, Santa Fe, NM 87501

Regional Society of Children's Book Writers, 29626 Cuthbert Road, Malibu, CA 90265 (inquire with SASE)

Religion Newswriters Association, *Times-Dispatch*, P.O. Box C-32333, Richmond, VA 23293 (inquire with SASE)

Rensselaer Polytechnic Institute, Phone (518) 276-8351, Fax (518) 276-8026, Technical Writers Institute, Troy, NY 12180-3590

Review and Herald's Writers Week, Phone (301) 791-7000, Fax (301) 791-7012, 55 West Oak Ridge Drive, Hagerstown, MD 21740

Rhinelander School of the Arts, Phone (608) 263-3494, University of Wisconsin—Madison, Suite 727, Lowell Hall, 610 Langdon Street, Madison, WI 53703

Rhode Island Council on the Arts, Phone (401) 277-3880, Fax (401) 521-1351, 95 Cedar Street, Suite 103, Providence, RI 02903-1034

Rhode Island Poetry Conference, Phone (203) 521-0358, 18 Woodrow Street, West Hartford, CT 06107

Rhodes College Writing Camp, 2000 North Parkway, Memphis, TN 38112 (inquire with SASE)

Robert Frost Place, Phone (603) 823-5510, Franconia, NH 03580

Robert Frost Poetry Celebration, Phone (305) 296-3573, 410 Caroline Street, Key West, FL 33040

Robert McKee's Story Structure, Phone (310) 312-1002, Two Arts, Inc., 12021 Wilshire Boulevard, Suite 868, Los Angeles, CA 90025

Rockport Writing Series, 1844 Bayshore Drive, Rockport, TX 78382 (inquire with SASE)

Rocky Mountain Conference Retreat, 815 West Fifth, Loveland, CO 80537 (inquire with SASE)

Rocky Mountain Fiction Writers, Conference, P.O. Box 260244, Denver, CO 80226-0244

Rocky Mountain Women's Institute, Phone (303) 871-6923, Fax (303) 871-6897, 7150 Montview Boulevard, Denver, CO 80220

Rocky Mountain Writers Guild, Inc., Phone (303) 444-4100, 837 15th Street, Boulder, CO 80302

Roger Williams Writers Conference, Phone (401) 254-3046, Roger Williams College, Bristol, RI 02809

Romance Writers of America, Phone (713) 440-6885, Fax (713) 440-7510, 13700 Veterans Memorial, Suite 315, Houston, TX 77014

Romantic Times Booklovers Convention, Phone (718) 237-1097, 55 Bergen Street, Brooklyn Heights, NY 11201

Rome Art and Community Center, Phone (315) 336-1040, 308 Bloomfield Street, Rome, NY 13440

Ropewalk Writers Retreat, Phone (800) 467-8600, University of Southern Indiana, Continuing Education, Evansville, IN 47713

Russian River Writers Guild, 167 North High Street, Sebastopol, CA 95421 (inquire with SASE)

S

Sacramento Area Literacy Coalition, Phone (916) 321-1799, The *Sacramento Bee,* P.O. Box 15779, Sacramento, CA 95852

Sagebrush Writers, Box 1255, Big Timber, MT 59011 (inquire with SASE)

Saint David's Christian Writers, Phone (717) 394-6758, 1775 Eden Road, Lancaster, PA 17601-3523

Saint Louis University Libraries Associates, Phone (314) 361-1616, Fax (314) 361-0812, 40 North Kingshighway, Saint Louis, MO 63108-1392

Saint Louis Writing Academy, Phone (314) 522-3718, 312 Saint Louis Avenue, Saint Louis, MO 63135

Salvation Army Central Territory Writers Conference, 10 West Algonquin Road, Des Plaines, IL 60016 (inquire with SASE)

San Diego County Christian Writers Guild, Phone (619) 748-0565, 14140 Mazatlan Court, Poway, CA 92064

San Diego Novel Writer Workshop, Phone (619) 462-5847, 8431 Beaver Lake Drive, San Diego, CA 92119

San Diego Writers/Editors Guild, 3235 Homer Street, San Diego, CA 92106 (inquire with SASE)

San Francisco Bay Area Book Festival, Phone (415) 861-BOOK, 555 DeHaro Street, Suite 220, San Francisco, CA 94107

San Francisco Foundation, Phone (415) 626-2787, 446 Valencia Street, San Francisco, CA 94103

San Jose Poetry Center, 110 South Market Street, San Jose, CA 95113 (inquire with SASE)

San Luis Obispo Poetry Festival, 2740 Grell Lane, Oceano, CA 93445-9164 (inquire with SASE)

Sandhills Writers' Conference, Phone (404) 731-7962, Augusta College, 2500 Walton Way, Augusta, GA 30904-2200

Sandy Cove Christian Writers Conference, Rural Delivery 6, Box 112, Coatesville, PA 19320 (inquire with SASE)

Sangamon State University Writers Conference, Phone (217) 786-6626, Academic Affairs, Springfield, IL 62794-9243

Santa Barbara Book Publishing Conference, Phone (805) 968-7277, Box 2206-62, Santa Barbara, CA 93118-2206

Santa Barbara Writers' Conference, Phone (805) 684-2250, P.O. Box 304, Carpinteria, CA 93013

Santa Clara Valley Christian Writers Seminar, 71 Park Village Place, San Jose, CA 95136 (inquire with SASE)

Santa Fe Writers Conference, Phone (505) 982-9301, Fax (505) 989-8608, Recursos, 826 Camino de Monte Rey, Suite A3, Santa Fe, NM 87501

Santa Monica College Writers Conference, Department of English, 1900 Pico Boulevard, Santa Monica, CA 90405 (inquire with SASE)

Sasquatch Writing Workshop, Phone (904) 867-0463, Box 194, Lowell, FL 32663

School of the Arts at Rhinelander, Phone (608) 263-3494, University of Wisconsin—Madison, 610 Langdon Street, Madison, WI 53703

Science Fiction and Fantasy Convention, CONduit 3, Box 201, Clearfield, UT 84015-0201 (inquire with SASE)

Science Fiction Fantasy Writers of America, Phone (518) 869-5361, Five Winding Brook Drive, Suite 1B, Guilderland, NY 12084

Science Fiction Research Association, Inc., Phone (512) 855-9304, 6021 Grassmere, Corpus Christi, TX 78415

Science Fiction Writers, 68 Countryside Apartments, Hacketstown, NJ 07840 (inquire with SASE)

Science Fiction Writers Group, Box 4335, Spartanburg, SC 29305 (inquire with SASE)

Science Fiction Writers Organization, Box 4236, West Columbia, SC 29171 (inquire with SASE)

Science Writers National Association, Phone (516) 757-5664, P.O. Box 404, Greenlawn, NY 11740

Scientists Institute for Public Information, 355 Lexington Avenue, New York, NY 10017 (inquire with SASE)

Scottsdale Cultural Council Poetry Series, 7383 Scottsdale Mall, Scottsdale, AZ 85251 (inquire with SASE)

Scottsdale/Paradise Valley YMCA Writers Voice, 6869 East Shea Boulevard, Scottsdale, AZ 85254 (inquire with SASE)

Screenwriting for the Independent Feature, United Video Features, 293 High Street, Candia, NH 03034 (inquire with SASE)

Screenwriting Workshop, Phone (800) 482-9748, 2730 Randolph Road, Charlotte, NC 28207

ScribbleFest Literary Group, Phone (213) 550-8522, 1880 Hill Drive, Los Angeles, CA 90041

Scripps Howard Foundation, Phone (513) 977-3035, P.O. Box 5380, Cincinnati, OH 45201-5380

Script Revision Workshops, 1223 Wilshire Boulevard, Suite A, Santa Monica, CA 90403 (inquire with SASE)

Sea Oats Writers Conference, Box 16101, Mobile, AL 36616 (inquire with SASE)

Seacoast Writers Association Conference, Phone (800) 974-6372, White Pines College, 40 Chester Street, Chester, NH 03036

Seattle Pacific Christian Writers Conference, Phone (206) 281-2036, Seattle Pacific University, Seattle, WA 98119

Self-publishing Seminar, 19918 Gulf Boulevard, #7, Indian Shores, FL 34635 (inquire with SASE)

Self-publishing Success Seminars, Box 546, El Cajon, CA 92022-0546 (inquire with SASE)

Seton Hall University Writers Conference, Phone (201) 761-9332, Bayley Hall, South Orange, NH 07079

Sewanee Writers Conference, Phone (615) 598-1141, 310R Saint Luke's Hall, 735 University Avenue, Sewanee, TN 37383-1000

Shawnee Hills Poetry Workshop, 403 South Sixth Street, Ironton, OH 45638 (inquire with SASE)

Shenandoah Playwrights Retreat, Phone (703) 248-1868, Pennyroyal Farm, Route 5, Box 167F, Staunton, VA 24401

Shenandoah Valley Writers Guild, Phone (703) 869-1120, Lord Fairfax Community College, P.O. Box 47, Middletown, VA 22645

Sierra Blanca Writers Workshop, Phone (609) 275-2947, Box 3098, Princeton, NJ 08543-3098

Sierra Nevada Writing Institute, Phone (702) 784-6865, University of Nevada English Department, Reno, NV 89557

Silicon Valley Writers Workshop, 1238 Prescott Avenue, Sunnyvale, CA 94089 (inquire with SASE)

Sinclair Writers Conference, Phone (513) 226-2594, Sinclair Community College, 444 West Third Street, Dayton, OH 45402

Sinipee Writers Workshop, Phone (319) 556-0366, P.O. Box 902, Dubuque, IA 52004-0902

Sirens Workshop Center, Phone (800) 9-MyAngel, Fax (508) 487-1605, Internet: gabrielsma@aol.com, 104 Bradford Street, Provincetown, MA 02657

Sitka Symposium, Phone (907) 747-3794, The Island Institute, P.O. Box 2420, Sitka, AK 99835

Ski Writers Association of the United States, Phone (518) 793-1201, Fax (212) 682-9185, Seven Kensington Road, Glens Falls, NY 12801

Skyline Writers Club, Phone (419) 935-1974, 13762 Oak Brook Boulevard, North Royalton, OH 44133

Small Press Center, Phone (212) 764-7021, 20 West 44th Street, New York, NY 10036

Small Press Genre Association, Phone (510) 254-7442, P.O. Box 6301, Concord, CA 94524

Small Press Traffic Reading Series, Phone (415) 285-8394, 3599 24th Street, San Francisco, CA 94110

Small Press Writers and Artists Organization, Phone (904) 672-3085, 167 Fox Glen Court, Ormond Beach, FL 32174

Smithsonian Institute Creative Writing Program, Phone (202) 357-4700, National Associate Program, 1100 Jefferson Drive, SW, Room 3045, Washington, DC 20560

Smokies in Springtime Writers Workshop, Phone (904) 867-0463, Box 194, Lowell, FL 32663

Snake River Institute, Phone (307) 733-2214, P.O. Box 7724, Jackson Hole, WY 83001

Snake River Writers Workshop, Phone (208) 799-LCSC, Lewis-Clarke State College, Lewiston, ID 83501

Society for Collegiate Journalists, Phone (804) 424-7000, Institute of Journalism, CBN University, Virginia Beach, VA 23462 (inquire with SASE)

Society for Scholarly Publishing, Phone (303) 422-3914, Fax (303) 422-8894, 10200 West 44th Avenue, Suite 304, Wheat Ridge, CO 80033

Society for Technical Communication, Phone (703) 522-4114, 901 North Stuart Street, Suite 304, Arlington, VA 22203

Society of American Business Editors and Writers, Phone (314) 882-7862, Fax (314) 882-9002, University of Missouri, P.O. Box 838, Columbia, MO 65205

Society of American Travel Writers, Phone (202) 429-6639, Fax (202) 775-4674, 1155 Connecticut Avenue, NW, Suite 500, Washington, DC 20036

Society of Authors Representatives, 10 Astor Place, Third Floor, New York, NY 10003 (inquire with SASE)

Society of Children's Book Writers, Phone (818) 888-8760, 22736 Vanowen Street, Suite 106, West Hills, CA 91037

Society of Midland Authors, 152 North Scoville, Oak Park, IL 60302

Society of Midland Authors, Phone (312) 337-1482, Ford-Choyke, 29 East Division Street, Chicago, IL 60610

Society of Professional Journalists, Phone (317) 653-3333, Fax (317) 653-4631, 16 South Jackson, Greencastle, IN 46135

Society of Southwestern Authors, Phone (602) 299-3523, Box 30355, Tucson, AZ 85751-0355

Songwriters Guild of America, 276 Fifth Avenue, Suite 306, New York, NY 10001 (inquire with SASE)

South Beach Writers Conference, Phone (305) 554-3421, Florida International University, North Miami, FL 33181

South Carolina Arts Commission, Phone (803) 734-8696, Fax (803) 734-8526, 1800 Gervais Street, Columbia, SC 29201

South Coast Writers, Phone (503) 247-2349, Box 909, Gold Beach, OR 99744

South Dakota Arts Council, Phone (605) 339-6646, Fax (605) 332-7965, 230 South Phillips Avenue, Suite 204, Sioux Falls, SD 57102-0720

Southeast Writers Conference, Phone (803) 366-5440, 782 Wofford Street, Rock Hill, SC 29730

Southeastern Writers Association, Phone (404) 288-2064, 4021 Gladesworth Lane, Decatur, GA 30035

Southern Baptist Writers Workshop, 127 Ninth Avenue North, Nashville, TN 37234 (inquire with SASE)

Southern California Writers, Phone (619) 278-4099, 2596 Escondido Avenue, San Diego, CA 92123

Southern Christian Writers Conference, Phone (205) 333-8603, Box 1106, Northport, AL 35476

Southhampton Writers Workshops, Phone (516) 287-8349, Long Island University, Southhampton, NY 11968

Southwest Christian Writers Association, Phone (505) 334-2258, Box 2635, Farmington, NM 87499-2635

Southwest Florida Writers Conference, Phone (813) 489-9226, Edison Community College, P.O. Box 06210, Fort Myers, FL 33906-6210

Southwest Mystery/Suspense Convention, 4502 South Congress Avenue, #338, Austin, TX 78745 (inquire with SASE)

Southwest Writers Workshop, Phone (505) 298-1653, P.O. Box 14632, Albuquerque, NM 87191

Space Coast Writers Guild, Inc., Phone (407) 727-0051, P.O. Box 804, Melbourne, FL 32902-0804

Spoleto, Italy, Writers Workshop, Phone/Fax (212) 663-4440, 760 West End Avenue, Suite 3-A, New York, NY 10025

Squaw Valley Community of Writers, Phone (916) 583-5200, P.O. Box 2352, Olympic Valley, CA 95730

Steamboat Springs Writers Group, Phone (303) 879-8079, P.O. Box 775063, Steamboat Springs, CO 80477

Steinbeck Festival, Phone (408) 758-7314, 110 West San Luis Street, Salinas, CA 93901

Stonecoast Writers Conference, Phone (207) 780-4291, University of Southern Maine, 96 Falmouth Street, Portland, ME 04103

Summer Seminar for Writers and Illustrators of Children's Books, Phone (312) 955-5597, 1321 East 56th Street, Chicago, IL 60637-1762

Summer Writing Workshop for Women, Phone (503) 236-9862, 622 SE 29th Avenue, Portland, OR 97214

Syvenna Foundation, Phone/Fax (903) 835-8252, Route 1, Box 193, Linden, TX 75563-9738

T

Taos Institute of Arts, Phone (505) 758-2793, Box 1389, Taos, NM 87571

Taos Poetry Circus Workshops, Phone (505) 758-1800, 5275 NDCBU, Taos, NM 87571

Taos School of Writing, Phone (505) 294-4601, P.O. Box 20496, Albuquerque, NM 87154

Taste of Chicago Writing Conference, Phone (312) 779-3300, Saint Xavier College, 3700 West 103rd Street, Chicago, IL 60655

Teachers and Writers Collaborative, Phone (212) 691-6590, Five Union Square West, New York, NY 10003

Technical Writers Institute, Phone (518) 276-8351, Fax (518) 276-8026, Rensselaer Polytechnic Institute, Troy, NY 12180-3590

Television Comedy Writing, Phone (202) 885-3409, Fax (202) 885-1075, American University, 4400 Massachusetts Avenue NW, Washington, DC 20016

Television Writers Summer Workshop, Phone (800) 999-4234, American Film Institute, 2021 North Western Avenue, Los Angeles, CA 90027

Telluride Talking Gourds Poetry, P.O. Box 160, Norwood, CO 81423 (inquire with SASE)

Telluride Writers Guild, Phone (303) 327-4767, Fax (303) 327-4898, Box 1008, Telluride, CO 81423

Tennessee Arts Commission, Phone (615) 741-1701, Fax (615) 741-8559, 320 Sixth Avenue North, Suite 100, Nashville, TN 37243-0780

Terre Haute Poet's Study Club, Phone (812) 234-0819, 826 S Center, Terre Haute, IN 47804

Texas Commission on the Arts, Phone (512) 463-5535, Fax (512) 475-2699, Box 13406, Austin, TX 78711

Texas Institute of Letters, Phone (512) 471-7213, Box 9032, Wichita Falls, TX 76308-9032

Texas Panhandle Romance Writers, P.O. Box 1343, Amarillo, TX 79105-1343 (inquire with SASE)

Texas Press Women Conference, P.O. Box 863, Sherman, TX 75090-0863 (inquire with SASE)

Texas Writers Association, 219 Preston Royal Shopping Center, Suite 23, Dallas, TX 75230-3832 (inquire with SASE)

Textbook Authors Association, Inc., Phone/Fax (904) 546-5419, Box 535, Orange Springs, FL 32182

Thalassa Writing Retreats, Phone (508) 487-6341, P.O. Box 1564, Provincetown, MA 02657

Third Coast Writers Conference, Phone (616) 387-2570, Western Michigan University, Department of English, Kalamazoo, MI 49008-5092

Thomas Worldwide Photojournalism Seminars, Phone (904) 867-0463, P. O. Box 194, Lowell, FL 32663

Three Rivers Writers Conference, P.O. Box 81536, Pittsburgh, PA 15217 (inquire with SASE)

Thunder Bay Literary Conference, Phone (517) 356-6188, Fax (517) 356-2765, Alpena County Library, 211 North First Avenue, Alpena, MI 49707

Thurber House, Phone (614) 464-1032, 77 Jefferson Avenue, Columbus, OH 43215

Tidewater Writers, 1415 Meads Road C, Norfolk, VA 23505 (inquire with SASE)

Toledo University Writing Workshops, Phone (419) 537-2696, Continuing Education, Toledo, OH 43606-3390

Travel Journalists Guild, P.O. Box 10643, Chicago, IL 60610 (inquire with SASE)

Travel Writing, Photography and Fiction Workshop, Box 9580, Coral Springs, Fl 33075 (inquire with SASE)

Traveling Poetry Exhibit, Phone (602) 621-3237, University of Arizona, Poetry Center, 1216 North Cherry Avenue, Tucson, AZ 85719

Trenton State College Writers Conference, Phone (609) 771-3254, CN 4700, Trenton, NJ 08650-4700

Truro Center for the Arts, Box 756, Truro, MA 02666 (inquire with SASE)

Tucson Poetry Festival, P.O. Box 44000, Tucson, AZ 85733 (inquire with SASE)

Tucson Writers Project, Tucson-Pima Library, P.O. Box 37470, Tucson, AZ 85726 (inquire with SASE)

Tulsa Arts and Humanities Council, Phone (918) 584-3333, 2210 South Main, Tulsa, OK 74114

Tulsa Christian Writers Club, Phone (918) 744-1876, Parkview Baptist Church, 5805 South Sheridan, Tulsa, OK 74105

TV and Screenwriting Conference, Phone (303) 443-4636, Writers in the Rockies, 1980 Glenwood Drive, Boulder, CO 80304

Twentieth Century Literature Conference, Phone (502) 588-6531, University of Louisville, Humanities 332, Louisville, KY 40292

Twin Elms Writers Center, 203 Drakes Corner Road, Princeton, NJ 08540 (inquire with SASE)

U

Ucross Foundation Residency Program, Phone (307) 737-2291, Fax (307) 737-2322, 2836 US Highway 14–16 East, Clearmont, WY 82835

United Arts, 411 Landmark Center, 75 West Fifth Street, Saint Paul, MN 55102 (inquire with SASE)

United States Ski Writers Association, Phone (518) 793-1201, Fax (212) 682-9185, Seven Kensington Road, Glens Falls, NY 12801

University of the Nations Writers Seminar, 1621 Baldwin Avenue, Orange, TX 92665 (inquire with SASE)

Unterberg Poetry Center of the 92nd Street YM-YWCA, Phone (212) 415-5760, 1395 Lexington Avenue, New York, NY 10128

Upper Peninsula of Michigan Writers Conference, Phone (609) 932-4716, 200 West Pewabic, Ironwood, MI 49938

Utah Arts Council, Literary Program, Phone (801) 533-5895, Fax (801) 533-6196, 617 East South Temple, Salt Lake City, UT 84102

V

Vermont Council on the Arts, Phone (802) 828-3291, Fax (802) 828-3233, 133 State Street, Montpelier, VT 05633-6001

Vermont Studio Center, Phone (802) 635-2727, Fax (802) 635-2730, P.O. Box 613 NW, Johnson, VT 05656

Villa Montalvo Center for the Arts, P.O. Box 158, Saratoga, CA 95071 (inquire with SASE)

Villanova Writers Workshops, Phone (215) 645-4620, Villanova University, Villanova, PA 19085

Virginia Center for the Creative Arts, Phone (804) 381-6142, Box VCCA, Sweet Briar, VA 24595

Virginia Commission for the Arts, Phone (804) 225-3132, 223 Governor Street, Richmond, VA 23219

238 ❑ The Complete Guide to Writers Groups, Conferences, and Workshops

Virginia Highlands Festival Creative Writing Days, Box 664, Route 1, Abingdon, VA 24120 (inquire with SASE)

Virginia Intermont College, Phone (703) 669-6101, Creative Writing Studies, Moore Street, Bristol, VA 24201

Voices International Poetry Conference, Phone (501) 225-0166, 1115 Gillette Drive, Little Rock, AR 72207

Volcano Art Center, Phone (808) 967-8222, Fax (808) 967-8512, P.O. Box 104, Hawaii National Park, HI 96718

W

Wallowa Lake Writing Workshops, P.O. Box 38, Enterprise, OR 97828 (inquire with SASE)

Walt Whitman International Poetry Center, Phone (609) 964-8300, Second and Cooper Streets, Camden, NJ 08102

Warren Wilson Program for Writers, Phone (704) 298-3325, Warren Wilson College, P.O. Box 9000, Asheville, NC 28815-9000

Washington Independent Writers, Phone (202) 347-4973, Fax (202) 628-0298, 220 Woodward Building, 733 15th Street, NW, Washington, DC 20005

Washington Romance Writers Retreat, 2357 Bedfordshire Circle, Reston, VA 22091 (inquire with SASE)

Washington State Arts Commission, Phone (206) 753-3860, 234 East Eighth Avenue, Olympia, WA 98504-2675

Weekend Writers Camp, 770 Tonkawa Road, Long Lake, MN 55356 (inquire with SASE)

Wells Writers Workshop, Phone (603) 225-9162, 69 Broadway, Concord, NH 03301

West Coast Science Fantasy Conference, Westercon 46, Box 24292, Seattle, WA 98124 (inquire with SASE)

West Marin Writers Conference, Phone (415) 381-5571, One Weatherly Drive, Mill Valley, CA 94941

West Virginia Department of Education and the Arts, Phone (304) 558-0220, 1900 Kanawha Boulevard East, Charleston, WV 25305

Westchester/Fairfield Writers Conference, Phone (914) 682-1574, 16 Lawrence Drive North, White Plains, NY 10603

Western Maryland Writers Workshop, Frostburg State University, Frostburg, MD 21532-1099 (inquire with SASE)

Western Michigan University Writers Conference, Phone (616) 387-2570, English Department, Kalamazoo, MI 49008-5092

Western Montana Writers Conference, Phone (406) 683-7537, Fax (406) 683-7493, Western Montana College, Dillon, MT 59725

Western New York Literary Center, Niagara-Erie Writers, Seven West Northrup Place, Buffalo, NY 14214 (inquire with SASE)

Western Reserve Writers and Freelance Conference, Phone (216) 943-3047, 34200 Ridge Road, #110, Willoughby, OH 44094

Western States Arts Federation, Phone (505) 988-1166, Fax (505) 982-9307, 236 Montezuma Avenue, Santa Fe, NM 87501

Western Writers of America, Phone/Fax (615) 791-1444, 1012 Fair Street, Franklin, TN 37064

Weymouth Center, 145 West Pennsylvania Avenue, Southern Pines, SC 28387

White River Poetry Intensives, Phone (501) 793-1766, Fax (501) 698-4622, Lyon College, P.O. Box 2317, Batesville, AR 72503-2317

Wildacres Writers, Phone (800) 635-2049, Internet: judihill@aol.com, 233 South Elm Street, Greensboro, NC 27401

Wildbranch Workshops, Phone (802) 586-7711, Sterling College, Craftsbury Common, VT 08527

Willamette Writers Conference, Phone (503) 452-1592, 9045 SW Barbur Boulevard, #5A, Portland, OR 97219

William Flanagan Memorial Creative Persons Center, Phone (212) 226-2020, 14 Harrison Street, New York, NY 10013

Wilmington Writers Workshop, Box 15505, Wilmington, DE 19850

Wisconsin Arts Board, Phone (608) 266-0190, Fax (608) 267-0380, 101 East Wilson Street, First Floor, Madison, WI 53703

Wisconsin Authors and Publishers Alliance Conference, 1209 South 36th Street, Manitowoc, WI 54220 (inquire with SASE)

Wisconsin Regional Writers Association, Phone (414) 668-6267, Route 1, Pebble Beach Road, Cedar Grove, WI 53013

Wisconsin Writers Retreat, Phone (608) 271-0433, 26 Lancaster Court, Madison, WI 53719-1433

Witter Bynner Foundation for Poetry, Inc., Phone (505) 988-3251, Fax (505) 986-8222, P.O. Box 10169, Santa Fe, NM 87504

Women in Communications, Inc., Phone (703) 528-4200, Fax (703) 528-4205, 2101 Wilson Boulevard, Suite 417, Arlington, VA 22201

Women in Scholarly Publishing, Phone (617) 253-5646, Fax (617) 258-6779, MIT Press, 55 Hayward Street, Cambridge, MA 02142

Women Writers Conference, Phone (606) 257-3295, University of Kentucky, 106 Frazee Hall, Lexington, KY 40606-0031

Women Writers West, Box 1537, Santa Monica, CA 90406 (inquire with SASE)

Women Writing Down the Colorado River, Phone (801) 259-7750, Canyonlands Field Institute, P.O. Box 68, Moab, UT 84532

Women's National Book Association, Inc., Phone (212) 675-7804, Fax (212) 989-7542, 160 Fifth Avenue, New York, NY 10010

Women's Wilderness Retreat Canoe Trips, Phone (505) 984-2268, P.O. Box 9109, Santa Fe, NM 87504-9109

Woods Hole Science Writing Program, P.O. Box 332, Woods Hole, MA 02543 (inquire with SASE)

Woodstock Guild, Phone (914) 679-2079, 34 Tinker Street, Woodstock, NY 12498

Wordwrights Writers Conference, 483 West Third Avenue, Roselle, NJ 07203 (inquire with SASE)

Working Writers Retreat, 2513 SE Taylor Street, Portland, OR 97214 (inquire with SASE)

Workshops at Pomotawh Naantam, Pomotawh Naantam Ranch, 26767 County Road 12, Somerset, CO 81434 (inquire with SASE)

World Congress of Poets, Phone (916) 626-4166, Fax (916) 626-5922, 3146 Buckeye Court, Placerville, CA 95667

World Mystery Convention, Phone (215) 925-0913, P.O. Box 49345, Philadelphia, PA 19102-9345

World of Freelance Writing, College DuPage, 22nd and Lambert Roads, Glen Ellyn, IL 60130 (inquire with SASE)

World Wide Writers Service, Inc., 186 North Coleman Road, Centereach, NY 11720 (inquire with SASE)

Write Associates Writers Conference, Phone (716) 839-2559, 471 Burroughs, Buffalo, NY 14226

Write for Success Workshop, Phone (813) 581-2484, 3748 Harbor Heights Drive, Largo, FL 34644

Write on the Sound Writers Conference, Phone (206) 775-2525, Edmonds Arts Commission, 700 Main Street, Edmonds, WA 98020

Write People: A Literary Conference, 2821 East Meisenheimer Road, Custer, MI 49405 (inquire with SASE)

Write Place, Phone (616) 949-5300, Grand Rapids Baptist College and Seminary, 1001 East Beltline Avenue, Grand Rapids, MI 49505

Write to Be Read Workshop, Phone (209) 335-2333, 260 Fern Lane, Hume, CA 93628-9999

Write to Sell, Phone (803) 366-5440, 782 Wofford Street, Rock Hill, SC 29730

Write to Sell Conference, Phone (619) 484-8575, 8465 Jane Street, San Diego, CA 92129

Write Touch, Box 1015, Brookfield, WI 53008 (inquire with SASE)

Writers Alliance, Phone (516) 751-7080, Box 2014, Setauket, NY 11733

Writers and Artists, Moore-Norman Vocational Tech, 4701 12th Avenue, NW, Norman, OK 73069 (inquire with SASE)

Writers and Books, Phone (716) 473-2590, 740 University Avenue, Rochester, NY 14607

Writers and Editors One-on-One, Phone (708) 729-0672, 2238 Henley Street, Glenview, IL 60025

Writers and Want to Be Writers, Phone (513) 933-0133, Box 353, #A, 123 Main Street, Lebanon, OH 45036

Writers at Work, Phone (801) 292-9285, P.O. Box 1146, Centerville, UT 84014-5146

Writers Bloc, 1278 Morgan Street, Santa Rosa, CA 95401 (inquire with SASE)

Writers' Block, Phone (415) 641-7513, 26 Crestline Drive, #2, San Francisco, CA 94131-1456

Writers Boot Camp, 1950 South Pelham, #1, Los Angeles, CA 90025 (inquire with SASE)

Writer's Center, Phone (301) 654-8664, 4508 Walsh Street, Bethesda, MD 20815-2004

Writers Conference in Children's Literature, P.O. Box 66296, Mar Vista Station, Los Angeles, CA 90066 (inquire with SASE)

Writers Conferences and Festivals, Phone (303) 759-0519, Fax (303) 759-0519, P.O. Box 102396, Denver, CO 80250

Writers Connection, Phone (408) 973-0227, Fax (408) 554-2099, 275 Saratoga Avenue, #103-A, Santa Clara, CA 95050-6664

Writers Consortium, Phone (619) 623-8414, Box 234112, San Diego, CA 92023

Writers Edge, Inc., Phone (407) 777-0977, Fax (407) 777-0997, 112 Neptune Court, Indialantic, FL 32903

Writers for Racing Project, Phone (609) 275-2947, Fax (609) 275-1243, P.O. Box 3098, Princeton, NJ 08543-3098

Writers Guild of America East, Inc., Phone (212) 767-7800, Fax (212) 582-1909, 555 West 57th Street, New York, NY 10019

Writers Guild of America West, Inc., Phone (310) 550-1000, Fax (310) 550-8185, 8955 Beverly Boulevard, West Hollywood, CA 90048

Writers Haven, Phone (619) 277-7302, 3745 Mount Augustus Avenue, San Diego, CA 92111

Writers House, Inc., Phone (212) 685-2400, Fax (212) 685-1781, 21 West 26th Street, New York, NY 10010

Writers-in-Exile, Phone (203) 397-1479, Fax (203) 737-4233, 42 Derby Avenue, Orange, CT 06477

Writers in Performance, Phone (212) 645-5848, Manhattan Theatre Club at City Center, 131 West 55th Street, New York, NY 10011-5835

Writers in the Rockies, Phone (303) 443-4636, TV and Screenwriting, 1980 Glenwood Drive, Boulder, CO 80304

Writers Information Network, Phone (206) 842-9103, P.O. Box 11337, Bainbridge Island, WA 98110

Writers Institute, Phone (800) 759-6737, Biola University, 13800 Biola Avenue, La Mirada, CA 90639

Writers Institute, Phone (608) 263-3494, University of Wisconsin, 222 Lowell Hall, 610 Langdon Street, Madison, WI 53703

Writers of Southern California, P.O. Box 19745, Los Angeles, CA 90019 (inquire with SASE)

Writers of Southern California, 130 Via Xanthe, Newport Beach, CA 72663 (inquire with SASE)

Writers on Writing, Phone (212) 854-7489, Barnard College, 3009 Broadway, New York, NY 10027-6598

Writers on Writing at Barnard, Phone (212) 280-2014, Barnard College, 3009 Broadway, New York, NY 10027-6598

Writers Productions, Phone (203) 227-8199, Fax (203) 227-6349, Box 630, Westport, CT 06881

Writers Refinery, Box 47786, Phoenix, AZ 85068-7786 (inquire with SASE)

Writers Resource Center, 2413 Collingwood, Toledo, OH 43620 (inquire with SASE)

Writers Retreat Workshop, Phone (508) 368-0287, P.O. Box 139, South Lancaster, MA 01561

Writers Retreat/Workshop, Phone (701) 857-3340, Minot State University, Minot, ND 58707

Writers Room, Phone (212) 807-9519, 153 Waverly Place, Fifth Floor, New York, NY 10014

Writers Roundtable, P.O. Box 127, Augusta, KY 41002 (inquire with SASE)

Writers Society of America, 11684 Ventura Boulevard, Suite 868, Studio City, CA 91604 (inquire with SASE)

Writers Software Conference, Writers Club, Prairie State College, 202 South Halsted Street, Chicago Heights, IL 60411 (inquire with SASE)

Writers Studio, Mercantile Library, 17 East 47th Street, New York, NY 10017 (inquire with SASE)

Writers Symposium, 1501 Broadway, Suite 302, New York, NY 10036 (inquire with SASE)

Writers Theatre, 145 West 46th Street, New York, NY 10036 (inquire with SASE)

Writers Unlimited, Phone (516) 736-6439, 186 North Coleman Road, Centereach, NY 11720

Writers Voice Project, Phone (518) 543-8833, Silver Bay, NY 12874

Writers' Workshop, Phone (704) 254-8111, P.O. Box 696, Asheville, NC 28802

Writers Workshop, 616 North Highland Avenue, Pittsburgh, PA 15206 (inquire with SASE)

Writers Workshop, Box 24001, Nashville, TN 37203 (inquire with SASE)

Writing Academy Workshops, Phone (206) 763-0710, 9001 Ninth Avenue, SW, Seattle, WA 98106

Writing and Selling to Hollywood Conferences, Phone (800) 833-5588, Fax (213) 785-1299, Hollywood Producer's Story Directory, 1900 Avenue of the Stars, #670, Los Angeles, CA 90067

Writing by the Sea, Phone (609) 884-7117, Cape May Institute, 1511 New York Avenue, Cape May, NJ 08204

Writing Camp and Conference, P.O. Box 664, Ottawa, KS 66067 (inquire with SASE)

Writing Center, Phone (619) 230-0670, 416 Third Avenue, San Diego, CA 92101-6803

Writing Enterprises International, Phone (415) 321-2808, Fax (415) 332-3322, 1150 Newell Road, Palo Alto, CA 94303

Writing for Children, 3707 Ridgeroad North, Little Rock, AR 72116 (inquire with SASE)

Writing in the Mountains, Drawer A, Ruidoso, NM 88345 (inquire with SASE)

Writing Institute Intensive Workshops, Phone (213) 224-0111, California State University at Los Angeles, 5151 State University Drive, Los Angeles, CA 90032

Writing on the Sea, Phone (904) 398-5352, 1358 Tiber Avenue, Jacksonville, FL 32207

Writing/Photography Seminar for Beginners, 9534 Guilford Drive, #A, Indianapolis, AZ 46240 (inquire with SASE)

Writing Programs, Phone (714) 251-1274, Screenwriting Center, 2034 East Lincoln, #300, Anaheim, CA 92806

Writing to Sell, Utah Valley Community College, 800 West 1200th Street South, Orem, UT 84058 (inquire with SASE)

Writing Today, Phone (800) 523-5793, Birmingham-Southern College, Birmingham, AL 35254

Writing With Your Whole Self, Suite 434-M, 20 Park Plaza, Boston, MA 02116 (inquire with SASE)

Writing Workshop for People Over 57, Phone (606) 257-8314, University of Kentucky, Ligon House, Lexington, KY 40506-0442

Writing Workshop for Photographers, Phone (904) 867-0463, P.O. Box 194, Lowell, FL 32663

Writing Workshops for Women, Phone (503) 236-9862, 622 Southeast 29th Avenue, Portland, OR 97214

Wyoming Arts Council, Phone (307) 777-7742, Fax (307) 777-7742, 2320 Capitol Avenue, Cheyenne, WY 82002

Wyoming Writers Conference, P.O. Box 160, Upton, WY 82730 (inquire with SASE)

Y

Yaddo, Phone (518) 584-0746, P.O. Box 395, Saratoga Springs, NY 12866

Yellow Bay Writers Workshop, Phone (406) 243-2094, Fax (406) 243-2047, University of Montana, Missoula, MT 59812

Yellowstone Institute, Phone (307) 344-7381, Yellowstone National Park, P.O. Box 117, Yellowstone National Park, WY 82190

Yosemite Field Seminars, Phone (209) 379-2321, Yosemite Association, P.O. Box 230, El Portal, CA 95318

Young Writers at Penn, Phone (215) 898-7507, University of Pennsylvania, Discovery Program, 3440 Market Street, #100, Philadelphia, PA 19104-3335

Z

Zen Monastery Writing Retreats, Phone (914) 688-2228, P.O. Box 197, Mount Tremper, NY 12457

Zobel Writing Seminars, Phone (415) 591-0300, Fax (415) 691-0700, 23350 Sereno Court, Villa 30, Cupertino, CA 95014